6/10/76   U

CORNELL UNIVERSITY PRESS
124 ROBERTS PLACE, ITHACA, N. Y. 14850

WE TAKE PLEASURE IN SENDING THIS
BOOK FOR REVIEW AND WILL BE GLAD
TO RECEIVE TWO COPIES OF THE NOTICE

PUBLICATION DATE—JUNE 30, 1976

LIST PRICE —$13.50

SHAW'S MORAL VISION
The Self and Salvation

SHAW'S MORAL VISION

The Self and Salvation

ALFRED TURCO, Jr.

Cornell University Press | ITHACA AND LONDON

First published 1976 by Cornell University Press.
Published in the United Kingdom by Cornell University Press Ltd., 2-4 Brook Street, London W1Y 1AA.

International Standard Book Number 0-8014-0965-9
Library of Congress Catalog Card Number 75-36524
Printed in the United States of America by York Composition Co., Inc.
Librarians: Library of Congress cataloging information appears on the last page of the book.

For Ellen and Jeffrey

Shaw, age 42:

Representative critics [complain] that my talent, though not unentertaining, lacks elevation of sentiment and seriousness of purpose. They can find, under the surface-brilliancy for which they give me credit, no coherent thought or sympathy, and accuse me, in various terms and degrees, of an inhuman and freakish wantonness; of preoccupation with "the seamy side of life"; of paradox, cynicism, and eccentricity, reducible, as some contend, to a trite formula of treating bad as good and good as bad, important as trivial and trivial as important, serious as laughable and laughable as serious, and so forth. As to this formula I can only say that if any gentleman is simple enough to think that even a good comic opera can be produced by it, I invite him to try his hand, and see whether anything resembling one of my plays will reward him.

—Preface, *Plays Pleasant*

Shaw, age 88:

Like Shakespear again, I was a born dramatist, which means a born artist-biologist struggling to take biology a step forward on its way to positive science from its present metaphysical stage in which the crude facts of life and death, growth and decay, evolution and reversion, consciousness and unconsciousness, selfpreservation and selfsacrifice, defy the methods of investigation we employ in our research laboratories, and have to be made apprehensible by fictions, pictures, and symphonies in which they are instinctively arranged in a manner which gives a mysterious pleasure.

—Postscript, *Back to Methuselah*

Contents

8   Contents

PART FOUR

Preface

▄▄

In Shaw's fourth novel, *Cashel Byron's Profession* (1882), the young pugilist-hero becomes so infuriated by a German professor's lecture on reforming society that he leaps onto a table and regales the audience of dilettantes with the most important speech Shaw had yet written:

—Executive power. . . . Thats a very good expression, gentlemen, and one that I can tell you a lot about. We have been told that if we want to civilize our neighbors, we must do it mainly by the example of our own lives, by each becoming a living illustration of the highest culture we know. But what I ask is, how is anybody to know that youre an illustration of culture? You cant go about like a sandwich man with a label on your back to tell all the fine notions you have in your head; and you may be sure no person will consider your mere appearance preferable to his own. You want an executive power: thats what you want. Suppose you walked along the street and saw a man beating a woman, and setting a bad example to the roughs. Well, you would be bound to set a good example to them; and, if youre men, youd like to save the woman; but you couldnt do it by merely living; for that would be setting the bad example of passing on and leaving the poor creature to be beaten. What is it that you need to know, then, so as to be able to act up to your ideas? Why, you want to know how to hit him, when to hit him, and where to hit him; and then you want the nerve to go in and do it. (87)

The skill with which Shaw has Cashel develop this core idea, for more than five pages, suggests that the novelist is doing more than merely exploiting the comic incongruity of having a boxer

9

deliver a quasi-philosophical disquisition. For while Cashel is in many ways a social innocent, his conviction that "a man's first duty is to learn to fight" (88) shows him equal to the task of making a closely reasoned exploration of the place of deeds in an ethical code. The speech on executive power in fact heralds the pragmatic perspective of many later Shavian works; for "fighting" here is a metaphor for action conceived as the mainspring of a philosophy based on judging principles by their effects. The very title of the novel presages those of later works that will similarly defend the positive *results* of apparently antisocial behavior—most notably, *Mrs Warren's Profession* and *Major Barbara* (which narrowly escaped being called *Andrew Undershaft's Profession*). Moreover, the naive Cashel is the prototype of the "wise fool" later to emerge in such apparently dissimilar characters as Marchbanks, Dick Dudgeon, and Joan of Arc. It is not really incongruous that the first metaphysician in Shaw's works—as eloquent as Don Juan and as efficient as Undershaft —is a prizefighter.

The reluctance of recent commentators to grapple with Shaw's works as instruments of philosophic inquiry is the paradoxical result of a critical tradition that goes back to the first decade of this century. I say "paradoxical" because the earliest critics were somewhat *too* eager to take on the "whole man," the artist-philosopher whose writings were primarily of interest as vehicles of some presumed broader significance. Almost certain to contain chapters called "The Artist and Philosopher" (Henderson 1911) or "The Poet and Mystic" (Burton 1916), such books in retrospect seem rather crude popularizations of a new prophet to a curious but ignorant public. Even later sympathetic treatments such as those by Collis (1925) and Colbourne (1931) were still basically concerned with reassuring Mr. Intelligent Everyman that beneath the glittering and baffling exterior of the by now world-famous "G.B.S.," there was indeed a "real" Shaw who had important things to say. As might be expected, hostile approaches shared with friendly ones this tendency to use Shaw's works to reveal the man behind them.

By 1930 there were already signs of a reaction against Shaw's reputation and popularity. The changing intellectual fashions that were beginning to make his once shocking ideas seem "dated" went hand in hand with the discrediting effect of Shaw's own strident pronouncements in support of totalitarian political regimes. It is no wonder that C. E. M. Joad's attempt during the 1940's to derive a systematic philosophy from the writings of this passé patriarch seemed a touching exercise in misplaced devotion. And it is equally understandable that when something approaching a critical revival began after the centenary (1956), the accent fell on the previously slighted concern with Shaw as a serious literary artist. Meisel's *Shaw and the Nineteenth-Century Theater* (1963) was concerned mainly with illuminating aspects of Shaw's dramatic method; while Crompton's *Shaw the Dramatist* (1969) resourcefully drew attention to the stature of individual plays. (A book published in 1973, Berst's *Bernard Shaw and the Art of Drama*, is the most fully developed and sophisticated version of this approach.)[1] Studies with a nonliterary emphasis tended to be more circumscribed than their predecessors, focusing on a particular facet of the man and his beliefs— for example, Shaw's view of women (Barbara Watson), the sources of his ideas (Julian Kaye), or the implications of his style (Richard Ohmann).[2]

The later phase described in this necessarily oversimplified

1. Despite our somewhat antithetical approaches, I think my own treatment of Shavian ideas is compatible with Berst's view that Shaw's "finest ideas are less fixed than fluid, more stimulative than definitive— moving, turning, mutating, and evolving through shifting dramatic perspectives. The ideas in his plays are as frequently tied to emotion and aesthetics as to reason. At their best they concurrently inform and are informed by dynamic theatre" (xvi).

2. Ohmann's is not primarily a literary analysis, but an investigation of the relationship between Shaw's "syntactic usages" and his "habitual patterns of thought" (xii–xiii).

account was generally a fortunate one: the scholarship of the last fifteen years has greatly increased our understanding of Shaw. Yet it is because earlier studies, whether panegyric or diatribe, grossly failed to fulfill their chosen task of discovering and evaluating the "artist-philosopher" that a resistance to acknowledging Shaw's intellectual seriousness and depth still lingers. Today's critics are not likely to join H. G. Wells in finding his thought to be "a jackdaw's hoard, picked up anyhow and piled together anyhow" (293).[3] But there is evidence of condescension when a nonspecialist critic such as David Daiches—in the very act of praising Shavian comedy as lively, entertaining, critical, and stimulating—holds that these admirable qualities derive "from the sparkle of Shaw's mind, not from a fully realized dramatic projection of a complex vision of life" (1107). I suspect a similar attitude behind the proclivity of specialist critics to treat inadequately (or ignore altogether) some basic problems. Why, for instance, is *The Quintessence of Ibsenism* so often viewed as a mere polemic instead of as an argument that will bear rigorous scrutiny? Why is there so little grasp of the fundamental importance of *The Perfect Wagnerite* in the evolution of Shaw's ideas? Why is it not understood that many Shavian characters are the same hero presented at different stages of their creator's awareness? Why do analyses of *Saint Joan* that deal very competently with the "tragic" body of the play jettison the epilogue as an unaccountable lapse into comedy? Why does even Colin Wilson, the writer who has made the most inflated claims for Shaw's philosophical significance, hold patronizingly that there are only three plays in which he was "completely in earnest" (153)? The present study of Shaw's view of self-realization and salvation aims to dispel the misconceptions to which such questions point.

An exploration of Shavian pragmatism as it emerges in *The Quintessence of Ibsenism* (1891) is essential. Once this most

3. Claiming that he knows his Shaw "fairly well," Wells goes on to complain that the dramatist "exalted the maker of enormous guns in 'Man and Superman'" (293).

important of Shaw's nondramatic works has been understood, one can readily see how the book was both a solution to the recurring dilemma of his novels (written from 1879 to 1883) and a harbinger of the ethical stance of plays such as *Mrs Warren's Profession* (1893–1894) and *Arms and the Man* (1894). From the vantage point he has thus established, Shaw begins to reach out tentatively toward a more comprehensive vision in *Candida* (1895), *The Devil's Disciple* (1897), and *Caesar and Cleopatra* (1898)—culminating in *The Perfect Wagnerite* (1898) as ideological successor to the *Quintessence*. *Man and Superman* (1901–1903) then stands forth clearly as a synthesis of the separate philosophical strands—pragmatism and heroic idealism—Shaw had struggled with during the late 1890's. This play is subsequently joined by *John Bull's Other Island* (1904) and *Major Barbara* (1905) to form a kind of trilogy dramatizing Shaw's attempt to preserve his grand design from newly perceived contingencies that threaten its destruction. The group becomes, in effect, a tetralogy with *Heartbreak House* (1916–1917), which reveals the Shavian vision coming full circle to achieve simultaneous completion and collapse. After indicating briefly how this reading might be extended to include the later plays, I will conclude with a general appraisal—from a modern perspective—of Shaw's insights into the human situation. My purpose throughout has not been to "prove" that Shaw is a philosopher by syncretizing his ideas into a formal metaphysic, but to depict as clearly as possible the process by which he endeavored to create an integrated vision of life through the medium of his art. And I have chosen to argue my case, not by means of a comprehensive "critical survey" of Shaw's writings, but by means of an *essay*, which focuses on the relatively few works that seemed crucial for plotting the trajectory of his intellectual growth.

Apart from a few parenthetical remarks, I have not attempted to relate Shaw to Bentham, Marx, Butler, and other thinkers who influenced him. Although the tracing of intellectual origins begun in Julian Kaye's *Bernard Shaw and the Nineteenth-Century Tradition* could profitably be carried further, my concern here is not with the origins of Shavian thought, but with its inner coherence. Ibsen and Wagner are discussed in great detail, not because they were necessarily more important in the evolution of Shaw's mind than, say, Schopenhauer and Nietzsche, but because elements from his analyses of the former pair are intricately woven into the fabric of Shavian drama. To wit: Shaw consciously mines Ibsen's plays and Wagner's operas for characters, situations, and themes which he then re-creates in his own works in order to explore further the philosophical issues that had intrigued him in writing the *Quintessence* and the *Wagnerite*. To give a sense of Shaw's imaginative transmutation of such pre-existing materials is more challenging than to recount already well-understood intellectual affinities between *Man and Superman* and Nietzsche, or between *Major Barbara* and Blake.

My critical approach may seem to run the risk of treating Shaw's plays as mines from which a specified thematic ore will be forcibly extracted. But this essay does not deal with "ideas" as static entities extrapolated from Shaw's works, but with the way ideas develop through those works to reveal overall and inherent patterns of meaning. What T. S. Eliot wrote of Shakespeare—that " 'the whole man' is not simply his greatest or maturest achievement, but the whole pattern formed by the sequence of plays"—applies with equal force to Shaw's writings. For while the meaning of *Hamlet* may not be in itself alone, that play stands *by* itself much more securely than *Major Barbara*, which can be fully understood only contextually in relation to the rest of Shaw's output. To say this is to suggest both the limitations of *Major Barbara* as a self-contained play and the richness of the larger sequence of which it is a part. Since it would be impossible within this essay to illustrate such thematic interrelationships by dealing with each work in terms of all the others, I have resisted the temptation to include material that would have merely extended the book's coverage without increasing its depth.

But I have tried to choose samples that, besides demonstrating my central premise, will also suggest how the method of this study might be extended to reveal Shaw's entire *oeuvre* as one great work of art, all the parts of which relate harmoniously to one another.

For helpful criticism and advice I am grateful to my former teachers Jerome Buckley and Robert Chapman, both of Harvard University; to my nonliterary friends Charles Capwell, John Hoffman, and Charles A. Miller; and to several colleagues in the English Department at Wesleyan University: William Coley, Geraldine Murphy, Carol Ohmann, Richard Ohmann, Joseph Reed, Victor Vogt, and Larry Vonalt. Stanley Weintraub of The Pennsylvania State University and Dan H. Laurence, Shaw's official bibliographer, have been diligent and patient in answering queries. I was fortunate also in having the services of two excellent undergraduate assistants—Keith Reierstad '70 and Jerry McGuire '76, both of Wesleyan. Finally, to the vital intellectual prodding of Ivan Waldbauer, professor of music at Brown University, I owe more than I can possibly acknowledge here.

Two sections of this book exist in article form. Chapter 1, on *The Quintessence of Ibsenism*, appeared in *Texas Studies in Literature and Language* (Winter 1976). Part of the discussion of *The Perfect Wagnerite* in Chapter 3 appeared in *The Shaw Review* (May 1974).

All quotations from Shaw's writings are used by permission of The Society of Authors and The Public Trustee.

ALFRED TURCO, JR.

Middletown, Connecticut

Note on Documentation

━━━

The sources of quotations from works by Shaw are identified by abbreviations, listed alphabetically here. Where a title is followed only by the date of composition, the volume is from the Standard Edition (London: Constable and Company); for books not in this edition, the list provides full bibliographical information. Page references in text citations are to the play itself unless there is notation to another part of the volume, such as the preface or postscript—for example, (*Mis* 4, Pref) refers to page 4 of the preface to *Misalliance*.

Works written from 1879 to 1929 (from *Immaturity* to *The Apple Cart*) were issued in the Standard Edition in 1931–1932; later volumes in the set continued to appear until 1950 as Shaw continued to write. The list of abbreviations does not provide dates of composition for collections, which were written over a period of time. The dates for prefaces, postscripts, and the like are those Shaw gives; where he made no indication, the date is that of first publication.

For all works written before 1906, the readings of the Standard Edition have been checked against the original versions for evidence of possible revision. (Of works discussed in this essay, *Major Barbara* [1905] is the last that Shaw altered significantly after the original text was published.) For all titles checked for possible variants, the list provides in brackets a shortened notation of sources used in collation. The bibliographical "References Cited" at the end of this volume contains full citations for these sources. In order to keep the search for variant readings within controllable bounds, the original version and the Standard Edition are the sole texts collated for all works except the three *Major Critical Essays,* where the intervening editions indicated were examined as well. In the interests of eschewing pedantry, the readings of the Standard Edition have been retained except in cases where this author judged revisions to be significant. Such changes have been called to the reader's attention by the following means. Where an entire quotation from the Standard Edition is a later addition, the abbreviation *n.o.t.* (*not in original text*) appears in parentheses after the words quoted: for example, "it is in Rufio's scabbard" (*Caes* 121, *n.o.t.*). If an added quotation is from one of the *Major Critical Essays,* a date appears in parentheses to identify the edition in which the passage first appeared: for example, "wicked people are allowed to commit crimes in the name of the ideal that would not be tolerated for a moment as open devilment" (*Quint* 96, *1913*). In more complex cases, where Shaw revised only *part* of a quotation—for instance, by adding, deleting, or altering a specific word, phrase, or sentence—pertinent explanations and earlier variants are provided in the footnotes.

All references in the text to other sources give the author's name and a page number. Complete information may be found in "References Cited." Where more than one work by a writer has been used, the inclusion of the date of publication distinguishes between them. Finally, I have followed Shaw's usage in regard to apostrophes and most other matters, but *not* his confusing habit of indicating italics by spaced letters or enlarged print.

And	*Androcles and the Lion,* 1912. Preface, 1915.
Arms	*Arms and the Man,* 1894. [Pub. Stone 1898, see *PP.*]
Art	*The Sanity of Art,* 1895. Preface, 1907. [(1) Ed. Laurence, see *NDW;* (2) Pub. Tucker 1908.]
Back	*Back to Methuselah,* 1918–1920. Preface, 1921; Postscript, 1944.

Barb	*Major Barbara,* 1905. Preface, 1906. [Pub. Brentano's 1907; see article by Dukore.]
Brass	*Captain Brassbound's Conversion,* 1899. Notes, 1900. [Pub. Stone 1901, see *TPP.*]
Bull	*John Bull's Other Island,* 1904. 1st Preface, 1906; 2d Preface, 1912; Postscript, 1929. [Pub. Brentano's 1907.]
Buoy	*Buoyant Billions,* 1947. Preface, 1947.
Caes	*Caesar and Cleopatra,* 1898. Notes, 1900. [Pub. Stone 1901, see *TPP.*]
Cand	*Candida,* 1894–1895. [Pub. Stone 1898, see *PP.*]
Cart	*The Apple Cart,* 1929. Preface, 1930.
Cash	*Cashel Byron's Profession,* 1882. Preface, 1901; Note on Modern Prizefighting, 1901. [Ed. Weintraub.]
Charles	*In Good King Charles's Golden Days,* 1939. Preface, 1945.
CL	*Collected Letters: 1874–1897.* Ed. Dan H. Laurence. New York: Dodd, Mead, 1965.
CP	*The Complete Prefaces of Bernard Shaw.* London: Hamlyn, 1965.
Crim	*Doctors' Delusions, Crude Criminology, and Sham Education.*
Disc	*The Devil's Disciple,* 1896–1897. Notes, 1900. [Pub. Stone 1901, see *TPP.*]
Doct	*The Doctor's Dilemma,* 1906. Preface, 1911.
EFS	*Essays in Fabian Socialism.* [(1) *Fabian Essays in Socialism,* 1889; (2) Kraus Reprint of *Fabian Tracts.*]
EPWW	*Everybody's Political What's What,* 1944.
Fanny	*Fanny's First Play,* 1911. Preface, 1914.
Far	*Farfetched Fables,* 1948. Preface, 1948–1949.
Gen	*Geneva,* 1938. Preface, 1945.
Heart	*Heartbreak House,* 1916–1917. Preface, 1919.
HMC	*How to Become a Musical Critic.* Ed. Dan H. Laurence. London: Hart-Davis, 1960.
Imm	*Immaturity,* 1879. Preface, 1921. [Microfilm of 1879 MS in National Library of Ireland.]
IWG	*The Intelligent Woman's Guide to Socialism,* etc., 1927.
Joan	*Saint Joan,* 1923. Preface, 1924.
Knot	*The Irrational Knot,* 1880. Preface, 1905. [Serialized in *Our Corner,* 1885–1887.]

Love	*Love among the Artists,* 1881. [Serialized in *Our Corner,* 1887–1888.]
Marr	*Getting Married,* 1908. Preface, 1911.
MCE	*Major Critical Essays* (contains *Art, Quint, Wag*). [Various editions, see under individual titles.]
Mill	*The Millionairess,* 1935. Preface, 1935.
Mis	*Misalliance,* 1909–1910. Preface, 1914.
Mrs W	*Mrs Warren's Profession,* 1893–1894. Preface, 1902. [(1) Pub. Stone 1898, see *PUP;* (2) *The Author's Apology,* pub. Brentano's 1905.]
NDW	*Selected Non-Dramatic Writings of Bernard Shaw.* Ed. Dan H. Laurence. Boston: Houghton Mifflin, 1965.
Over	*Overruled,* 1912. Preface, 1916.
P&P	*Platform and Pulpit.* Ed. Dan H. Laurence. New York: Hill & Wang, 1961.
Phil	*The Philanderer,* 1893. [Pub. Stone 1898, see *PUP.*]
PP	*Plays Pleasant* (contains *Arms, Cand, Tell*). Preface, 1898. [Pub. Stone 1898.]
PUP	*Plays Unpleasant* (contains *Mrs W, Phil, Wid*). Preface, 1898. [Pub. Stone 1898.]
Pyg	*Pygmalion,* 1912. Preface, 1916.
Quint	*The Quintessence of Ibsenism,* 1891. 1st Preface, 1891; 2d Preface, 1912–1913; 3d Preface, 1922. [(1) Pub. Tucker 1891; (2) pub. Brentano's 1913.]
Rocks	*On the Rocks,* 1933. Preface, 1933.
RS	*The Religious Speeches of Bernard Shaw.* Ed. Warren S. Smith. University Park: Pennsylvania State University Press, 1963.
Simp	*The Simpleton of the Unexpected Isles,* 1934. Preface, 1935.
SR	*Shaw on Religion.* Ed. Warren Sylvester Smith. New York: Dodd, Mead, 1967.
SSS	*Sixteen Self Sketches.*
ST	*Shaw on Theatre.* Ed. E. J. West. New York: Hill & Wang, 1958.
Super	*Man and Superman,* 1901–1903. Epistle Dedicatory, 1903; The Revolutionist's Handbook, 1903; Maxims for Revolutionists, 1903. [Pub. Brentano's 1904.]
Tell	*You Never Can Tell,* 1895–1896. [Pub. Stone 1898, see *PP.*]
Theat I	*Our Theatres in the Nineties,* Vol. I.

TPP	*Three Plays for Puritans* (contains *Brass, Caes, Disc*). Preface, 1900. [Pub. Stone 1901.]
True	*Too True to Be Good*, 1931. Preface, 1933.
Unsoc	*An Unsocial Socialist*, 1883. Preface, 1930; Postscript, 1887. [Ed. Laurence, see *NDW*.]
Wag	*The Perfect Wagnerite*, 1898. 1st Preface, 1898; 2d Preface, 1901, 3d Preface, 1913; 4th Preface, 1922. [(1) Pub. Stone 1899; (2) pub. Constable 1902; (3) pub. Brentano's 1909; (4) pub. Tauchnitz 1913.]
Wid	*Widowers' Houses*, 1885, 1892. [Pub. Stone 1898, see *PUP*.]

PART ONE

1   *The Quintessence of Ibsenism*

▄▀

Rudiments of a Shavian Ethic

Of the three main categories of men distinguished by Shaw in the second chapter of *The Quintessence of Ibsenism* (1891), the first and most important is designated by an unusual use of the word "idealist":

We have seen that as Man grows through the ages, he finds himself bolder by the growth of his courage: that is, of his spirit (for so the common people name it), and dares more and more to love and trust instead of to fear and fight. But his courage has other effects: he also raises himself from mere consciousness to knowledge by daring more and more to face facts and tell himself the truth. For in his infancy of helplessness and terror he could not face the inexorable; and facts being of all things the most inexorable, he masked all the threatening ones as fast as he discovered them; so that now every mask requires a hero to tear it off. The king of terrors, Death, was the Arch-Inexorable: Man could not bear the dread of that. He must persuade himself that death can be propitiated, circumvented, abolished. How he fixed the mask of personal immortality on the face of Death for this purpose we all know. And he did the like with all disagreeables as long as they remained inevitable. . . . The masks were his ideals, as he called them; and what, he would ask, would life be without ideals? Thus he became an idealist, and remained so until he dared to begin pulling the masks off and looking the spectres in the face—dared, that is, to be more and more a realist. But all men are not equally brave; and the greatest terror prevailed whenever some realist bolder than the rest laid hands on a mask which they did not yet dare to do without. (25)[1]

1. Shaw was thirty-six years old when the book appeared in 1891; a

What, according to Shaw, is an ideal? An illusion. A pretense.
A lie. The strategy of this peculiar definition will become clear
if the *Quintessence* is viewed within the context of nineteenth-
century assumptions about social progress. The social reformer
is nearly always dubbed an "idealist" by the man in the street
who rationalizes his preference for the status quo by proclaiming
himself a "realist." The *Quintessence* turns the tables on such
a man—the Shavian realist is the critic of society, the Shavian
idealist is the conventional person. Taking the reactions of a
hypothetical "community of one thousand" to the British family
system, Shaw asserts that the seven hundred comprising the
majority will be satisfied with the system as it is: these are the
Philistines. Because the two hundred and ninety-nine who are
dissatisfied with the system can be coerced by the others into
accepting it, they will "accordingly try to persuade themselves
that, whatever their own particular domestic arrangements may
be, the family is a beautiful and holy natural institution" (27).
The members of this higher level of society, though more intelligent than the seven hundred, are called idealists because the
family conceived along such lines "is only a fancy picture . . .
invented by the minority as a mask for the reality, which in its
nakedness is intolerable to them" (27).

What will happen, then, when the "one man" representing
the highest level, thus far unexplained (27), removes the mask?

---

revised edition was published in 1913. The main difference between the
two is the result of Shaw's subsequent inclusion of new chapters dealing
with the last plays of Ibsen, which postdated the original book. Since
the second edition was mainly an expansion and clarification of the first,
I have treated the enlarged version as being essentially of a piece with its
predecessor. The appropriate indications (see Note on Documentation—
pp. 16–20), however, have been made in all cases where passages were
either added after 1891 or else involved *substantive* alteration of the
original text. In the above quotation, for instance, the word "personal"
(in the sixth sentence) first appeared in the 1913 edition. For all passages
cited, the 1913 edition is a final text identical to the Standard Edition
of 1932.

"This thing [says the realist] is a failure for many of us. It is insufferable that . . . human beings, having entered into relations which only warm affection can render tolerable, should be forced to maintain them after such affections have ceased to exist, or in spite of the fact that they have never arisen. The alleged natural attractions and repulsions upon which the family ideal is based do not exist; and it is historically false that the family was founded for the purpose of satisfying them. Let us provide otherwise for the social ends which the family subserves, and then abolish its compulsory character altogether." What will be the attitude of the rest to this outspoken man? The Philistines will simply think him mad. But the idealists will be terrified beyond measure at the proclamation of their hidden thought—at the presence of the traitor among the conspirators of silence—at the rending of the beautiful veil they and their poets have woven to hide the unbearable face of the truth. They will crucify him, burn him, violate their own ideals of family affection by taking his children away from him, ostracize him, brand him as immoral, profligate, filthy, and appeal against him to the despised Philistines, specially idealized for the occasion as Society. (27–28)

Having begun as a mere pretense, ideals must rapidly become moral imperatives if they are to be rescued from destruction at the hands of a bolder spirit. In short, conventionality must become self-righteous, a deliberate attempt to poke out the mind's eye: "The policy of forcing individuals to act on the assumption that all ideals are real, and to recognize and accept such action as standard moral conduct, absolutely valid under all circumstances, contrary conduct or any advocacy of it being discountenanced and punished as immoral, may therefore be described as the policy of Idealism" (27). Determined to protect the convention from exposure, society next converts it into a principle, which the individual has a duty to uphold. Other persons may then be used as means to the end of safeguarding this absolute— in contradiction to Shaw's belief that "to treat a person as a means instead of an end is to deny that person's right to live" (37).

Since ideals originate in the lack and dread of self-knowledge, it will come as no surprise that "people are led to do as mischievous, as unnatural, as murderous things by their religious and moral ideals as by their envy and ambition" (117). In fact, the absolutizing power of ideals as reflected in social institutions and religious doctrine enables vicious persons to deceive themselves with virtuous impunity. The outcome is that "wicked people are allowed to commit crimes in the name of the ideal that would not be tolerated for a moment as open devilment" (96, *1913*). The resulting "man of principle" will be a great advocate of duty (that is, the duty of others to himself); the society in which he lives will commend the nobility of self-sacrifice (the sacrifice of the citizen to the State); the virtues of obedience will be lauded by those who desire to be obeyed; God and country, justice and honor will become the casual verbiage of vested interests bent on manipulating individuality for their own ends while concealing their will to power. Such persons need not even be depraved: since idealism contradicts what really *is*, even the most charitable and well-intentioned idealist will eventually be forced to "sacrifice" another in order to maintain his own illusions. Invoking Isaiah and Malachi as forerunners to the modern prophet Ibsen, Shaw offers the words "idols" and "idolatry" as synonyms for "ideals" and "idealism" (7, 2d Pref), and warns his readers that "our ideals, like the gods of old, are constantly demanding human sacrifices" (123).

The allusion to the Bible is but one indication of Shaw's awareness of the similarities between "idealism" and the motives underlying conventional religiosity. Like primitive religion, duty "arises at first, a gloomy tyranny, out of man's helplessness, his self-mistrust, in a word, his abstract fear" (23). The idealist is analogous to the believer in original sin, who thinks that "human nature, naturally corrupt, is held back from ruinous excesses only by self-denying conformity to the ideals" (31). But in an age when belief in a transcendent deity has become untenable, it is no longer possible to view all the evil in the world as the result of man's will, and all the good as a result of divine intervention: human will and passion, not God and reason, are the forces that shape events.[2] Viewed from this perspective, " 'original sin' is the will doing mischief. 'Divine grace' is the will doing good. Our fathers, unversed in the Hegelian dialectic, could not conceive that these two, each the negation of the other, were the same" (20n).[3]

Reason, then, is not a modern successor to divine grace, that is, a beneficent force that will save humanity from its own will. Shaw's attack on "idealism" is rooted in an anterior attack on rationalism—reason is valuable because it enables us to fulfill our will, but "faith in reason as a prime motor is no longer the criterion of a sound mind, any more than faith in the Bible is the criterion of righteous intention" (22). It is because "the will to change our habits and thus defy morality arises before the intellect can reason out any racially beneficent purpose in the change" (122, *1913*) that Ibsen claims the "right of private judgment in questions of conduct" (125). Far from being a

2. Compare the following: "We can now, as soon as we are strong-minded enough, drop the pessimism, the rationalism, the supernatural theology, and all the other subterfuges to which we cling because we are afraid to look life straight in the face and see in it, not the fulfilment of a moral law or of the deductions of reason, but the satisfaction of a passion in us of which we can give no rational account whatever" (310). This passage is from *The Sanity of Art*, which often provides an interesting running commentary on issues dealt with more obliquely in the *Quintessence*. In the original version published as a magazine article ("A Degenerate's View of Nordau," in *Liberty*, ed. Benjamin R. Tucker [New York: 27 July 1895]), this passage began "We can now, as soon as we are strong-minded enough, drop the Nirvana nonsense, the pessimism, the rationalism, the theology . . ." and ended " . . . of which we can give no account whatever" (*NDW* 359-360). The word "supernatural" was added when Tucker subsequently published the work as a book in 1908. But "the Nirvana nonsense" was deleted—and "rational" was added—only in the Standard Edition text (1932).

3. "Passion is the steam in the engines of all religious and moral systems. . . . The difference between Caliban and Prospero is not that Prospero has killed passion in himself whilst Caliban has yielded to it, but that Prospero is mastered by holier passions than Caliban's" (*Art* 303-304). In the 1895 edition, the second sentence read: "The difference between Caliban and Prospero is that Prospero is mastered by holier passions." The revised text first appears in the 1908 edition.

digression, the long discussion of rationalism (18–22) is the core of the book. In Shaw's ethic, the syllogism takes its place beside Jehovah as an external illusion cleverly concealing the operation of human instincts.[4]

To the dutiful, self-sacrificing, reasoning idealist, Shaw opposes the "selfish" realist who follows the dictates of his own will: "The idealist, higher in the ascent of evolution than the Philistine, yet hates the highest and strikes at him with a dread and rancor of which the easy-going Philistine is guiltless. The man who has risen above the danger and the fear that his acquisitiveness will lead him to theft, his temper to murder, his affections to debauchery: this is he who is denounced as an archscoundrel and libertine, and thus confounded with the lowest because he is the highest" (30). In other words, the idealist projects the moral anarchy within himself onto the realist. He assumes that the latter must be committing all the depraved acts that he himself would commit if not restrained by fear of the legal and divine sanctions that stand ready to be invoked in the name of ideals. But since experience shows that "self-surrender" in practice has a "repulsive effect" (34), the realist is actually more constructive as well as more daring than his idealistic counterpart: "No one ever feels helpless by the side of the self-helper; whilst the self-sacrificer is always a drag, a responsibility, a reproach, an everlasting and unnatural trouble with whom no really strong soul can live. Only those who have helped themselves know how to help others, and to respect their right to help themselves" (34). The realist, in short, "has come to have a deep respect for himself and faith in the validity of his own will" (31); and while Shaw never claims that the man who follows his own will is automatically beneficent, we shall see later that his analysis of *Emperor and Galilean* (49–59) does look forward to a time

4. For cogent expressions of Shaw's view of the relative functions of reason and will—written exactly contemporaneously with the publication of the *Quintessence*—see his letters to E. C. Chapman (29 July 1891) and William Archer (25 October 1891), both in *CL* 300–303, 315–318.

when the personal will and the "world will" (he does not yet know the term *Life Force*) will be reconciled through dialectical synthesis.

To expand this rudimentary account and come to grips with the Shavian perspective more concretely, it will be helpful to deal with several objections that might reasonably occur to someone reading the *Quintessence* skeptically: first, that its thinking involves a trite inversion of traditional formulas; second, that its underlying premises are naively utopian; third, that its ethics are indiscriminately relativistic. After defending the book against these plausible but mistaken charges, I will suggest a major respect in which Shaw's argument is open to valid criticism.

Shaw's assertion that morality is only a pretentious name people give to their habits invites the countercharge that "realism" is simply a pretentious name Shaw gives to the violation of tradition. In fact he is not so simplistic:

The reader must therefore discount those partialities which I have permitted myself to express in telling the stories of the plays. They are as much beside the mark as any other example of the sort of criticism which seeks to create an impression favorable or otherwise to Ibsen by simply pasting his characters all over with good or bad conduct marks. If any person cares to describe Hedda Gabler as a modern Lucretia who preferred death to dishonor, and Thea Elvsted as an abandoned, perjured strumpet who deserted the man she had sworn before her God to love, honor, and obey until her death, the play contains conclusive evidence establishing both points. If the critic goes on to argue that as Ibsen manifestly means to recommend Thea's conduct above Hedda's by making the end happier for her, the moral of the play is a vicious one, that, again, cannot be gainsaid. If, on the other hand, Ghosts be defended, as the dramatic critic of Piccadilly did defend it, because it throws into divine relief the beautiful figure of the simple and pious Pastor Manders, the fatal compliment cannot be parried. When you have called Mrs Alving an emancipated woman or an unprincipled one, Alving a debauchee or a victim of society, Nora a fearless and noble-hearted woman or a shocking little liar and an unnatural mother, Helmer a selfish hound or a model husband and father, according to your bias, you have said something which is at once true and false, and in both cases perfectly idle. (120–121)

While it is clear that Shaw's sympathies are with Thea, Mrs. Alving, and Nora, the above passage moves beyond partisanship to the rejection of all generalization. The sets of laudatory and disparaging epithets are equally pointless because both substitute the abstract for the concrete. If on the simplest level an ideal is a pretense or convention, and on a deeper level an ideal is an absolute or principle, then on the deepest level an ideal becomes any abstraction that attempts to constrict what Shaw sees as life's concrete particularity.[5] Take, for instance, Shaw's insistence upon the importance of "being always prepared to act immorally" (121–122). In this context, "immoral" is used in a special sense to describe any behavior that violates convention; even so, Shaw's assertion stops short of recommending systematic nonconformity. His argument is that immorality "does not necessarily imply mischievous conduct: it implies conduct, mischievous or not, which does not conform to current ideals" (121). Indeed, the observation that merely to defy conventional standards would be

5. See *Quint* 73, 119–120; and *Art* 304. A better grasp of Shaw's point here would have saved a number of Ibsen's interpreters from serious blunders. For instance, it is a sclerotic cliché of Ibsen criticism that *The Wild Duck* (1884) is a "retraction" of *Ghosts* (1882). The reasoning inevitably boils down to some variant of the following: Mrs. Alving insists that one should live in accordance with truth and is a sympathetic character; Gregers Werle also insists on the truth and is a revolting character who produces a catastrophe: ergo, the latter play repudiates the position of the former. But this argument ignores the fact that the word "truth" designates a concept that does not have the same *specific* meaning in both plays. Mrs. Alving's "truth" is a belief in the primacy of the concrete over the abstract and the relative over the absolute; Werle's "truth," on the other hand, is itself abstract and absolute. The parallel characters in these two plays are not Mrs. Alving and Werle, but Manders and Werle; note that both the latter praise ideals (called "illusions" in the first play and "lies" in the second—hardly a change of position), seek strength from sources outside themselves, and take a fanatically "all or nothing" view of duty, morality, and self-sacrifice. Far from being a reversal of *Ghosts*, *The Wild Duck* dramatizes the same theme from another angle of vision.

as naively idealistic as to submit to them is an insight which
should be credited to Shaw rather than directed against him by
his critics. Shaw is no Byronic iconoclast who violates conventional judgments in order to feel gloriously wicked; his analysis
of *Hedda Gabler* deplores the "unlooked-for reaction of idealism,
this monstrous but very common setting-up of wrong-doing as
an ideal" (89). Richard Ohmann's view that the argument of
the *Quintessence* amounts to a "semantic sleight-of-hand—morality is immoral"—(44) would be a more accurate statement of
Shaw's position if rephrased to read "morality is *a*moral,": that
is, conduct that merely conforms to ideals is, in Shaw's words,
"purely conventional and of no ethical significance" (135, *1913*)
one way or another.[6] Shaw realizes that ideals may be necessary
as a practical matter (25–26), but he wants to alert readers to
the dangers inherent in them. He does not deny that "ideals are
sometimes beneficent, and their repudiation sometimes cruel"
(96, *1913*); he only warns that "thoughtless conformity to
[ideals] is constantly producing results no less tragic than those
which follow thoughtless violation of them" (121).[7] The same
point appears in many other places in his writings—when he
observes that even a man of genius "accepts a hundred rules for
every one he challenges" (*Art* 306);[8] when he cautions that "artificial morality is not . . . to be condemned offhand. In many
cases it may save mischief instead of making it" (*Over* 158,
Pref); when he reminds the overly zealous that "revolutionary
movements attract those who are not good enough for established

6. In *The Sanity of Art,* Shaw attacks "those habits of the majority
which it pretentiously calls its morals" (302). (In the 1895 and 1908
editions, this passage read: "what the majority consider to be 'right' in
conduct or overt opinion"). Likewise law "deadens the conscience of
individuals by relieving them of the ethical responsibility of their own
actions" (*Art* 307). In a later work he describes morality as "the substitution of custom for conscience" (*Fanny* 247, Pref).

7. The phrase "thoughtless violation of them" (1913) originally read:
"the violation of ideals which are still valid" (1891).

8. The word "hundred" (1908) originally read "thousand" (1895).

institutions as well as those who are too good for them" (*And* 146); when he insists that "only fools and romantic novices imagine that freedom is a mere matter of the readiness of the individual to snap his fingers at convention" (*Mis* 67, Pref).[9] It is the perception that iconoclasm is no more than inverted conformity that gives pith to such Shavian maxims as "He who slays a king and he who dies for him are alike idolaters" (*Super* 211, Maxims), or Candida's blunt "How conventional all you unconventional people are!" (118).

The source of such later insights is found in the *Quintessence* itself:

We have already seen both Ibsenites and anti-Ibsenites who seem to think that the cases of Nora [in *A Doll's House*] and Mrs Elvsted [in *Hedda Gabler*] are meant to establish a golden rule for women who wish to be "emancipated": the said golden rule being simply, Run away from your husband. But in Ibsen's view of life, that would come under the same condemnation as the ecclesiastical rule, Cleave to your husband until death do you part.[10] Most people know of a case or two in which it would be wise for a wife to follow the example of Nora. . . . But they must also know cases in which the results of such a course would be as tragi-comic as those of Gregers Werle's attempt in The Wild Duck to do for the Ekdal household what Lona Hessel did for the Bernick household. (125)

Critics seem not to have understood that being a realist, far

9. Shaw cautions his readers against assuming the possibility of unlimited freedom: "A ready-made code of conduct for general use will always be needed as a matter of overwhelming convenience by all members of communities. . . . The moral evolution of the social individual is from submission and obedience as economizers of effort and responsibility, and safeguards against panic and incontinence, to wilfulness and self-assertion made safe by reason and self-control" (*Art* 307–308). (In the 1895 edition, this passage read: "a ready-made code of conduct for general use will be used more or less as a matter of overwhelming convenience by all members of communities. . . . The whole progress of the world is from submission and obedience as safeguards against panic and incontinence, to wilfulness and self-assertion made safe by reason and self-control." The revised text first appears in the 1908 edition.)

10. The word "ecclesiastical" (1913) originally read "conventional golden" (1891).

from providing an opportunity to do what one pleases and go to the devil in haste, is going to be a very demanding job indeed. Writing of the *Quintessence,* William Irvine observes that, while seemingly an anarchist, Shaw actually "does not face the issue [of unlimited freedom] so squarely. He praises self-control in the artist Marie Bashkirtseff" (140). Yet Shaw's praise of Marie indicates how squarely he does face the issue; he brings her forth, not as a qualification of his argument, but as a demonstration that the realist is a person who must demand a good deal more of himself than his idealistic counterpart. For self-realization is impossible without the self-restraint the idealist lacks ("ideals are in practice not so much matters of conscience as excuses for doing what we like"—96, *1913*); without the self-scrutiny the idealist fears ("We still cannot bring ourselves to criticize our ideals, because that would be a form of self-criticism"—3, 3d Pref); without the inner control which is a very different matter from the sort of "conscience" that merely internalizes externally imposed norms.[11] If this is understood, it will be clear why in his later preface to *Immaturity* Shaw argues that the "grace of God"—conventionally seen as the source of moral values—must be deliberately rejected before a person's "birth of moral passion" can take place (xix–xx).

Contemporary readers are less likely to charge Shaw with being a flippant nonconformist than with being a naive progressive. To this second major objection one can reply that, while the purpose of the *Quintessence* undoubtedly was to legitimize the advocacy of programs for reforming late Victorian society, Shaw's implications allow little comfort to any reformer so rash

11. In Shaw's ethic, self-control is supremely important as a precondition for human development: "increased command over himself [is] the only sort of command relevant to [man's] evolution into a higher being" (*Caes* 197–198, Notes). Thinking out "the great central truth of the Will to Power . . . , [Nietzsche] had no difficulty in concluding that the final objective of this Will was power over self, and that the seekers after power over others and material possessions were on a false scent" (*Back* lii). (See also *Super* 183n, Rev Hdbk).

as to make this meaty little book his Bible. Once again, the matter hinges on the primacy of the concrete over the abstract. Any "ism" or doctrine must have a substantive content. Idealism and realism, however, have as much to do with the perspective in which beliefs are held as with the substance of such beliefs. The mere fact that Peer Gynt and Brand have opposite views does not make one a realist and the other an idealist: Shaw sees the two characters as different sides of the same coin of idealism. Similarly, when in the analysis of *Enemy of the People* Shaw inveighs against society's claim to collective authority over the individual, he warns his readers not to confuse his position with anarchism, which is "the idealization of the repudiation of Governments" (75).[12] A few years later in *The Perfect Wagnerite* (1898) he goes so far as to entitle a section "Panacea Quackery, Otherwise Idealism," in which he argues that the advocacy of *any* doctrine as a panacea is a form of idealism (216–217).

Since to the layman the word "Shavian" still connotes an attitude of cynical clownishness about things in general combined with the espousal of panaceas designed to produce Utopia, there is a common tendency to exaggerate the extent to which Shaw is a victim of his own "isms" and shibboleths. But his Fabian essays and tracts of the late 1880's and early 1890's hardly support this impression: for all the stylistic fireworks, they are cautionary and prudent documents. In them Shaw makes clear that "the state is not merely an abstraction; it is a machine to do certain work" (*EFS* 47); that "Socialism to me has always meant, not a principle, but certain definite economic measures which I wish to see taken" (*EFS* 65); that "no individual or society can possibly be absolutely and completely right . . . if

12. Basic statements of the Shavian attack upon anarchism may be found in "The Impossibilities of Anarchism" (*EFS* 65–99), the section of *The Perfect Wagnerite* called "Anarchism No Panacea" (222–223), the segment of *The Sanity of Art* called "Why Law is Indispensable" (304–309), the part of the preface to *Misalliance* called "The Provocation to Anarchism" (101–103), as well as in *IWG* 29–30 and *EPWW* 338.

we try to figure to ourselves a forcible reconstruction of society on lines rigidly deduced either from the Manchester School or from State Socialism, we are at a loss to decide which of the two would be more intolerable and disastrous" (*EFS* 115–116). A piece called "The Illusions of Socialism" (1896) attempted to force socialists themselves to come to terms with myths (for example, "the working class as a virtuous hero . . . in the toils of a villain called 'The Capitalist' "—*NDW* 415) they had generated concerning their own doctrines. Certainly readers of the plays will recall that the most typically Shavian heroes—men like Bluntschli, Caesar, Undershaft, and Magnus—succeed not because they believe in this or that "right" system, but because of their ability to respond resourcefully and without the prejudices that arise from a reliance upon "systems." Shaw is not advocating that we solve problems merely by substituting one formula for another: the "quintessence [of Ibsenism] is that there is no formula" (125). In short, he is at this stage of his career a thoroughgoing pragmatist.

As for the third major charge, that the *Quintessence* is a polemic in favor of indiscriminate relativism, the answer can only be that the book is, on the contrary, a protest against undiscriminating moralism:

There can be no question as to the effect likely to be produced on an individual by his conversion from the ordinary acceptance of current ideals as safe standards of conduct, to the vigilant open-mindedness of Ibsen. It must at once greatly deepen the sense of moral responsibility. Before conversion the individual anticipates nothing worse in the way of examination at the judgment bar of his conscience than such questions as, Have you kept the commandments? Have you obeyed the law? Have you attended church regularly? paid your rates and taxes to Caesar? and contributed, in reason, to charitable institutions? It may be hard to do all these things; but it is still harder not to do them, as our ninety-nine moral cowards in the hundred well know. . . . Substitute for such a technical examination one in which the whole point to be settled is, Guilty or Not Guilty? one in which there is no more and no less respect for virginity than for incontinence, for subordination than for rebellion,

for legality than for illegality, for piety than for blasphemy: in
short, for the standard qualities than for the standard faults, and
immediately, instead of lowering the ethical standard by relaxing
the tests of worth, you raise it by increasing their stringency to a
point at which no mere Pharisaism or moral cowardice can pass
them.   (123–124)[13]

While this passage is clearly related to what has been said already
about the nature of moral choice and the rejection of abstraction, it also makes clear that Shaw is not advocating the kind of
relativism that denies the possibility of values in life: what is
needed is *vigilant* open-mindedness, not the refusal to make judgments but the ability to judge without conventional preconceptions.[14] His frame of reference is that of humane values: the
case of such patently vicious behavior as murder is dismissed as
"too obvious in its ethics to leave any room for discussion" (135–
136, *1913*).[15]

The point is not that any act should be permitted, but that
"conduct must justify itself by its effect upon life and not by its
conformity to any rule or ideal" (125).[16] To say that behavior
should be judged by its effect clearly implies that there is a
shared assumption concerning what good effects are, and that
murder, theft, and rapine do not produce them:

It is enormously important that we should "mind our own business"
and let other people do as they like unless we can prove some dam-

13. In this passage, "virginity" originally read "chastity"; "qualities"
originally read "virtues"; and "faults" originally read "vices." The revisions first appear in the 1913 edition.
14. "The advantages of living in society are proportionate not to the
freedom of an individual from a code, but to the complexity of and
subtlety of the code he is prepared not only to accept but to uphold as a
matter of such vital importance that a lawbreaker at large is hardly to be
tolerated on any plea" (*Barb* 237, Pref).
15. Though specifically dealing with vivisection, Shaw's speech "The
Dynamitards of Science" (*P&P* 31–36) is an attack on all forms of extreme or indiscriminate relativism.
16. The word "life" (1913) originally read "happiness" (1891). The
significance of this change will be discussed below (p. 96).

age beyond the shock to our feelings and prejudices. It is easy to put revolutionary cases in which it is so impossible to draw the line that they will always be decided in practice more or less by physical force; but for all ordinary purposes of government and social conduct the distinction is a commonsense one. The plain working truth is that it is not only good for people to be shocked occasionally, but absolutely necessary to the progress of society that they should be shocked pretty often. But it is not good for people to be garotted occasionally, or at all. That is why it is a mistake to treat an athiest as you treat a garotter, or to put "bad taste" on the footing of theft and murder. (122, *1913*)

Other works by Shaw show the centrality of this point of view to his outlook on life. In his first surviving literary attempt, *My Dear Dorothea* (1878), he had in a few words struck off a definition of duty in the only sense that word ever had any legitimate meaning for him, that is, a "consideration for the consequences of one's acts" (26). Many times throughout his life he repeated the equivalent of the conviction that there is no test of the morality of an act "except the test of its effect on human welfare" (*Marr* 203, Pref). Many of his sharpest insights derive their pungency from the way a concrete morality of deeds belies abstract conviction: "What a man believes may be ascertained, not from his creed, but from the assumptions on which he habitually acts" (*Super* 217, Maxims).

The last quotation should remind us that all men—idealists, realists, or Philistines—rely on assumptions of some kind. Shaw's failure to make this explicit in the *Quintessence* invites the valid objection that the book's ethics are more sophisticated than the epistemological underpinnings from which they are supposedly derived. Even someone who agrees wholeheartedly with Shaw that "there is no golden rule" (125) can hardly deny that this very point is expressed by a special kind of rule: to wit, "all generalizations are invalid except this one." Similarly, it may indeed be the case that the test of a line of conduct should be its effect on life rather than its conformity to a formula; far from jettisoning principle, however, this standard attempts to prescribe a principle which is considered more valid than those usually invoked to decide ethical questions. Such logical sleights-of-hand result not from Shaw's lack of awareness of his own presuppositions, but from his rhetorical habit of exaggerating the contrast between his claims and those of his ideological adversaries. The reader of the *Quintessence* must be willing to exercise a corrective function to compensate for its author's fondness for transforming these differences in degree into differences in kind. I do not suggest that this tendency seriously impairs the force of Shaw's critique. But the trait goes far to explain why, despite his frequent claim to test, discard, and replace outworn creeds, Shaw's ideas are today less germane to those who believe in a radical restructuring of society than to those interested in making intelligent modifications of traditional value systems.

Shaw's apparent lack of concern for the logical problems raised by his rhetorical strategy can probably be explained by the topical nature of his essay on Ibsen; for when it was first published in 1891, the *Quintessence* was a work he could expect to ride the crest of the *Zeitgeist*. The book's social context is the assertion of individual rights against Victorian ideals of duty and respectability; its intellectual context is the Romantic primacy of the intuitive over the rational and of the immanent over the transcendent; its scientific context is the acceptance of evolutionary theories from which its special brand of relativism derives; its philosophical context suggests affinities with various figures from Hegel to William James.[17] One extract can fairly represent the tone of the whole: "[Ibsen] protests against the ordinary as-

17. The latter greatly admired Shaw's work: "Have you read B. Shaw's last volume, *John Bull's Other Island* [and *Major Barbara*]—the *most* utterly delightful body of truths I've ever had in my hands" (Perry II, 467). When Eric Bentley in *A Century of Hero-Worship* linked the names of Shaw and James (283–284), philosopher Sidney Hook expressed outrage in *The Nation* (October 7, 1944). But Bentley pressed his point in *The Playwright as Thinker* (340–341); and the treatment by Julian Kaye (86–100) has established beyond cavil the deep affinity between the two men.

sumption that there are certain moral institutions which justify all means used to maintain them, and insists that the supreme end shall be the inspired, eternal, ever growing one, not the external, unchanging, artificial one; not the letter but the spirit; not the contract but the object of the contract; not the abstract law but the living will" (122).[18] The reader who senses an inspirational quality in the cadencing of that language is quite correct. Though Shaw rejects both the primitive worship of Jehovah and the expiatory salvation of Christianity, his very attack on these and other forms of idealism affirms his belief that "all religions begin with a revolt against morality" (121) and that "Ibsen's attack on morality is a symptom of the revival of religion, not of its extinction" (121). The book's several references to Bunyan (see also 52, 121, 147–148), its praising of parable and revelation as ongoing processes (147–148), its recommending of the finest contemporary drama and philosophy as a modern contribution to Scripture (148), its affirming that rational formulations attempting to disprove religious doctrine are not in themselves adequate to answer ultimate questions (50)—all of these suggest the extent to which Shaw's pragmatism is prologue to a religious quest.

The Way of the World

Despite a persistent gibe to the contrary, the *Quintessence* cannot be dismissed simply as the quintessence of its author; and much of the criticism that has been directed against it is beside the point. We have been told, for instance, by Edmund Wilson (in Kronenberger, 142) that Shaw emphasized Ibsen's social significance at the expense of his art—an objection that would be more pertinent had Shaw not already explained that he is dealing with a single aspect, not the total accomplishment, of

18. In the 1891 edition, this passage read as follows: "[Ibsen] protests against the ordinary assumption that there are certain supreme ends which justify all means used to attain them; and insists that every end shall be challenged to show that it justifies the means." The revised text first appears in the 1913 edition.

his subject (12, 42). Others, such as Robert Brustein, complain that the use of the term "ideal" to mean a convention is mere "semantic confusion" (44n). Anticipating this criticism, Shaw argues that this usage was necessitated by Ibsen's own habit of having "harped on conventions and conventionalists as ideals and idealists" (29)—an observation that settles the matter finally because it happens to be true.[19]

It is easy to exaggerate the distortion Shaw made in the interests of distilling Ibsen's social "message" (42). Admittedly, the text is sprinkled with asides such as that which introduces his commentary on *John Gabriel Borkman:* "Poverty is mainly the result of organized robbery and oppression (politely called Capitalism)" (105, *1913*). But this polemical point is not central to Shaw's analysis of the play: his discussion has more to do with abuse of personal relationships than with social injustice on a broader plane. And even if such were not the case, the problem of the individual versus society is one upon which the thinking of these two men is very similar. For instance, Ibsen's distrust of "duty" and "self-sacrifice," his loathing of "expiatory" schemes of salvation, his affirmation of the joy of life and the purification of the will, even the eschatological implications of such symbols as the "button moulder" and the "Third Empire"—such ideas are so central to both Shaw and Ibsen that it is a waste of time to speculate about which dramatist's "quintessence" they are.

If Shaw had possessed a scholarly temperament, he could have

19. A case in point is the famous exchange between Parson Manders and Mrs. Alving in *Ghosts:* "MANDERS. . . . Have you forgotten that a son ought to love and honour his father and mother? MRS. ALVING. Do not let us talk in such general terms. Let us ask: Ought Oswald to love and honour Chamberlain Alving? MANDERS. Is there no voice in your mother's heart that forbids you to destroy your son's ideals? MRS. ALVING. But what about the truth? MANDERS. But what about the ideals? MRS. ALVING. Oh—ideals, ideals! If only I were not such a coward!" (VII, 222). There are also the famous tag lines—Rörlund's "banner of the ideal" in *Pillars of Society* (mentioned by Shaw), and Gregers Werle's "claim of the ideal" in *The Wild Duck.*

amassed considerable documentation to substantiate his view of Ibsen. Instead, he is so prone to strike off insights in a white heat of argument that he actually overlooks evidence to support his position. Ibsen once wrote, for example, "I have sometimes been called a pessimist: and indeed I am one, inasmuch as I do not believe in the eternity of human ideals. But I am also an optimist, inasmuch as I fully and confidently believe in the ideals' power of propagation and of development" (V, xv). That passage, not mentioned by Shaw, might easily have served as the motto of his own book on Ibsen in all respects but one; for despite Shaw's social meliorism, he does not—at *this* stage of his career—share the confidence Ibsen has placed in man's potential for self-development through ideals.

The basic soundness of Shaw's approach needs underscoring because much of the remainder of this chapter will deal with his distortions of Ibsen instead of his insights. It is hardly a novel premise that the particular way in which he distorts Ibsen tells us some significant things about Shaw himself; nonetheless, the attempt to specify precisely where his analysis goes awry will result in some surprises. The *Quintessence* implies more than it states. Some of what it implies even contradicts what it states.

It is first necessary to look more closely at the main terms: Philistine, idealist, and realist. Though these expressions do well enough as rule-of-thumb distinctions (and I shall occasionally make use of them in this way), to apply them rigidly either to Shaw's thought or to his plays is to idealize the very terminology Shaw marshaled in his attack upon idealism. To point out that human beings cannot really be categorized in this abstract manner is to affirm, not reject, the essence of the *Quintessence*. The fact that idealism seizes "on the weaknesses of the higher types of character" (118) suggests that the term will be rich in implications. To begin with, Shaw's book operates within the conceptual framework of evolutionary assumptions: "The need for freedom of evolution is the sole basis of toleration" (122, *1913*). Thus the Philistine, idealist, and realist should be understood not as static classifications, but as persons at different points on the same maturational journey. Moreover, the terms need not be used to pigeonhole people, but to suggest stages of development *within* a person—witness that in several of his discussions of Ibsen's plays, Shaw emphasizes characters (Nora Helmer, Rebecca West, Alfred Allmers) whose relation to the categories changes in the course of their respective dramas. There is no such thing as *the* realist in the abstract; it is rather "a case of 'The ideal is dead: long live the ideal!' And the advantage of the work of destruction is that every new ideal is less of an illusion than the one it has supplanted" (40). The Philistine and the idealist are potential realists at an earlier stage of development—in the very process of describing a man and woman who resort to illusions to mask the nature of their sexual passion, Shaw is careful to acknowledge that "the germ of the highest love is in them both" (37). The terms are not a series of disjunct categories, but a calculus of increasing self-knowledge, awareness, and mastery.

Shaw's writings supply a good deal of ancillary support for the hypothesis that it is possible for a man to be a Philistine in one way, an idealist in another, and a realist in a third. No author ever took more care to warn readers of the risks involved in drawing too sweeping conclusions from necessarily finite data. In his plays Shaw is fond of portraying persons who have profound insight and ability in one particular area of human endeavor—for instance, Higgins in phonetics or Isaac Newton in mathematics—but who are by no means free from prejudices and vanities in other respects. In real life he cautions us that "no eminence in a specific department implies even ordinary ability in any other . . . I may fairly claim to be an adept in literature; but in dozens of other departments I am a duffer" (*Far* 82, Pref; cf. *True* 9, Pref). These caveats regarding technical skills find their counterparts in the moral realm when Shaw insists that "no specific virtue or vice in a man implies the existence of any other specific virtue or vice" (*Super* 218, Maxims), or when he holds that very few men have more than one point of honor (*Super*

216, Maxims; *True* 61; *SSS* 103)'. In each of these instances, Shaw emphasizes the necessity of concrete differentiation. Thus to approach Shaw's own plays, as some critics have, by attempting to classify the characters neatly according to the terminology of the *Quintessence* is to indulge in precisely the kind of labeling that he tries to discourage. Because it contains three main characters, *Candida* has often been abused by this method. Morell, Marchbanks, and Candida have been debated endlessly in terms of *who* is the realist, the idealist, or the Philistine, with quite insufficient attention given to the possibility that any of the three characters can be seen as occupying any of those three categories depending both upon one's point of view and upon which particular scene one wishes to discuss.

The reader of the *Quintessence* who understands the specificity of the Shavian terminology will not be confused, as others have been, by an important passage, which seems to contradict itself by showing that the realist himself is a certain kind of idealist:

Here the admission that Shelley, the realist, was an idealist too, seems to spoil the whole argument. And it certainly spoils its verbal consistency. For we unfortunately use this word ideal indifferently to denote both the institution which the ideal masks and the mask itself, thereby producing desperate confusion of thought, since the institution may be an effete and poisonous one, whilst the mask may be, and indeed generally is, an image of what we would fain have in its place. If the existing facts, with their masks on, are to be called ideals, and the future possibilities which the masks depict are also to be called ideals—if, again, the man who is defending existing institutions by maintaining their identity with their masks is to be confounded under one name with the man who is striving to realize the future possibilities by tearing the mask and the thing masked asunder, then the position cannot be intelligently described by mortal pen. (29)

We need to bear in mind, to begin with, that both types of idealist have in common a view of how things ought to be. In the reactionary case, the idealist is saying that human nature *ought* to be fitted to ideals; in the progressive case, that ideals *ought*

to be fitted to human nature. For one, the emphasis is upon
conformity to absolutes in the past; for the other, loyalty is to an
ultimate in the future.[20] It is the difference between Parson Manders insisting that children *ought* to love their parents regardless
of the latter's virtues, and Brand assaulting conformity with a
vision of "things as they ought to be" in his battle for the perfect
Adam.

Both Manders and Brand are idealists in the sense that their
respective allegiances involve illusions. Manders's ideals, however, are mere lies—instances of what Shaw in "The Illusions of
Socialism" would call *flattering* illusions: those which enable us
to avoid painful realities and "reconcile us to the discomfort of
our lot or to inevitable actions which are against our consciences"
(*NDW* 407). Brand's ideals, on the other hand, are goals—instances of what Shaw would come to call *necessary* illusions:
those which are "the guise in which reality must be presented
before it can arouse a man's interest, or hold his attention, or
even be consciously apprehended by him at all" (*NDW* 408–
409). Thus Shelley is a realist because his ideals are "future possibilities" (goals) rather than "masks" (lies). Idealism has its
progressive and heroic—as well as its conventional and reactionary—side. Unfortunately, Shaw sometimes invites confusion by not making explicit whether he is using the term *ideal*
in the negative sense to describe self-deception that seeks to escape
"naked reality" (*NDW* 407) or in the positive sense to denote
"cheerful . . . incentives to men to strive after still better realities" (*NDW* 407). But while his chosen strategies of expression
in this matter are open to criticism, the substance of Shaw's
argument is both complex and, contrary to the usual charge,
logically consistent.[21]

20. I have taken the absolute/ultimate distinction from William James's
Pragmatism, 106.
21. To avoid confusion in developing my own argument, I shall hence-
forth use adjectives such as "progressive" or "heroic"—and "conventional"
or "reactionary"—to specify which variety of idealism is meant in the
few instances where the context does not make it apparent.

A deeper problem, however, arises when the subtlety of the insights summarized thus far is not carried forth into the actual analysis of Ibsen's drama. Shaw does not proceed, as one might expect from him on the basis of the quotation just discussed, to distinguish between Society and Shelley, between Manders and Brand, between the man "defending existing institutions" and the man "striving to realize the future possibilities"—in short, between the exemplars of the two kinds of illusions (flattering and necessary), which he would so carefully separate and contrast five years later. On the contrary, he seems determined to discredit all kinds of idealism—including that which is a manifestation of realism; and thus his real meaning flies directly in the face of his apparent message.

This will become clearer if we begin with what Shaw correctly saw as the first of Ibsen's major plays, *Brand*. To Shaw, Brand is an idealist, "a villain by virtue of his determination to do nothing wrong" (42). That such a phrase is an expected description of an idealist, but not quite of *this* idealist, is apparent from Shaw's own description: "Brand the priest is an idealist of heroic earnestness, strength, and courage. Conventional, comfortable, and sentimental churchgoing withers into selfish snobbery and cowardly weakness before his terrible word. 'Your God,' he cries, 'is an old man: mine is young'; and all Europe, hearing him, suddenly realizes that it has so far forgotten God as to worship an image of an elderly gentleman with a well-trimmed beard, an imposing forehead, and the expression of a headmaster" (42).[22] The interesting point about this passage is that Brand seems more like the Shavian realist than the idealist Shaw proceeds to make him out to be. If it is replied that Brand's idealism consists not in his views but in the fanaticism with which he pursues his ideal of the perfect Adam, the answer is that the Shavian realist has something of this quality too. Is there really much difference, for example, between the previously quoted

22. Only the first sentence of this passage appeared in the 1891 edition. The remainder was added in 1913.

"one man in a thousand" being ostracized and burned because he tells the others the embarrassing truth about the marriage system, and Brand being ostracized and stoned because he tells the people some embarrassing truths about their religion? Shaw attacks Brand for being the champion not of "things as they can be made, but of things as they ought to be" (42); but it is hard to find any criterion—except sheer emotional fiat—by which Shaw's own models of realism (Blake, Shelley, Ruskin, among others—30) are not open to the same charge. Ibsen himself had mixed feelings about his hero's call of "All or Nothing," seeing it as egotistical but nonetheless admirable. Shaw's sympathies, on the other hand, are at this point more with the various "imperfect Adams" in the play—those who continue to live their mundane lives and are steadfast only in their refusal to sacrifice themselves to Brand's exalted vision.

Shaw's bias is most pronounced in his handling of the last act. Nowhere, not even in *Enemy of the People,* does Ibsen present more viciously satirical portraits of stupid, self-interested bourgeois officialdom than in the dean, schoolmaster, sexton, provost, and mayor—with their inflated self-importance, their pompous moralizing ("When God desires a man to fall / He makes him an Original"—III, 204), and their use of religion as a means of controlling others (" 'Good Christians' means 'good citizens' "—III, 200). These are the idealists in comparison to whom Brand is heroic—for Ibsen. But here in its entirety is Shaw's description of the fifth act: "[Brand] is hailed by the people as a saint, and finds his newly built church too small for his congregation. So he calls upon them to follow him to worship God in His own temple, the mountains. After a brief practical experience of this arrangement, they change their minds, and stone him. The very mountains themselves stone him, indeed; for he is killed by an avalanche" (43–44). Brand's despair, his perception that the forces of respectable society use him as a tool, his loss of a congregation through the trick of a malicious lie, his struggle alone and upward into the avalanche—all of these for Shaw become "after a brief practical experience of this arrangement"! Of the dean, sexton, and schoolmaster, he says nothing.

Before suggesting why Shaw is reluctant for Brand to appear noble, it will be helpful to consider an even more peculiar analysis. Shaw's unsympathetic treatment of Mrs. Alving makes his essay on *Ghosts* the most distorted in the book. Like several other of Ibsen's plays, *Ghosts* might be said to begin at the edge of an abyss in the past—by the time the curtain rises, Oswald is doomed to die of venereal disease. An intelligent character, which his mother certainly is, can only hope to face the outcome stoically, but not to alter it. Yet Shaw chooses to tell the events of the history in the present tense without informing the reader exactly where the play as such begins: to read his analysis one might think, for instance, that Captain Alving was an actual character who died in the first act of the drama. The result of this method is that Mrs. Alving, instead of seeming the enlightened victim of mistakes in the dim past, seems like a person in complete control of her destiny at every point, who has only herself to thank for her final predicament.

Shaw's point of emphasis is rather strange, to say the least: "Ghosts, as it is called, is the story of a woman who has faithfully acted as a model wife and mother, sacrificing herself at every point with selfless thoroughness. Her husband is a man with a huge capacity and appetite for sensuous enjoyment. Society, prescribing ideal duties and not enjoyment for him, drives him to enjoy himself in underhand and illicit ways" (66). It is true that Mrs. Alving finally comes to understand that she was not simply a wronged woman, but was herself partially responsible for the Captain's degeneracy. For Ibsen, her growth into this full awareness is the main action and does not, in fact, emerge until late in the play. But Shaw places the above quotation at the very *beginning* of his discussion of *Ghosts*—as if the realization to which Mrs. Alving slowly and painfully comes were a self-evident truth that she ought to have known in the first place. In doing so, he ignores the woman's resistance from the beginning to the actions forced upon her by Manders, under-emphasizes what it indeed must have been like to have to live with Captain Alving (whom Shaw sees as brimming with *joie de vivre*), and makes Oswald's return too exclusively a catalyst for his mother's new awareness. Just as in discussing *Brand* Shaw overlooks the conventional idealism of the townspeople, so in *Ghosts* the obvious idealist (Manders) is mentioned only once in passing. But here the reason is not hard to find. Since by the beginning of the play events have already gone too far for Mrs. Alving's enlightenment to make any real difference in the outcome of the action, Shaw emphasizes the result of her former sub-servience to ideals instead of the process by which she grows into full awareness. By this means, he is able to dissociate that educative process from the tragic conclusion of the play. In short, preventable idealism has replaced incurable syphilis as the fatal element.

In a third example, *The Master Builder,* the tone of Shaw's comment is completely wrong. How many readers of Ibsen will feel that Shaw does full justice to Halvard Solness: "The Master Builder is a dead man before the curtain rises: the breaking of his body to pieces in the last act by its fall from the tower is rather the impatient destruction of a ghost of whose delirious whisperings Nature is tired than of one who still counts among the living" (91, *1913*). While one may grant that Solness is a hero who borders on the grotesque, surely he is not so con-spicuously cadaverous as this description would lead us to think. Although past his prime, Solness's unimpaired charisma is no mere "ghostly" reminder of his former vitality. And what of Shaw's selective summary of the action: "The play begins ten years after the climbing of the tower. The younger generation knocks at the door with a vengeance. Hilda, now a vigorous young woman, and a great builder of castles in the air, bursts in on him and demands her kingdom; and very soon she sends him up a tower again (the tower of the new house) and waves her scarf to him as madly as ever. This time he really does break his neck; and so the story ends" (96, *1913*). Granted that Ibsen's hero has a ruthless streak (as shown in his mistreatment of Kaia Fosli, the Broviks, and his wife) that makes him in one way an idealist, nevertheless Shaw's account ignores evidence of both Solness's self-insight and self-struggle in order to make him look merely ludicrous. While the ascent of the tower is partly an act of *hubris,* most readers will share to some extent Hilda's conviction that the master builder's final act is "terribly thrilling." But one finds no trace of heroism in the callous comedy of Shaw's précis.

If Shaw's main interest in the *Quintessence* had been to advocate progressive social doctrines, one would have expected characters such as the dean and mayor, Manders, and Mrs. Solness (not to mention Hjalmar Ekdal and Kroll) to be dealt with very harshly. Admittedly, Shaw is not enthusiastic about them; but these ready-made idealists figure hardly at all in his discussion of the plays. Instead, he is interested in exposing the errors of Ibsen's heroic idealists—Brand, Solness, Mrs. Alving, Rubeck—persons who in terms of his own prior definition have as much claim to be considered realists. To a point, Shaw's approach is commendable. Expressing concern for all people, not just the exceptional person, the *Quintessence* rebukes the "one man in a thousand" for his tendency to ignore the claims of common human nature and its unheroic failings.[23] And one can

23. This concern has been obscured by misunderstanding of Shaw's subsequent advocacy of the Superman. It should be noted that Shaw never believed in a cult of isolated great men, but rather in a "Democracy of Supermen" (*Super* 185, Rev Hdbk). He makes this point forcefully and consistently in *Wag* 214–215; *Super* xxxvii; *Barb* 207, Pref; *EPWW* 336–344; and *Back* 266, Post. Shaw naturally sees some persons as having capabilities immensely beyond the average. The proper role of the extraordinary individual, however, is not to dominate and exploit other people, but to use his gifts to raise the level of the mass of men (*EFS* 278). Even Andrew Undershaft, who makes no secret of despising the mob, explains that Cusins, Barbara, and he himself "must stand together above the common people" in order to "help their children to climb up beside us"

hardly urge as a defect that the resultant emphasis falls on Ibsen's most significant characters at the expense of straw men like Manders and Kroll. At the same time, one cannot help wondering why Shaw seems so determined to expose virtually every aspiring character in Ibsen as an idealist. Since the categories—Philistine, idealist, realist—are not absolutes, and no person yet living is free of illusion in all respects, why does Shaw so emphasize defects instead of positive qualities in discussing persons whose self-understanding considerably *exceeds* the average?

Intellectually aware of both his approach and the dangers it involves, Shaw constantly reminds his readers of "Ibsen's deep sympathy with his idealist figures" (118). He grants that Brand, "made terrible by the consequences of his idealism to others, is heroic" (48); that Julian was "on the way" to realizing the third empire (58); that Rosmer's "nature is a fine one" (78); and that Rubeck is "as able an individual as our civilization can produce" (111, *1913*). (Surely Shaw cannot intend such terms of praise to refer to the 29.9% of the population he has previously described as "idealists"!) He goes on to insist that Ibsen's heroes are "far above the criticism that sneers at idealism from beneath, instead of surveying it from the clear ether above, which can only be reached through its mists" (118–119). He even apologizes to the reader because he has himself "suggested false judgments by describing the errors of the idealists in the terms of [that is, from the perspective of] the life they have risen above rather than in those of the life they fall short of" (119). But it is not convincing for Shaw to claim that this procedure was necessary to make himself intelligible—the difference between the two methods is not one of intelligibility but one of tone. To survey idealists from above in terms of the life they fall short of would be to acknowledge their heroic aspirations toward the higher life. In contrast, to survey idealists from below in terms of the life

---

(*Barb* 288). During the 1930's and 1940's, however, Shaw's long-term democratic humanitarianism betrayed him into short-term reactionary politics.

they have risen above is to negate this heroic struggle by viewing it through Philistine glasses.

In the first part of this chapter, I dealt with a number of common objections to the *Quintessence* and countered them by showing that the underlying assumptions of Shaw's essay were not utopian but pragmatic. In my view, what Shaw finds so disturbing in his analysis of the specific plays is that idealism, even *heroic* idealism, is impractical. Brand may die a saint, but he has "caused more intense suffering by his saintliness than the most talented sinner could possibly have done with twice his opportunities" (44). Mrs. Alving may become fully enlightened, but nonetheless, at the final curtain, stands at the mercy of cruel alternatives that offer no hope. Solness may hear "harps in the air," but he is killed in the fall from the tower. Julian and Maximus may aspire "to build Brand's [rainbow] bridge between the flesh and the spirit" (54), but at the end Julian is dead and Maximus simply mistaken. Rosmer may wish to make his countrymen noble by "freeing their minds and purifying their wills" (IX, 42); may insist that with people who are emancipated "morality may be an instinctive law of their [own] nature" (IX, 65); may speak of "every mind, every will pressing forward—upward—each by the path its nature prescribes for it" (IX, 105)—all good Shavian precepts unmentioned by Shaw in his essay because at the play's end both Rosmer and Rebecca lie drowned beneath the mill bridge. Rubeck and Irene may climb the mountain, but they complete the circle begun by Brand and are crushed in the avalanche that concludes *When We Dead Awaken*. Heroic idealism does not pass the pragmatic test. What these men aspired to be, and were not, condemns them—in Shaw's mind.

But Ibsen is more of two minds on the matter. According to Shaw, readers "have sometimes so far misconceived [Ibsen] as to suppose that his villains are examples rather than warnings, and that the mischief and ruin which attend their actions are but the tribulations from which the soul comes out purified as gold from the furnace" (42). Yet Ibsen's heroic idealists are both examples *and* warnings; it is Shaw who sees them only as warnings. Although he will praise Don Quixote, Brand, and Peer Gynt because they are "all . . . men of action seeking to realize their ideals in deeds" (48), Shaw in fact, if not quite openly, believes that the dangers inherent in such attempts outweigh the likelihood of success. The price of idealism is that heroes will come to a point where "they ignore the real—ignore what they are and where they are" (48). Their kingdom is not of this world.

Thus it comes about that Shaw the pragmatist is far more interested in mounting an attack on *all* forms of "idealism" than in observing distinctions between progressive and reactionary varieties: "Whether, like Brand, we make such claims [of the ideal] because to refrain would be to compromise with evil, or, like Gregers Werle, because we think their moral beauty must recommend them at sight to every one, we shall alike incur Relling's impatient assurance that 'life would be quite tolerable if we could only get rid of the confounded duns that keep on pestering us in our poverty with the claims of the ideal' " (78). Here the lumping together of Brand and Werle brings the Shavian point of view to the clearest possible focus. The two characters are similar in that both impose themselves on other people, but while Werle's neurotic meddlesomeness is the essence of his personality, Brand's zealousness is a flaw in an otherwise noble nature. The perspective that sees the contrast between the two men as less striking than the similarity is identical with that which later rejoices when Irene and Rubeck climb upward into the avalanche: "That is the end of them and of the plays of Henrik Ibsen. The end too, let us hope, of the idols, domestic, moral, religious and political, in whose name we have been twaddled into misery and confusion and hypocrisy unspeakable. For Ibsen's dead hand still keeps the grip he laid on their masks when he first tore them off; and whilst that grip holds, all the King's horses and all the King's men will find it hard to set those Humpty-Dumpties up again" (115–116, *1913*). This wholesale housecleaning of idealism condemns not only the conventional idealist, but also the Ibsenite realist who is a heroic idealist. Shaw intuits that the prospect of implementing his own reformist goals will depend upon an ability to resist grand designs foredoomed to failure by the nature of the world. This is certainly the quintessence of what Shaw learned from Ibsen, though he was not quite fair to call it the quintessence of Ibsenism. Hence the disparity between the book's forcefulness as an expression of Shaw's own pragmatist ethic and its weakness as an exposition of the thought of Ibsen's drama. It is one thing to claim, as Peer Gynt does, that a hovel is a castle; but Ibsen never implies, as Shaw does, that *every* castle is a castle in the air.

2   Executive Power

▪▪

"Sonny" Transmogrified (The Novels)

In Shaw's first novel, *Immaturity* (1879), two minor characters debate the proper principles of child-rearing. Appealing
to scripture, Mrs. Watkins's view is "spare the rod and spoil the
child." In response to her more lenient husband's question—
"Who says that in the Bible [?]"—she answers Solomon. "Ah!"
Mr. Watkins chides, "Perhaps youll tell us what sort of fist [*sic*]
Solomon made of bringing up his own son" (240).[1] A few pages
later, a gifted artist named Cyril Scott is being told by the conventional Mrs. Summers that the deceased father of Harriet
Russell (the book's heroine) was a "dreadful" man. When Cyril
reminds Mrs. Summers of her own previous statement that the
gentleman had treated both his wife and his daughter very
kindly, she hastens to provide the clarification that Mr. Russell
was not dreadful "in worldly ways. But he believed in nothing."
Scott responds contemptuously, "Oh! Is that all?" (245). Still
later, Robert Smith, the book's young hero, is trying to improve
the mind of the shallow Belle Woodward, who asks if he really
believes "that virtue is its own reward in this world." Smith's
prompt reply: "If it were not . . . it would be vice" (384).

1. Rehoboam, Solomon's son and successor, was an inept despot who
provoked the northern tribes to secede from the kingdom of Israel. His
arrogant reply to the supplicating tribesmen suggests that he had bettered
the instruction received at his father's hands: "My father made your
yoke heavy, and I will add to your yoke; my father also chastised you
with whips, but I will chastise you with scorpions" (I Kings 12:14).

These examples illustrate Shaw's conviction that the value of a concept can be measured only by the concrete results it produces. Whereas Solomon's generalization may have sounded wise, it failed the pragmatic test of producing a virtuous son. Mr. Russell may have been evil according to the labels of conventional idealism, but his humane treatment of his family vindicates him. And Smith's answer is so bumptiously utilitarian that he incorporates virtue's being "its own reward in this world" as part of the definition of virtue. The other novels offer similar instances of Shaw's attempt to undermine abstract categories— when Conolly, the hero of *The Irrational Knot,* defines *truth* as "all that we know" (242), and when Cashel Byron protests his rejection from respectable society by asking what *harm* he has done by practicing his supposedly "anti-social and retrograde" profession of boxing (135–136). As these examples will serve to suggest, my main aim here is not to consider the novels as literary works, but to use them as preparation for coming to terms with the ethical stance of early Shavian drama. Like *The Quintessence of Ibsenism,* Shaw's fiction advocates a strongly pragmatic perspective—mainly (again like the *Quintessence*) by polemical use of negative counterexamples. *Immaturity* is particularly striking in this regard; for young Smith, the most aware and articulate character in the book, is a hopelessly impractical person.

Intelligent, literate, and very much at sea, Smith is incapable of decisive action. The closest he comes is his resignation from his position as a clerk for a carpet firm, but this climactic event one-third of the way through the book leads only to a secretaryship to an M.P., and finally to an application for entrance into the Civil Service. Shaw is very aware of his young anti-hero's "inveterate sententiousness" (266),[2] his tendency to attitudinize

2. The words "inveterate sententiousness" (Standard Edition) originally read "conceits" (1879). (I am grateful to Stanley Weintraub, editor of *The Shaw Review,* for the loan of a microfilm of Shaw's holograph manuscript of *Immaturity.*)

("Wretched sycophant that I am"—48), and his priggishness
("Women have no moral sense"—375). Indeed, it is hard to
know whether the portrait should be taken as the writer's attempt
as self-definition or self-parody. There are times when the author
and his hero seem similar—many of the observations of the
omniscient narrator (an authorial surrogate who is very close to
Shaw himself) would need only to be reworded in the first person to be taken for speeches of Smith. At other times, however,
the narrator comments sarcastically on the central character's
snobbery and callowness. Shaw even lures the reader into em-
pathizing with an utterance of Smith, only suddenly to draw
back and indicate that the sentiment was intended ironically.

"You dont mean to say that you are an atheist" said Isabella,
with sudden interest and a complete change of tone.
"Atheist is a bad counter for interpreting between us; for it probably conveys an entirely different impression to each of us. Further
it implies affirmation. My position is one of pure negation. I am an
Agnostic." He felt like Professor Tyndall or Mr Huxley as he spoke.
(269)[3]

While the torpedo in the concluding statement is a later addition,
there are many instances of the same technique in the original
version. I have simply chosen the example that most strikingly
illustrates this device.

The nature of Smith's dilemma is dramatized most concretely
in a debate with Harriet Russell, the efficient dressmaker to
whom he is attracted early in the book, concerning the merits of
a surveyor:

"I rather liked him [said Harriet]. He seemed a quiet, sensible
man, used to practical work."
"Which means" said Smith, "that he is exactly as narrow as his
profession."
"Or perhaps that he has had the energy to learn a profession that
suits him."

3. The last sentence of this passage (Standard Edition) was not in
Shaw's manuscript (1879).

"It may be so. He was fortunate to have had the chance of doing so."

"I do not see anything to prevent anybody from doing the same. . . . Push yourself; and get into business on your own account."

"That notion of 'pushing' yourself" said Smith dogmatically, "is a popular delusion—"

"Now, what is the use of your talking like that?" said Harriet, interrupting him deprecatingly, and almost impatiently. . . .

"Bosh!" said Smith. "I will prove to you in the clearest manner—"

"There is no use in your proving anything in the face of common sense. I know that people who set themselves out to do it can push themselves on and make their way in the world."

"True; but suppose it is not worth your while to set yourself out to do it. Suppose you enjoy yourself more in keeping out of the rush than scrambling in it, spending your life pushing and being pushed."

"You will be left behind, and laughed at, and be sorry afterwards. That's all." (92–93)

Smith's problem should not be confused with mere laziness, for he is as conscientious a clerk as Harriet is a seamstress. His difficulty is that, unlike Harriet, he cannot be content with a routine divorced from a sense of vocation. We may extol the discontent that leads Smith to "persuade himself that it was elevation of taste, and not want of capacity, that had led him to contemn his daily occupation" (93). But whereas the Standard Edition of 1931 allows us the option of concurring with Smith's high opinion of himself, the original manuscript (which reads "flatter" for "persuade") has an unambiguously negative force. In both versions of the work, the many comic juxtapositions of Smith's pretensions with his accomplishments express Shaw's view that mere refusal to fit into society is not enough.

The very opposite of Smith, Harriet lacks all conceptual ability, cannot assimilate the isolated facts she grasps so well (55), and responds to her friend's literary tutelage by concluding that Shelley is "a good book, only fit for children" (56). The "idealization of matter-of-fact" (257), she dwells alone and earns her living (in spite of the objections of relatives), is able to "sympathize . . . with worldly prosperity" (46), and can "appreciate a commercial argument" (191–192). Clearly attracted to these qualities of "matured self-possession" (298), Smith is from the start "awed by the impression of power which he received from her fine strong hands and firm jaw" (13). Although Smith's cultural and intellectual pretensions lead him to an "unjustifiable contempt" for his employers, who are "within their scope, useful if prosaic men" (11),[4] he is willing to overlook Harriet's lack of refinement because "it is the unconsciously acquired culture which comes from a lonely struggle with the world that really individualizes her" (220).

This last comment is one of many signals that Shaw does not regard Harriet as the drudge she has struck some critics as being. In the only book published on Shaw's novels so far, R. F. Dietrich argues that Harriet is "limited by the scope of the practical" (31) and that it is only her superiority to the affectation and rigidity of some of the minor characters that prevents readers from seeing her as "the Philistine she really is" (38). Dietrich's view seems reasonable enough—on the basis only of the long passage quoted above, one might easily conclude that Smith and Harriet are opposite sides of the same coin; that is, if he is aspiration without practicality, she is practicality without aspiration. Shaw of course might have written his novel to make exactly this point; in later works such as *John Bull's Other Island,* he would strongly criticize such unfortunate compartmentalizations of valuable human qualities. But that is not his purpose in *Immaturity,* where reader response is controlled so that Harriet's virtues undercut Smith's deficiencies without the process being reversible.

Shaw's strategy for accomplishing this feat is twofold. First, by having Harriet often described as "natural" (223), "unconventional" (223), "original" (258), "unique" (296), and so forth,

4. The words "if prosaic" (Standard Edition) were not in Shaw's manuscript (1879).

he makes it difficult to take her as a precursor of the 70 per cent of the population he went on to classify as Philistines in *The Quintessence of Ibsenism*. Since (as Smith avers) one "would never dream of referring [Harriet] to any standard outside herself" (223), she has without conscious effort achieved the self-realization for which Smith struggles in vain. Her charming qualities are not blunted by efficiency; rather her efficiency is humanized by charm. Shaw renders her character further immune to unfavorable comparison with Smith's by suggesting that, if she is not the Philistine she may seem to be, Smith *is* in some ways the Philistine he does not seem to be. Referred to as "matter-of-fact" (359), "Philistine" (414, *n.o.t.*), and "more like two yards of tape than anything else" (182), Smith's inability to practice Harriet's virtues by no means exempts him from sharing more pretentious versions of her faults. For instance, Harriet's prejudice that a female ballet dancer must be immoral (82) is no more snobbish than his own fear that some respectable acquaintances may spy him at the ballet hall he frequents. As Harriet is fond of passing off Smith's *bon mots* as her own, so many of his statements in turn sound like inadvertent quotations from controversial literature he has read. While her superiority to him in certain areas is very real, his superiority to her in others is only apparent.

Shaw's approval of Harriet is nicely pointed up in the book's final pages, when Smith pays her a last visit after she has passed him by and married Cyril Scott. Once again, her prosaic wisdom undercuts his probing skepticism:

"Is marriage really a success?" [inquired Smith.]

"What is the use of asking that? What else is there to do if you are to have a decent home? But it is not fit for some people; and some people are not fit for it. And the right couples dont often find one another as Cyril and I did. The routine for most is, one year of trying to persuade themselves that they are happy, six months of doubt, and eighteen months of conviction that the marriage is a miserable mistake. Then they get tired of bothering themselves over it, and settle down into domestic commonplace, quite disenchanted, but not tragically unhappy." (423)[5]

Harriet can only encourage Smith in the hope that some day he will "get away from [his] books and come to know the world and get properly set" (423, *n.o.t.*). He is, she concludes, a "bad case of immaturity" (423, *n.o.t.*). Harriet's last comment makes explicit the point of the novel—that Smith's "immaturity" is defined not in terms of his ideas and perceptions (which are in fact startlingly mature compared to those of the other characters), but in terms of his inability to translate his vision into action.

In his preface (1921) to *Immaturity,* Shaw analyzed the personal problems he was facing at the time the novel was written. It is not necessary here to summarize the account given of his boyhood, family, relatives, upbringing, employment as a clerk, and emigration to London at age twenty; suffice it to say that for all the hilarity of the piece, he appears as a lonely young man greatly disturbed by the same ineffectuality that plagued the jejune hero of his first book. Living an intense mental life as a boy, "Sonny" Shaw felt uncomfortable when he "had to come out of the realm of imagination into that of actuality" (xliv). Although certain he would some day be a great man, Shaw "remained diffident as ever" because he was still "incompetent as ever" (xxiv). In a fifty-page letter written in 1905 to authorized biographer Archibald Henderson, he is blunter still about the

5. A comparison of the Standard Edition with the holograph manuscript reveals that, in addition to heavily revising the body of the text, Shaw provided a new ending to replace the original's indecisive meandering to a close. Everything from "Is marriage really . . ." to " . . . Cyril and I did" is a later addition. The next sentence of Harriet's speech originally read: "The routine with most women is, one year of trying to persuade themselves that they are happy, six months of doubt, and eighteen months of conviction that marriage is an utter and miserable mistake." (The concluding sentence is identical in both versions.) I have retained the passage because Shaw's revisions clarify rather than alter the sense of the original.

nature of his difficulties during this period: "What was wrong with me then was the want of self respect, the diffidence, the cowardice of the ignoramus & the duffer. What saved me was the consciousness that I must learn to do something—that nothing but the possession of skill, of efficiency, of mastery in short, was of any use" (Henderson 57). Given the natural tendency for a person to exaggerate the value of qualities he lacks, it is understandable that Shaw would think Harriet's skill, efficiency, and mastery easily outweigh her lack of Smith's high mental attributes. Thus while it may be true that, seen objectively, Harriet is a Philistine, this judgment cannot be sustained in terms of the moral universe of the book itself. When Dietrich defends his own evaluation of Harriet by noting that Shaw never tired of "making the point that some Philistines, especially those unconventionally raised, are easily mistaken for Shavian 'realists' " (38), he overlooks that Shaw's fondness for making this point may have resulted in part from having fallen prey earlier in life to the identical error himself. Furthermore, if my first chapter is correct in finding pragmatism an indispensible component of realism, then to some extent *every* realist contains a healthy residue of Philistine.

Taking Shaw's fiction as a whole, Dietrich offers the theory that "what is being developed in these novels is not so much the art of the novel as the art of being Bernard Shaw" (52). In his view, Shaw begins with "the impregnation of the Shavian idea— Robert Smith being appropriately fetal in his undefined shapelessness" (193)—and then attempts in the heroes of later novels to redefine Smith's character in more satisfactory terms. These experiments at first produce little success. For instance, Conolly of *The Irrational Knot* (1880) is "a monster of the mind" (that is, of fanatical rationalism—89); Owen Jack in *Love among the Artists* (1881) is "a monster of the body" (of unconscious instinct—113). But the marriage of Lydia Carew and the prizefighter in *Cashel Byron's Profession* (1882) is, Dietrich contends, a symbolic union of mind and body; and *An Unsocial*

Socialist (1883) completes the process by recording "the birth of a relatively complete human being" (193), Sidney Trefusis. In this progression from novel to novel, the young writer "molded the soft clay of immaturity into the man and superman that everyone took for granted in the later Shaw" (52).

Although one may doubt the likelihood that five early books written during as many years could present their author's entire spiritual autobiography in microcosm, Dietrich's thesis has at least an initial plausibility. For in claiming that "every man who entertains a belief, or a disbelief, has a right to become a propagandist, both for the sake of testing himself and enlightening others" (414), the hero of Shaw's first novel would seem to anticipate perfectly the working method of the hero of his final one. I am almost tempted to think of the refined, shy Smith imagining himself to be the brash, flamboyant Trefusis, much as an inept sculptor might go to bed and dream of being Michelangelo. Thoroughly convinced of the value of work as "sustained and intelligently directed effort resulting in the production or attainment of some worthy end" (267), Smith lacked a clear set of beliefs to which he could dedicate himself. Trefusis's socialism compensates for such a defect with a vengeance: "With my egotism, my charlatanry, my tongue," crows Sidney, "I am fit for no calling but that of saviour of mankind" (104). Smith awkwardly attempted to assume a magisterial air with Harriet and Isabella; Trefusis unhesitatingly acts as tutor to the world. Smith's personal rebellion against "that arch scoundrel . . . Figgis, the carpet fiend, to whose depravity I have too long pandered" (164) sounds like a neophyte's version of Sidney's virtuous tirades against the whole society of which Figgis is a respectable member.

The attempt of "Don Juan Lothario Smith" (411) to flirt with Isabella foreshadows the more vigorous susceptibility of Trefusis to any woman within reach. In this area, too, the difference between the two men is that between a wish and its fulfillment. Which is precisely the problem: there is something suspiciously "neat" about the way Trefusis relates to Smith like a picture to a negative. This is not to deny that the novels reveal a progressive maturation of understanding, but one must redefine what it is Shaw has come to understand. In his handling of the heroes of *Immaturity* and *An Unsocial Socialist*, I would hold that the deepening of insight lies not in the contrast between the two characters themselves, but in Shaw's perception that Trefusis's relation to Smith is *not* that of an oak to an acorn. For despite the apparent force of his personality in comparison to Smith's, Trefusis has disguised rather than resolved the immaturity of his impractical predecessor.

In his treatment of *Immaturity*, Dietrich correctly argues that "if Shaw were interested only in propagandizing Shelleyan ideas, he most certainly would not have made his spokesman look foolish and immature in the expression of those ideas" (42). But this applies with even greater force to Trefusis, whom Shaw debunks by a similar method of luring the reader into taking him seriously and then suddenly shifting tone so that the character's pretentiousness is spoofed. Sidney lectures Henrietta, the overly amorous wife he has fled to devote himself utterly to his calling:

"Modern English polite society, my native sphere, seems to me as corrupt as consciousness of culture and absence of honesty can make it. A canting, lie-loving, fact-hating, scribbling, chattering, wealth-hunting, pleasure-hunting, celebrity-hunting mob, that, having lost the fear of hell, and not replaced it by the love of justice, cares for nothing but the lion's share of the wealth wrung by threat of starvation from the hands of the classes that create it. If you interrupt me with a silly speech, Hetty, I will pitch you into the canal, and die of sorrow for my lost love afterwards. You know what I am, according to the conventional description: a gentleman with lots of money. Do you know the wicked origin of that money and gentility?"

"Oh, Sidney; have you been doing anything?"   (67)

Viewed as set pieces, Trefusis's arguments can be cogent and spirited; but their context more often than not makes Sidney look ridiculous. Who else would seize upon Henrietta's death (of which he was the indirect cause) as an occasion to attack her distraught parent for being able to "bear death and misery with perfect fortitude when it is on a large scale and hidden in a back slum" (125)? The incongruity of means to ends also diminishes Sidney when he pursues his messianic frivolities on a huge income inherited from his capitalist father. His compulsive immersion in his socialistic credo is not a resolution of the problem posed by Smith's directionlessness, but a swing of the pendulum to an equal and opposite extreme. Far from being a completely realized human being, Trefusis is the ideological counterpart of the fanatical rationalism of Conolly and the fanatical impulsiveness of Owen Jack.

This is not to suggest that Trefusis is treated as a merely ludicrous figure. His rudeness to Jansenius after Harriet's death can be seen as the result of a displaced release of painful emotions. His defense of preaching socialism while practicing capitalism is in fact the same argument that Shaw himself repeatedly offered later in life whenever naive idealists asked him why he did not donate his fortune to the poor.[6] Although Sidney talks like a wild-eyed revolutionary predicting the smash-up of society, he acts like a bustling Fabian licking postage stamps and printing up handbills. The object of Shaw's satire here is less Trefusis himself than the tendency of respectable society to mistake political radicals for incarnate devils. Fully aware of the conventional reaction to him, Trefusis parodies its absurdity by deliber-

6. In addition to Sidney's defense of himself (212–213), see also *EFS* 44n; *Cash* 248–249, Note; *Super* 191, Rev Hdbk; *Barb* 220, Pref; *Mis* 67–68, Pref; *And* 51–52, Pref; *Back* lvii; *IWG* 95–99; *Cart* 180–181, Pref; and *Rocks* 185, Pref. Shaw's basic points are that socialism will be instituted by law and not personal righteousness, that a rich person who literally gives his wealth to the poor would render himself a pauper without making any lasting difference to the plight of others, and that an individual is more realistically engaged in working to implement socialism by constitutional means than in attempting to act as if he were king of some imaginary realm where a snap of the fingers would bring in the millennium. In Shaw's view, even beneficent charity (as distinguished from the patently self-serving philanthropy satirized later in *Major Barbara*) plays into the hands of privilege.

ately exaggerating the satanic role the average man assumes is his true nature.

Still, for all his cleverness, Trefusis cannot be said to pursue his goals effectively. The key to his weakness is not in what he does say, but in what he does not do. What we know of his history is not very promising—for instance, that he once ran for a seat in Parliament and "came out at the foot of the poll with thirty-two votes" (170). And what concrete results does he produce in the book itself? He brings a shepherd whose house has been blown down in a storm to the doors of a boarding school and requests (with didactic vehemence) that the proprietress give the man's family shelter for the night. He persuades the wealthy Charles Brandon to sign a petition supporting workers' rights to the fruit of their labors. (Sir Charles signs not because he has been convinced by Trefusis's arguments but because he wants an introduction to Donovan Brown, an eminent artist who has already joined the socialist cause.) Lastly, he marries Agatha Wylie, the book's attractive young heroine. But Lady Brandon's remark that Agatha "has taken enough trouble to catch" him (228) suggests that the firebrand may well end up with more than the "genial partner for domestic business" (248) he had bargained for, especially since Agatha privately regards him as "obstinate in his Socialistic fads" (244)!

This record of accomplishments suggests that Trefusis is not a transformed but a transmogrified Smith. The shy, mildly eccentric, and deftly satiric nature of the clerk has become the brash, sardonic, and militant façade of the revolutionary. Both men illustrate in different ways the problems inherent in trying to bring one's imagination to bear effectively upon life. Dietrich may indeed be right in viewing the novels as the expression of Shaw's ongoing experiment to discover a viable personality, as well as in arguing that Trefusis's character marks the creation of the theatrical image that Shaw himself was to exploit as a public man. But the hero of *An Unsocial Socialist* should not be seen as a prefiguration of the matrix of attributes which would later comprise the Superman, but rather as a prophetic critique of the ultimate failure of Shaw's public persona. For if Smith bears the same relation to Trefusis that "Sonny" Shaw bore to "G.B.S.," then the projected solution turned out to be an elaborately contrived restatement of the problem. The same frail spirit has merely been decked out in a garish new set of clothes.

As one might expect from Shaw's later analysis of Ibsen's plays, the novels are less concerned with exposing conventional idealists who use illusions to protect themselves against painful realities than with analyzing failed realists who cannot come to grips with a world that must take precedence even over the most noble idealism. The educative process that characters undergo in the novels is apt to move from high aspiration to blasé acceptance of things as they are. Mary Sutherland in *Love among the Artists* wants to set herself "aside from the ordinary world to live a higher life than most of those about me," but comes to feel that "I was born into the world: I have lived all my life in it: I have never seen or known a person or thing that did not belong to it. How can I be anything else than worldly?" (80). A hint of why Shaw's novels insistently foreshadow the *Quintessence*'s advocacy of the primacy of concrete action over abstract principles may be gathered from another character's suggestion that "all quixotism is tainted with spiritual vainglory" (*Love* 42). The more exalted the vision of a person, the more likely he is to be lured into committing the errors of those high-minded Ibsenite idealists who forget "what they are and where they are" (*Quint* 48). It is in protest against aspiration's undermining of efficiency that Shaw's novels tend to give a happier fate to the typically pedestrian person than to the visionary who is not enough of a Philistine to be a realist.

Realists, Militant and Triumphant (*Widowers' Houses, Mrs Warren's Profession, Arms and the Man*)

In 1892 Shaw completed his first play, *Widowers' Houses*. Drama textbooks have been content to follow the author's own description of this rough piece of work as a "grotesquely realistic exposure of slum landlordism" (*PUP* x). The spring of the action is the discovery made by young Harry Trench that the father of his fiancée, Blanche Sartorius, has made his money by renting out slum tenements. The scene in which Trench attempts to confront Sartorius with the moral implications of his occupation provides the first anticlimax in Shavian drama. Sartorius patiently responds that the good doctor is "a very young hand at business" (40) and proceeds to explain that if he were to repair the houses they would be wrecked by their occupants within a week. The point Sartorius ostensibly wants to make is that "when people are very poor, you cannot help them, no matter how much you may sympathize with them" (41). But the slum landlord is in fact stalking bigger game:

SARTORIUS. . . . And now, Dr Trench, may I ask what your income is derived from?

TRENCH (*defiantly*) From interest: not from houses. My hands are clean as far as that goes. Interest on a mortgage.

SARTORIUS (*forcibly*) Yes: a mortgage on my property. When I, to use your own words, screw, and bully, and drive these people to pay what they have freely undertaken to pay me, I cannot touch one penny of the money they give me until I have first paid you your seven hundred a year out of it. . . . It is because of the risks I run through the poverty of my tenants that you exact interest from me at the monstrous and exorbitant rate of seven per cent, forcing me to exact the uttermost farthing in my turn from the tenants. And yet, Dr Trench, you, who have never done a hand's turn of work in connection with the place,[7] you have not hesitated to speak contemptuously of me because I have applied my industry and forethought to the management of our property, and am maintaining it by the same honorable means. . . .

TRENCH (*dazed*) Do you mean to say that I am just as bad as you are? . . .

7. The words "you, who have never done a hand's turn of work in connection with the place" (Standard Edition) were not in the first edition of *Plays Pleasant and Unpleasant* (1898).

Sartorius. . . . If, when you say you are just as bad as I am, you
mean that you are just as powerless to alter the state of society,
then you are unfortunately quite right.   (41–42)[8]

In response Trench only "hangs his head and gazes stupidly at
the floor, morally beggared" (42) by his own attitude of complacent despair.

At the very least, this passage reveals a remarkable willingness
to give the devil his due. As Shaw was to point out in his preface
(1902) to *Mrs Warren's Profession,* "When the virtuous young
gentleman [in *Widowers' Houses*] rose up in wrath against the
slum landlord, the slum landlord very effectually shewed him
that slums are the product, not of individual Harpagons, but of
the indifference of virtuous young gentlemen to the condition of
the city they live in." (165). The scene is disturbing because we
have naively expected the engaging but shallow Trench (ironically
a doctor by profession) to rise to Sartorius's challenge with something more than a throb of conscience followed by a relapse into
comfortable acquiescence in the perpetuation of social diseases.
Sartorius remains despicable in his self-serving pessimism about
the inevitability of poverty; and Shaw in real life is the firm
advocate of a society organized to make his kind of livelihood
impossible. But in spite of that, the passage betrays a grudging
admiration for the efficient sinner who "very effectually" understands his position in the world and is not afraid to act upon it.
The dramatist's own comments confirm his admiration of Sartorius's "valuable executive capacities and even high moral virtues

8. Jerald Bringle's unpublished doctoral dissertation (New York University, 1970) illuminates the difficult textual problems of *Widowers'
Houses.* While Shaw made no important changes in the play after 1898,
the text printed in *Plays Pleasant and Unpleasant* of that year was itself
a revision of an earlier version published in 1893. Moreover, the first two
acts were drafted in 1884 and reworked in 1887. The important point here
is that Shaw's original 1884 shorthand draft contains a readily recognizable
—if crude—version of the "reversal scene," which I quote from the
Standard Edition of nearly half a century later. Hence the *ideas* this passage contains belong to the period immediately following composition of
An Unsocial Socialist in 1883.

in their administration" (*PUP* xxiii). In an appendix to a special preface written in 1893, he claims to have drawn Sartorius "as a man of strong and masterful character, unscrupulous but not a law-breaker, a kind and unselfish father, and much more reasonable and even magnanimous with Trench than the typical villa owner" (*CP* 706). A letter Shaw contributed to the press controversy aroused by the play tended further to discomfit his critics:

They denounce Sartorius, my house-knacking [*sic*] widower, as a monstrous libel on the middle and upper class, because he grinds his money remorselessly out of the poor. But they do not (and cannot) answer his argument as to the impossibility of his acting otherwise under our social system; nor do they notice the fact that though he is a bad landlord he is not in the least a bad man as men go. . . . I will not ask those critics who are so indignant with my "distorted and myopic outlook on society" what they will do with the little money their profession may enable them to save. I will simply tell them what they *must* do with it, and that is follow the advice of their stockbroker as to the safest and most remunerative investment.   (*CP* 709–710)

Shaw pays his efficient villain the compliment of insisting that he be taken seriously. But he goes further in portraying Sartorius as a man whose perceptions are valid as far as they go. In his ability to see through idealistic obfuscation, his understanding that *all* money is tainted, and his subtly cogent justification of his own actions, Sartorius resembles a preliminary sketch for the character of Andrew Undershaft. His lack of the underlying compassion that leavens Undershaft's apparent brutality does not alter the fact that the later hero's achievement rests firmly on this predecessor's foundations. As we shall see, it is not possible to understand more than Sartorius without first understanding as much. For the time being, it will suffice to recognize in the central figure of Shaw's first play a projection of the failed novelist's intuition that it is better for an individual to have executive power without noble ideals than the reverse.

Like *Widowers' Houses, Mrs Warren's Profession* deals with a moneyed parent confronted by a daughter's accusation concerning the unsavory sources of the family income. This parallel provides the first example of what is to become a typical Shavian device of relating plays to one another dialectically. When Shaw finds that he has written himself into an unforeseen problem, he will often return in a later work to an analogous situation in order to come to grips intellectually with the product of his artistic intuition. After *Widowers' Houses* he may well have been chagrined to have produced the venal Sartorius as a solution to his search in the novels for an exemplar of self-reliance and efficiency. It would next be necessary to distinguish vicious from responsible pragmatism—and to do so without resorting to a hero whose radiant beneficence would lure audiences into uncritical acceptance of his ethical premises. In *Mrs Warren's Profession* Shaw creates a heroine in some ways as anti-social as Sartorius and attempts to justify her actions as the tenable response of an ordinarily well-disposed nature to a cruel social predicament. His aim is not to recommend this woman's specific behavior as a model for emulation, but to attack the society which in effect left her no alternative course of action. Nonetheless, by providing Mrs. Warren with a strong ideological adversary—a daughter endowed with greater mental resources and moral awareness than the snobbish Blanche—Shaw forces himself to define, clarify, and defend his own positive attitude toward the ethical assumptions (as distinct from the *occupation*) of his disreputable heroine.

In order to render her more sympathetic than his impressive slumlord, Shaw details the sordid circumstances of Mrs. Warren's early life. While Sartorius referred at one point to his mother's standing "at her wash-tub for thirteen hours a day" (56), nowhere in *Widowers' Houses* did Shaw suggest that privation was the scourge that drove his hero to a vicious occupation. Whereas Blanche smugly dismissed the plight of her grandmother, Vivie pays serious attention to *her* grandmother's predicament in trying to support four daughters on the income from a fried-fish shop. By the time Mrs. Warren describes how her half-sister died of poisoning in a whitelead factory where she was employed for starvation wages, we almost applaud the decision of her sister Liz and herself to avoid a similar fate by becoming prostitutes and eventually setting up a syndicate of brothels. Mrs. Warren's apology constitutes a condensed recapitulation of much that Shaw had been trying to say since he began writing: "I always thought that oughtnt to be. It *cant* be right, Vivie, that there shouldnt be better opportunities for women. I stick to that: it's wrong. But it's so, right or wrong; and a girl must make the best of it. . . . Dont you be led astray by people who dont know the world, my girl" (212). Here the common ideals of what is "right" and what "ought" to be are juxtaposed with the reality of the "world" and what "is." Like the Shavian realist described earlier, Mrs. Warren has violated the canons of morality not from a taste for nonconformity, but from a conviction that the ethics of a line of conduct can be tested only pragmatically. She readily admits that she "always wanted to be a good wo-man," but recognizes that the effect of attempting to act on this principle was to be "slave-driven until I cursed the day I ever heard of honest work" (246). Thus when Vivie sentimentally asks if her mother would not have advised her to go into the factory if they too had been poor, Mrs. Warren replies indig-nantly: "Of course not. What sort of mother do you take me for! How could you keep your self-respect in such starvation and slavery? And whats a woman worth? whats life worth? without self-respect!" (212).

This Shavian realist's self-esteem comes from an intuitive conviction of the validity of her own will, not from a conscience that is only the internalization of conventional norms. When Vivie, responding to her mother's claim to despise people with no character, asks whether it isn't "part of what you call character in a woman that she should greatly dislike such a way of making money," Mrs. Warren blandly replies: "Why, of course" (211). In other words, the ethical worth of her choice of vocation can only be decided on the basis of the special circumstances that provoked the decision and the results it subsequently produced. While Mrs. Warren has committed acts that would outrage many, she nonetheless has deep moral passion. It is precisely because she is not a woman of principle that she can be a woman of integrity.

While Mrs. Warren believes in knowing "what the world is really like" (243), the basically humane impulses motivating her relativism prevent our confusing her with a crass Philistine like her wealthy "partner," George Crofts (the Sartorius-figure of the play). More of a challenge is involved, however, in defending her from the charge that she is an idealist—in her conventional notions about her parental "rights," for example ("Treat my own daughter with respect! What next, pray!"—186). But since we have already shown that Shaw's definition of the *Quintessence*'s ethical categories does not preclude a person's being an "idealist" in one respect and a "realist" in another, Mrs. Warren's clear-sightedness concerning her own rights is not discredited because she is blinded by convention in regard to her daughter's. The matter is complicated because Vivie, while certainly a more large-minded person than her mother, is in some ways an idealist too. She is not immune from her own illusion, a "fancy picture" (*Quint* 27) of herself as taut, tough, and imperturbable. Though she is proud that others can depend upon her "not to cry and not to faint" (238), her claim seems defensive in view of the maudlin quality of her "baby-talk" love scenes with Frank Gardner (211), her pointing a rifle at her breast and telling Frank "Fire now. You may" (228) after being disillusioned by Crofts, and her somewhat excessive contempt for her mother's "cheap tears" (245) in the final scene. There is heavy irony in Vivie's declaiming that people can make their own circumstances (209) without realizing that her relative freedom has been made possible only by the opportunities her parent provided. In pointing out that Mrs. Warren is "not a whit a worse woman than the reputable daughter who cannot endure her" (*Mrs W* 165, Pref), Shaw makes explicit that neither character can be regarded as his spokesman in an absolute sense.

Since Vivie herself is not free of sentimental idealism, we must carefully scrutinize her grounds for rejecting her mother at the end of the play. The gist of her argument is given in the following speech: "If I had been you, mother, I might have done as you did; but I should not have lived one life and believed in another. You are a conventional woman at heart" (246). One reason for Vivie's conclusion is the discovery that her now well-to-do parent still practices the "profession," partly from a love of material comforts and partly because it offers work and excitement to a woman who now has nothing better to do (244–245). Yet Vivie's legitimate antipathy on this point is the instrument not of Shaw's negative judgment of his heroine, but of his outrage against the civilization ultimately to blame for her maimed vitality. In the preface Shaw holds that "though it is quite natural and *right* for Mrs Warren to choose what is, according to her lights, the least immoral alternative, it is none the less infamous of society to offer such alternatives" (166). That she has become so inured to prostitution as to be not "fit" for anything else (244) keeps firmly before us the narrowing of potential that has resulted from her relatively correct decision.[9] But a more sympathetic person than Vivie might have found such a waste tragic rather than disgusting.

Still, the main basis for Vivie's charge that her mother is a "conventional woman at heart" is to be found in Mrs. Warren's plea to her: "Havnt I told you that I want you to be respectable? Havnt I brought you up to be respectable?" (243). This contradiction between the woman's own life and her ambitions for Vivie has convinced one critic that she is "a thorough hypo-

9. This narrowing occurs whenever human beings act in such a way that their characters become defined primarily in terms of a single attribute instead of a harmonious balance of qualities. As we shall see, such psychic compartmentalization amounts practically to a definition of Shaw's conception of tragedy.

crite; that is, a thorough idealist" (Nethercot 39). In evaluating this claim, we must first note the context of Mrs. Warren's remark—an offer she has just made to give Vivie an opportunity to "make friends" with some of her influential acquaintances. Sensing that Vivie may misinterpret her motive, she immediately adds: *"I dont mean anything wrong:* thats what you dont understand . . . Havnt I told you that I want you to be respectable?" (243—italics mine). She invokes respectability to prevent Vivie from misinterpreting her offer as an indirect invitation to enter the business. But to deal directly with Nethercot's charge of hypocrisy, the *Quintessence* has already shown us that a belief in uniform application of ethical principles is itself an *idealist* syndrome, and that often the apparent hypocrisy of a resourceful inconsistency is the only weapon the realist has to wield against the real hypocrisy of society's moral absolutism. After all, Mrs. Warren's quarrel had never been with the *professed* ideals of respectable people, but with society's sanctimoniousness in stigmatizing her as a "bad" woman because she refused to allow those ideals to be used to manipulate her into a false position. For Mrs. Warren to be a prostitute and want her daughter to be respectable would be hypocritical only if her original motive for entering the "profession" had been an innate love for it, rather than a realization that solid material foundations are the precondition for any hope of a better life. And since the poignancy of her situation depends on her having had the strength to embrace a repugnant course of action because she felt it to be pragmatically unavoidable, there can hardly be valid objection to her having insured that Vivie will never need to commit a similar outrage against her own nature.

It is of course true that Mrs. Warren is attempting to use her daughter to consolidate her own position as a respectable mother, and from that demand Vivie must necessarily break free. But it is also true that the middle-aged woman who wants her daughter to be reputable is no more "conventional" than the former young girl who would rather "have gone to college and been a lady if

I'd had the choice" (208). Strictly speaking, Mrs. Warren could only have avoided her daughter's charge of "conventionality" if she had sent Vivie into a whore-house. *That* was the alternative to respectability—in the real world. But Vivie can no more understand this than Barbara can later understand Undershaft when he claims to have "saved her soul" by saving her from physical privation. Unable to break free from inflexible moral categories, Vivie falls back on being "right" (246), only to leave herself open to her mother's pertinent reply: "Lord help the world if everybody took to doing the right thing!" (247). By attacking her parent as morally inconsistent, Vivie reveals her own idealistic presuppositions as well as her lack of understanding of the real nature of Mrs. Warren's pragmatism. But readers of the early novels and the *Quintessence* should not make the same mistake.

In *Mrs Warren's Profession* Shaw's defense of his heroine was the instrument of a powerful satirical attack on the wrongs of society. But in his next play, *Arms and the Man*, the affirmation of a heroic relativist becomes his *primary* purpose. To this end, a shift from an "unpleasant" to a "pleasant" ambiance is necessary. Despite *Arms and the Man*'s exposure of the fraudulence of military ideals, the grim realities of warfare are rarely allowed to intrude into the play's genial atmosphere. The innocuous pretensions of Bulgarians who pride themselves on washing their hands daily and installing an "electric bell" in their home can hardly arouse the wrath we felt when Sartorius fired his assistant for spending twenty-four shillings to repair a staircase. Moreover, Captain Bluntschli, the amiable pragmatic hero, does not invite the objections even a sympathetic reader might make to Mrs. Warren's more overtly domineering character. By concentrating on human foibles instead of human crimes, the playwright is able to subordinate satirical elements to his main end of creating a hero who embodies the moral position Shaw had been defining in his previous novels, essays, and plays. One convenient way to dramatize this concrete ethic is simply to have Bluntschli act directly as spokesman for it. But the real force of Shaw's attack on abstraction lies in the way the action of the drama unfolds. After arousing our expectations that his stage-types will act according to certain obvious behavioral principles, Shaw lets the real human beings start bursting through the play's own artificial comedic scaffolding. Thus he makes his doctrinal point brilliantly by using art to subvert doctrine.

Captain Bluntschli is a "professional" soldier who fights for cash, runs away from battles, and carries chocolate creams in his cartridge case. His "professional point of view" allows no room for honor, valor, or other idealistic pretensions. When the young lady into whose bedroom he has escaped accuses him of being afraid to die, he charmingly offers his soldier's credo: "It is our duty to live as long as we can" (8). When Raina, the young lady in question, later insists that she has lied only twice in her life, Bluntschli replies, "Dear young lady: isnt that rather a short allowance? I'm quite a straightforward man myself; but it wouldnt last me a whole morning" (49). When asked to "judge" the eavesdropping servant Louka, he refuses: "I musnt judge her. I once listened myself outside a tent when there was a mutiny brewing. It's all a question of the degree of provocation" (63). Bluntschli's reaction to a dueling challenge from Sergius Saranoff, the heroic attitudinizer who is Raina's betrothed, is characteristic:

SERGIUS (*gravely, without moving*) Captain Bluntschli.
BLUNTSCHLI. Eh?
SERGIUS. You have deceived me. You are my rival. I brook no rivals. At six o'clock I shall be in the drilling-ground on the Klissoura road, alone, on horseback, with my sabre. Do you understand?
BLUNTSCHLI (*staring, but sitting quite at his ease*) Oh, thank you: thats a cavalry man's proposal. I'm in the artillery; and I have the choice of weapons. If I go, I shall take a machine gun. (58)

Later Sergius calls off the duel and is amazed that Bluntschli doesn't care why: "I didnt ask the reason when you cried on; and I dont ask the reason now that you cry off. I'm a professional soldier: I fight when I have to, and am very glad to get out of it when I havnt to" (61). Two pages later when Bluntschli averts an argument between Raina and Sergius, the latter wants to describe his intervention as "Swiss civilization nursetending Bulgarian barbarism" (63). Bluntschli's reply: "Not at all . . . I'm only very glad to get you two quieted" (63). Upon what is Sergius's foolishness based? Illusions. Principles. Abstractions. Ideals. Upon what is Bluntschli's success based? In his own words: "Instinct, and experience of the world" (50)'.

The triumph of the pragmatist over the idealist is also the triumph of instinct over rationalism. While this point follows naturally from the premises of the *Quintessence,* it has not been fully appreciated because readers are apt to follow the lead of Sergius, who is as certain that he is passionate as he is that Bluntschli is mechanistic:

> SERGIUS. I refuse to fight you. . . . The reason is that it takes two
>   men—real men—men of heart, blood and honor—to make a gen-
>   uine combat. I could no more fight with you than I could make
>   love to an ugly woman. Youve no magnetism: youre not a man:
>   youre a machine.
> BLUNTSCHLI (*apologetically*) Quite true, quite true. I always was
>   that sort of chap. I'm very sorry.   (61)

The verbal abstraction upon which all idealization depends makes it difficult to grasp what it really means to follow one's own impulses. The proverbial "man of honor" who kills his wife upon discovering that she is unfaithful is considered passionate; does this mean that the man who wishes his wife no harm under the same circumstances is to be judged "unfeeling"?[10] In fact the

10. In the futuristic "As Far as Thought Can Reach," a scientist named Pygmalion manufactures two "artificial human beings" (Shaw's ironic description of normal twentieth-century man). These creatures can make love, spew rhetoric, imagine they are kings and queens, know that those who differ from them are damned, and consider themselves passionate; but Martellus explains that the two are in fact "automata" who only respond to external stimuli: "Give them a clip below the knee, and they will jerk their foot forward. Give them a clip in their appetites or vanities

"passionate" man in question is only acting out a socially conditioned response; it is the second man who may have impulses that are not reducible to mere postulates of external forces. The world, however, flatters its crimes by reversing this judgment—and indeed, whenever characters come along in Shaw's plays who, in R. J. Kaufmann's phrase, "take their emotional . . . cues from themselves" (2), the other characters in the play (not to mention the critics) will almost inevitably find such persons to be possessed by a cold, inhuman rationalism.

As a case in point, take Bluntschli's reply quoted above: "I always was that kind of chap. I'm very sorry." Sergius can no more see that this response expresses feeling than Alan Jay Lerner could see that in *Pygmalion* it is Eliza's *refusal* to marry Higgins that makes her a passionate woman.[11] It is Sergius himself, for all his conscientious intensity, who is automatic; for he is an emotionless repository of stock reflexes, a man whose little quirks and mannerisms (such as folding the arms grandly and intoning, "I never withdraw . . . I am never sorry") follow a logic as predictable as the movements of a toy soldier. He reacts, in Shaw's words, "like a repeating clock of which the spring has been touched" (66). And it is Bluntschli who, in his calm reasonableness, leaves room for impulse in life and thus becomes, as he says at the play's climax, a man of "incurably romantic disposition" (68). Again, the abstract use of a term like "romantic"

---

or any of their lusts and greeds, and they will boast and lie, and affirm and deny, and hate and love without the slightest regard to the facts that are staring them in the face, or to their own obvious limitations" (*Back* 227). The climax of the scene results from the mechanical female having an angry fit, in which she kills Pygmalion. When the denizens of the future react to this deed by regarding her with loathing and disgust, the male figure turns on them and whines: "Have you no hearts?" (234).

11. See "Pygmalion and My Fair Lady," *Shaw Review,* I, 10 (1956), 4–7. The best rebuttal to Lerner's rationale for his emasculated ending was provided by Shaw himself fifty years earlier in one sentence of the preface to *Mrs Warren's Profession:* "The clamor for naturalness and human feeling, raised by so many critics when they are confronted by the real thing on the stage, is really a clamor for the most mechanical and superficial sort of [stage] logic" (168).

misleads readers—they look upon this revelation as an indication that Bluntschli himself is discovered to be a fool. There is a grain of truth in this, as we shall see; but Shaw's point is rather that, as a result of his pragmatism, Bluntschli can be romantic without being ridiculous. For the kind of romance Sergius embodies is a susceptibility to romantic *illusion;* Bluntschli's, in contrast, is simply an openness to the full range of life's zany possibilities: "I ran away from home twice when I was a boy. I went into the army instead of into my father's business. I climbed the balcony of this house when a man of sense would have dived into the nearest cellar. I came sneaking back here to have another look at the young lady . . . " (68). By its very "Anti-Romantic" (*PP* xix) quality this drama gives full play to the romance of life. Bluntschli may be the compleat Utilitarian, but his never resisting temptation suggests that his character owes more to Blake than to Bentham.

Besides being a man of impulse, Bluntschli is a splendid instance of the hero as a man without preconceptions rather than one who insists upon his individuality. It is true that the play abounds in epigrams of egotistical disillusionment, such as, "you are right to take this huge imposture of a world coolly" (63), or "give me the man who will defy to the death any power on earth or in heaven that sets itself up against his own will and conscience: he alone is the brave man" (56). But the cream of the jest here is that these very Shavian-sounding sentiments are actually spoken by the Byronic ass Sergius, who quite accurately describes Bluntschli as "a commercial traveller in uniform. Bourgeois to his boots" (30). No wonder the latter does not scruple to admire Nicola, the wily and self-effacing servant who owes his prosperity entirely to the expertise with which he plays the role of underling.[12] In Shaw's view it is Bluntschli, the casual man

12. Nicola is the first example of a group of characters in Shavian drama who might be dubbed "superservants." These include the impeccably effective William the waiter in *You Never Can Tell;* the "admirable" Bashville in Shaw's play of that name; Collins in *Getting Married;*

of the world, who is the individualist; it is Sergius, the studied individualist, who is conventional.

Sergius's saving grace is that even his folly is only an attitude; in point of fact he is no more taken in by romantic and military ideals than Bluntschli. He is constantly reveling in the fraudulence of his own military attainments; and as for the "higher love" he espouses, his beloved Raina needs only to leave the stage for him to observe that it is indeed a "very fatiguing thing to keep up for any length of time" (33)—so fatiguing that he eventually marries a practical servant to escape from her, just as Raina marries the practical soldier to escape from him. Sergius's problem is not stupidity but scorn. Seeing just as clearly as Bluntschli that ideals are in conflict with things as they are, he does not have the sense to scrap the ideals but instead resorts to misanthropy directed against everyone (beginning with himself). Whereas Bluntschli sees the discrepancy between the ideals and the world and concludes (as it were) "so much the worse for the ideals," Sergius sees the same discrepancy and concludes "so much the worse for the world." As Shaw points out in a revealing aside,

---

Juggins in *Fanny's First Play;* and Private Meek in *Too True to Be Good.* All of the superservants are pragmatists who have mastered their profession totally; their effectiveness does not involve individualistic aspiration; quite the contrary, they become flustered *only* when circumstances threaten to remove them from their strictly servile footing. (Cf. "The perfect servant, when his master makes humane advances to him, feels that his existence is threatened, and hastens to change his place"—*Super* 217, Maxims.) Thus Nicola, when accused of having "the soul of a servant," replies: "Yes: thats the secret of success in service" (23–24); William feels "at a great disadvantage" when the appearance of his son (Bohun the barrister) at the hotel throws him off his "proper footing" (279); Collins, though really an alderman, knows that his "secret in business" is that his customers "can always spot" him as a greengrocer (*Marr* 259–260); Juggins, after the discovery that he is of noble birth, calms his middle-class employers by insisting that he "should be treated as a footman" (*Fanny* 310); Meek "could be an emperor if he laid his mind to it: but he'd rather be a private. He's happier so" (*True* 93) because he is indispensable in that position. Hence Shaw's respect for persons who succeed by mastering their circumstances within the conventional system.

"his jejune credulity as to the absolute validity of his concepts and the unworthiness of the world in disregarding them" (27) has led him into a cynical Byronism which is only the mirror image of standard conformity. Sergius observes that "everything I think is mocked by everything I do" (58) and concludes that the world is a farce; Bluntschli simply asks him to reconsider what he thinks: "Now that youve found that life isnt a farce, but something quite sensible and serious, what further obstacle is there to your happiness?" (61). And since Sergius is actually an incipient pragmatist without the courage of his convictions, he can rise to sense just as Bluntschli can fall into nonsense. Bluntschli will eventually praise his rival's decision to marry Louka: "My congratulations. These heroics of yours have their practical side after all" (67), just as Sergius will greet Bluntschli's massive miscalculation concerning Raina's age and feelings: "Bluntschli: my one last belief is gone. Your sagacity is a fraud, like everything else. You have less sense than even I" (69). For pragmatism involves the rejection of formulae, including the formula that says the pragmatist is always correct.

With *Arms and the Man*, Shaw completes the first full phase of his exploration of the problem of self-realization. The novels had expressed an urgent conviction of the primacy of action. The pressing nature of the problem for which neither *Immaturity* nor *An Unsocial Socialist* had found a solution would greatly influence the meaning attributed to "idealism" and "realism" in *The Quintessence of Ibsenism* several years later. The realism which at the beginning of that essay seemed to denote what in normal parlance would be called noble idealism turned out in the ensuing analysis of Ibsen's plays to connote a steadfast pragmatism. Thus it is not suprising that the efficient slumlord of Shaw's first play became more confidently self-justified than was quite advisable for the point the drama was trying to make. Realizing the pitfalls inherent in the very plausibility of Sartorius's adroit ethical cant, Shaw in *Mrs Warren's Profession* sought to distinguish his heroine's realism from both the crass Philistinism of

Sartorius and the hypocritical idealism for which some critics have mistaken it. Having thus clearly defined his ethical position, Shaw in his next work depicts a paragon who actively embodies its success. I do not mean to suggest that *Arms and the Man* should be viewed as a climax in his development; for it will soon become apparent that the play avoids coping with difficulties that would have made the triumph less complete. But it is typical of the searching quality of Shaw's mind that, having made his case with *Arms and the Man,* he immediately began to re-examine, qualify, and develop it further in his next plays. Before we go on to these works, however, it will be helpful to recapitulate briefly the main line of argument concerning the nature of Shavian pragmatism.

The Pilgrim as Pragmatist

In his preface to the *Plays Pleasant* (1898) Shaw wrote: "I have acquired the politician's habit of regarding the individual, however talented, as having no choice but to make the most of his circumstances" (xiv). The same piece insists: "Now I am no believer in the worth of any mere taste for art that cannot produce what it professes to appreciate" (vi).[13] (That the criterion implied here would require the scrapping of some fine criticism—including Shaw on music—shows the lengths to which Shaw would go to espouse his ethic of action.) Whenever Shaw is talking about art, morality, or politics, the same point is emphasized. Concrete action is preferable to unfounded aspiration: "It is not enough to know what is good: you must be able to do it," says Zoo in *Back to Methuselah* (159). This is the view of a Shavian lifetime. Years before, in *The Sanity of Art*'s defense of nineteenth-century art against the charge of "degeneration," Shaw had not only been concerned with the moralistic error of Max Nordau's attack, but also with rebutting his suggestion that men like Wagner and William Morris were ineffectual dreamers.

13. The word "mere" (Standard Edition) was not in the original text (1898).

To be sure, Wagner wrote theoretically about music dramas and the way to present them; the point, however, is that he "not only shewed this on paper, but he successfully composed the music dramas, built a model theatre, gave the model performances, *did* the impossible" (329–330). Morris objected to the ugliness of the life around him: "Well, did he sit down, as Nordau suggests, to rail helplessly at the men who were at all events getting the work of the world done, however inartistically? Not a bit of it"—and there follows a description of Morris's achievements as decorator, artist, printer, businessman, and poet (330).

Although in the *Quintessence* Shaw wrote that no act has any moral character apart from the will behind it, he seems to have believed implicitly that no will has any moral character apart from the action in which it results. The deed is simply a realization: it is "*effective* will" (*Wag* 184—italics mine). The process is described to Eve by the serpent in the Garden of Eden: "You imagine what you desire; you will what you imagine; and at last you create what you will" (*Back* 9). Though the world's best talker, Shaw is at pains to make clear that he does not believe "the world can be saved by talk alone" (*True* 108). He had always respected "big achievers" (*CL* I, 655).

Shaw's habitual emphasis on concrete results explains why, on turning to socialism during the mid- and late 1880's, he came to reject the revolutionary and doctrinal absolutism of the (Marxist) Social Democratic Federation and gravitated instead toward the "sane tacticians" (*EFS* 130) in the more moderate Fabian Society. Spurning the barricades of the catastrophists, the Fabians resolved to "turn heroic defeat into prosaic success" (*EFS* 292). This group's two main tenets were *gradualism* (the pursuit of social changes piecemeal through already established democratic processes such as elections) and *permeation* (the attempt to exert an influence unobtrusively on nonsocialist organizations such as the traditional political parties). As Shaw observes, the Society eschewed dogmas such as that of class war, and instead defined ideological issues pragmatically as a struggle between "those who have more to gain than to lose by Collectivism, solidly arrayed against those who have more to lose than to gain by it" (*EFS* 149–150). Thus they tended to concentrate on specific proposals —the eight-hour day, graduated income tax, municipalization of utilities—that would "make it as easy and matter-of-course for the ordinary respectable Englishman to be a Socialist as to be a Liberal or a Conservative" (*EFS* 292). Taking their name from the general Fabius Cunctator who kept Rome's hopes alive by avoiding direct confrontation with the superior forces of Hannibal, the members' first rule, Shaw notes approvingly, was "not to try and deceive ourselves as to our power" (*EFS* 156–157). His description of the group as one that "lived by its wits, and by its wits alone" (*EFS* 142) and whose "tactics" always depended on its "strength at the moment" (*EFS* 156) call to mind the pragmatic heroes of his own early plays.

Though more militant leftists ridiculed the Fabians as "armchair Socialists . . . of the gas-and-water variety" (*EFS* 137, 153), Shaw's own view was that the Society's unspectacular empiricism promised to bridge the gap between "ideal Socialism and practical Social Democracy" (*EFS* 66). His political writings from this period reveal a very situational polemicist. In an election leaflet entitled "Vote! Vote!! Vote!!!" he advised readers that "even if you think that both candidates are fools, make the best of it by voting for the opponent of the bigger fool of the two" (Henderson 241). In pieces such as "The Economic Basis of Socialism" (*EFS* 3–29) and "Socialism and Superior Brains" (*EFS* 261–283), he examined the major dogmas of nineteenth-century liberalism (that laissez faire capitalism, for instance, provides equality of opportunity and rewards each man according to his ability) and attempted to show how these plausible abstractions break down in practice. Replying in "The Transition to Social Democracy" to those who envisioned a transfer of political power in a revolution taking twenty-four hours, he noted drily that "you cannot convert first and third class carriages into

second class . . . by merely singing the Marseillaise" (*EFS* 43).
He enjoyed recounting how more rigorous socialists were miffed
by the Fabians' preference for "practical suggestions and criticisms . . . not to mention our way of chaffing our opponents in
preference to denouncing them as enemies of the human race"
(*EFS* 127). In his own Fabian tracts, he tried to deal with
theoretical issues in a practical manner, choosing titles such as
"The *Impossibilities* of Anarchism" or "The *Common Sense*
of Municipal Trading" (*EFS* 65–99, 161–248—italics mine).

In politics as well as in other areas of life, such a persistently
utilitarian perspective could not help but seem pedestrian at
times.[14] A friend of Shaw's once commented that the Philistines
seemed to be converting him much faster than he was converting
the Philistines (Farmer 203). The grain of truth in the remark
derives from its perception of the extent to which Shaw is more
concerned with pragmatic problems than with lofty aims. Although this attitude would later become strikingly modified, it
never ceased to be a factor in his outlook on life. His preface to
Getting Married includes a revealing section on Samuel Butler,
who "preached the Gospel of Laodicea,[15] urging people to be
temperate in what they called goodness as in everything else"
(196). Agreeing with Butler, Shaw insists that lofty aspirations
produce a moral strain that is harmful:

What people call goodness has to be kept in check just as carefully
as what they call badness; for the human constitution will not stand
very much of either without serious psychological mischief, ending
in insanity or crime. . . . A life spent in prayer and almsgiving is
really as insane as a life spent in cursing and picking pockets: the

14. For a discussion of Bentham's role as the "intellectual godfather" of
Sidney Webb and the Fabians, see McBriar 149–155.
15. A wealthy city in Asia Minor. "And to the angel of the church in
Laodicea write: . . . I know your works: you are neither cold nor hot.
Would that you were cold or hot! So, because you are lukewarm, and
neither cold nor hot, I will spew you out of my mouth. For you say, I
am rich, I have prospered, and I need nothing; not knowing that you are
wretched, pitiable, poor, blind, and naked" (Rev. 3:14–17).

effect of everybody doing it would be equally disastrous. . . . It is desirable that the normal pitch of conduct at which men are not conscious of being particularly virtuous, although they feel mean when they fall below it, should be raised as high as possible; but it is not desirable that they should attempt to live above this pitch any more than that they should habitually walk at the rate of five miles an hour or carry a hundredweight continually on their backs. . . . What we do want is a higher quality for our normal: that is, people who can be much better than what we now call respectable without self-sacrifice. (197–198)

The above excerpt is not a unique example. In his preface to *Major Barbara* Shaw also advocates "a conscientious Laodicean- ism" (216). And in a later passage satirizing the worldly ma- jority, he reminds us that while the Philistines he criticizes may not be the salt of the earth, "they are the substance of civilization; and they save society from ruin by criminals and conquerors as well as by Savonarolas and Knipperdollings" (*And* 10, Pref). Although obviously with some reluctance, Shaw often feels that a narrowing of vision is the price one must pay to reduce exis- tence to manageable proportions.

That the Shavian emphasis upon effectiveness ("executive power") has its dangerous side is not to be denied. To say that "the world is ruled by deeds, not by good intentions, and . . . one efficient sinner is worth ten futile saints and martyrs" (*Wag* 245, *1909*) is true only as far as it goes; and advice such as "the only really simple thing is to go straight for what you want and grab it" (*Super* 153) may be taken to heart by Jack the Ripper as well as by Ann Whitefield. There are times when Shavian love of efficiency leads to a dangerous idealization of the efficient:

It was as easy for Marx, with his literary talent,[16] to hold up Thiers as the most execrable of living scoundrels, and to put upon Gallifet a brand indelible enough to ostracize him politically for ever, . . . as it was for Victor Hugo to bombard Napoleon III from his paper

16. The words "with his literary talent" (Standard Edition) were not in the original text of this chapter (1909). For more on this subject, see Chapter 7, note 10 below.

battery in Jersey. It was also easy to hold up Félix Pyat and Delescluze as men of much loftier ideals than Thiers and Gallifet; but
the one fact that could not be denied was that when it came to actual shooting, it was Gallifet who got Delescluze shot and not Delescluze who got Gallifet shot, and then when it came to administering
the affairs of France, Thiers could in one way or another get it
done, whilst Pyat could neither do it nor stop talking and allow
somebody else to do it.   (*Wag* 240, *1909*)

A critic turning to Shaw's work to document this outlook will
find himself in the midst of an embarrassing plenitude of examples. In them one sees the basis of Shaw's flirtation, during
the 1920's and 1930's, with dictators and fascists. Frustration
does strange things to people; and the result of Shaw's measuring
merit by the *effect* of actions led him to assume, as the world
for which he had held such high hopes grew steadily worse, that
if good people could not get something done, then the people
who could get something done must be good. It had been all
very well, in a play in the 1890's, to hail Nicola as the ablest man
in Bulgaria (*Arms* 66); it was quite another matter, in real life
in the 1930's, to hail Mussolini as the ablest man in Italy.

But an attack on the excesses of Shaw's position is not necessarily a criticism of the plays I have been discussing, for his
dramatic heroes and heroines are by and large humane persons
who cannot be accused of using their practical efficiency for evil
ends. Bluntschli can admit to telling more lies in a morning than
Raina has told in a lifetime—no matter, he is more truthful
than she.[17] Lady Cicely Waynflete, the heroine of *Captain Brassbound's Conversion* (1899), may be unscrupulous, yet she

17. In "A Dramatic Realist to His Critics" (1894) Shaw dismisses as
irrelevant the charge that Raina herself is a minx and liar: "I have
nothing to do with that: the only moral question for me is, does she do
good or harm? If you admit that she does good, that she generously saves
a man's life and wisely extricates herself from a false position with
another man, then you may classify her as you please—brave, generous,
and affectionate; or artful, dangerous, and faithless—it is all one to me:
you can [not] prejudice me for or against her by such artificial categorizing
. . . " (*ST* 22). This is the Shavian moral position in a nutshell.

charmingly sets right the affairs of those who are *too* scrupulous. These characters are not moral purists, but they do act with respect for others—they are pragmatists not because they have no values but because persons are their values. Thus the question of unscrupulous behavior by genuinely vicious people does not arise (except possibly in the case of Sartorius). Undeniably, however, Shaw sometimes oversimplifies thematic issues by taking advantage of theatrical conventions that will go unquestioned because they are standard elements of comic technique. J. B. Priestley has a point when he argues that someone who ignored danger as blithely as Lady Cicely in *Brassbound* might not have lasted long in the actual circumstances she confronts (349). Similarly in *Arms and the Man* the hero survives as much by luck as by cunning. In real life, fleeing soldiers cannot assume that the bedrooms into which they find their way will contain attractive young ladies eager to receive them. Bluntschli's father is even so cooperative as to die at just the right moment for his son to dazzle his future parents-in-law with an inheritance. Such events are acceptable within (and *only* within) the traditional comedic framework Shaw adopts. The chocolate creams in Bluntschli's cartridge case are what really give the show away— the real Shavian soldier would have carried an *extra* supply of bullets.

With these reservations noted, let us conclude by returning briefly to Shaw's analysis in *The Quintessence of Ibsenism* of the origin of ideals in fear of self-knowledge. To accept such illusions involves implicitly a commitment to disregard facts which contradict them. By a process of generalization, concrete reality will be ignored in favor of what ought to be. Next "ought" and "is," instead of being seen in terms of illusion and reality, come to be viewed in terms of "right" and "wrong." Thus ignorant fears acquire an ethical sanction: the ideal becomes a principle. Such moral sanctities need in turn only be attributed to a source outside the self (god or the Volk) to emerge as a Church (actual or surrogate), complete with zealots in search of the external "enemies" an ideology requires to save its devotees from the task of confronting their own limitations. Since dogmatic absolutes inevitably reflect the state of mind of those who invent them, idolaters are finally enabled to glorify as humility the projection of their own ignorance on a cosmic scale, and to make fulfillment of their own egotism an act of supreme self-abnegation.

One can of course distinguish among those who create this system, those who love it bovinely as part of the natural order, and those who manipulate it for their own ends. The psychology of each attitude is different; the practical result is that same "sacrificial" mentality which results in the abolition of persons: "All abstractions invested with collective consciousness or collective authority, set above the individual, and exacting duty from him on pretence of acting or thinking with greater validity than he, are man-eating idols red with human sacrifices" (*Quint* 75). And of one thing we may be certain: if the mob calls its savage barbarism by the name of patriotism, its repressed self-hatred by the name of morality, and its ignorant superstition by the name of religion, then the world is obviously not going to be a very pleasant place for the individual who is not imposed upon by these delusions. How such a person manages to lead his life without getting his throat slit is the pivotal issue in Shaw's plays.

Misled by Shaw's public image as outsider and seer, prospective readers have sometimes come to these dramas expecting to find a procession of iconoclastic rebels before whose strength the forces of prejudice and reaction crumble into dust. Surely there are heroes such as Dick Dudgeon and Julius Caesar (both to be considered in the next chapter) who might be seen in this light. But an equally typical Shavian character is apt to be a matter-of-fact, well-fed person whose success results from a realization that what an individual must face in this life is not a stupendous moral issue, but a prosaic resolution of unsatisfactory alternatives. In a note defending the professions of Cashel Byron and Mrs. Warren, Shaw wrote that "the word prostitution should either not be used at all, or else applied impartially to all persons who do things for money that they would not do if they had other assured means of livelihood" (*Cash* 247, Note). Abjuring moral labels, which simply "beg all the most important questions in life for other people" (248), Shaw states his case for the unheroic truth:

It must be remembered that it is an exceedingly difficult and doubtful thing for an individual to set up his own scruples or fancies (he cannot himself be sure which they are) against the demand of the community when it says, Do thus and thus, or starve. It was easy for Ruskin to lay down the rule of dying rather than doing unjustly; but death is a plain thing: justice a very obscure thing. . . . No doubt, if you are a man of genius, a Ruskin or an Ibsen, you can divine your way and finally force your passage. . . . But if you are an ordinary person you take your bread as it comes to you, doing whatever you can make most money by doing. And you are really shewing yourself a disciplined citizen and acting with perfect social propriety in so doing. Society may be, and generally is, grossly wrong in supporting the existing political structure; but this only means, to the successful modern prizefighter, that he must reform society before he can reform himself. A conclusion which I recommend to the consideration of those foolish misers of personal righteousness who think they can dispose of social problems by bidding reformers of society reform themselves first.   (*Cash* 248–249, Note)

At first this may sound like a counsel of political passivity—as if Shaw were urging each person merely to accept the existing order and turn it to his own advantage. Yet his point is rather that, for the man or woman already trapped in a given situation, no other course is possible. His last two sentences make clear that those who have managed to secure freedom of action in spite of the political system should by all means strive to change a form of societal organization that wastes the lives of all. But that is not a choice the *victims* of the system are free to exercise. For the person in the latter position who sees concretely, life becomes a challenge to achieve viability within an established, arbitrary, and sometimes vicious framework called the world.

If today's readers do not respond very enthusiastically to Shaw's dramatizations of this ethic, it is partly because in our world ultimate questions and catastrophes seem more imminent than they were for Shaw. Contemporary fashion in literature is concerned with epiphany, apocalypse, and magnificent atrocities. But perhaps there is more to be said for Shaw here than his posterity will admit. What he perceives is that neither Armageddon nor utopia is of much use as a working hypothesis. Things may collapse, but probably not tomorrow; things may improve, but not very dramatically, and also probably not tomorrow. Meanwhile one must go on living. The individual can count on nothing except that the world will disillusion him, and Shaw sees the creative confrontation of that disillusionment as the crucial step in the process of self-realization.

Like Ibsen before him, Shaw attempts to explore the nature of ethical choice. But there is one important difference. Ibsen's vision is bleak indeed—he portrays Mrs. Alving's life long after she had made the wrong decision. Shaw's vision is more hopeful —he does not want to show how nobly a woman can endure an appalling fate, but rather how such a fate can be avoided. He wants to go back to the point *before* Mrs. Alving made the fatal choice, to show us a Mrs. Warren who made the viable choice, and then to dramatize the (relative) rightness of that decision. No doubt Mrs. Warren's profession leads to problems, including the loss of her daughter; but it does not lead to the problem of dying, like her half-sister, of "phossy jaw." It is as if Shaw takes the question of Christian in *The Pilgrim's Progress* (his favorite book)—"What shall I do to be saved?"—and transforms it into a bleakly modern equivalent: "What shall I do to *survive?*" That question is central not only in the plays already discussed, but also in such later ones as *Major Barbara, Heartbreak House, Saint Joan, The Apple Cart,* and *In Good King Charles's Golden Days.* The right to survival is the root premise of Shavian drama.

Sartorius, Mrs. Warren, Captain Bluntschli—each of these characters from the earliest plays is instinctive rather than cerebral, practical rather than principled, prosaic rather than lofty, and (again excepting Sartorius) humane rather than moral. How often the characters whom Shaw admires turn out not to be coxcombs like Leonard Charteris (*Phil*), iconoclasts like Sergius Saranoff (*Arms*), or intellectuals like Mrs. Clandon (*Tell*), but rather menials, materialists, or crusty middle-aged ladies—all intuitive pragmatists with a talent for making the best of things. No more than Bluntschli would any of them be offended by the accusation of having "a low shopkeeping mind" (*Arms* 52). Through these personages the Shavian spirit, anticipated in the novels and made explicit in the *Quintessence,* has become flesh. And while Shaw often uses such figures to point up defects in the political organism that he hopes his writings will help to reform, the personal force of his characters finally overshadows the intended "message." In his polemical tracts, of course, Shaw was quick to claim that socialism "is as honest as it is inevitable" (*EFS* 40), that there are "no cruelty and selfishness outside Man himself; and . . . his own active benevolence can combat and vanquish both" (*EFS* 28), that the necessary reforms would involve only "extensions of practices already in full activity [which are] all sure to come" (*EFS* 60). But now it is as if his own *dramatis personae* had appeared to him in a nightmare and said, "See here, Shaw, we've read these Fabian Essays of yours, and this palaver about the coming of a just society and the improvement of man may be all very well; but what on earth are *we* supposed to do in the meantime?" It is because these dramas are about precisely that and because their heroes remember "what they are and where they are" (*Quint* 48) under all circumstances that the plays remain vital in an age when most of their creator's social and political ideals have themselves been relegated to the realm of wishful utopianism.

PART TWO

3 The Pragmatist as Pilgrim

▪▪

Candida, The Devil's Disciple, Caesar and Cleopatra

In quoting Wagner's self-analytical remark that "seldom has there taken place in the soul of one and the same man so profound a division and estrangement between the intuitive or impulsive part of his nature and his consciously or reasonably formed ideas" (*Wag* 247), Shaw cited an insight that applies equally to himself. His own pragmatic convictions are subverted by impulses of a very different kind. He tells us on the one hand that efficiency is all, but on the other reminds us that "if life is crowned by its success and devotion in industrial organization and ingenuity, we had better worship the ant and the bee" (*Caes* 198, Notes)—which he by no means proposes to do. He tends to idealize state power, yet he also warns us that "there is nothing worse than government by defectives who wield irresistible powers of physical coercion" (*Back* xiv). He allows Epifania the millionairess to assert, "I have to take the world as I find it," only to have the Egyptian doctor she will marry retort, "The wrath of Allah shall overtake those who leave the world no better than they found it" (*Mill* 195). And although he often denigrates authoritarian religion, he also reminds us that all the world is the temple of the Holy Ghost, that there is a "soul . . . hidden in every dogma" (*Back* lxxiii), that a common faith and shared beliefs are essential if civilization is to survive (*True* 16, Pref), that all conceptions (sexual) are immaculate and all ground consecrated: in short, that religion is not a compartment of life but the motive power behind life itself.

Shaw's religion should not be confused with statements he made *about* religion in his capacity as personal publicity agent for the Life Force, the Superman, or Creative Evolution as the supposed faith of the future. It is not the terms themselves that matter, but what they signify; for the Shavian catchwords are only external manifestations of an internal search for a dimension of reality he had shunned earlier in life. Nothing could seem more compulsively mundane than his youthful novels, where aspirations exist only for the purpose of being discarded once their illusory nature has been exposed. Yet even the pragmatic ethic of *The Quintessence of Ibsenism* foreshadows a religious quest. Shaw starts out in a ruthlessly practical frame of mind, and then as he grows older begins to search for solid ground beneath and beyond the contingencies of existence. But he does not cease to be practical.

The Perfect Wagnerite marks a turning point in its author's intellectual development. But the direction Shaw's thought was about to take can also be inferred from several of the later plays of his first dramatic flowering (1892–1899). A hint of the process can be gathered from the fact that in the first edition of the *Quintessence* Shaw had written that "conduct must justify itself by its effect on happiness and not by conformity to any rule or ideal" (125), but in later editions the word "happiness" was replaced by "life." He begins with the British utilitarian position that the achievement of happiness is the moral end of a person's life, but then moves to the position that the advancement of life's purpose is the moral end of any meaningful human happiness. While this new vitalistic context still needs to be defined, there is a clear difference in emphasis between happiness as an end and life as an end. Happiness is a purely personal affair; life relates the individual to the cosmos.

The shift in emphasis first occurs in *Candida* (1895), the conclusion of which involves a double paradox. The first is that the

immature boy is "stronger" than the manly husband. Candida
is wife, mother, and sister, in short, "the sum of all loving care"
(140), to Morell. She is none of these to Marchbanks, because
he is capable of standing alone. (This importance placed upon
self-reliance and independence follows directly from what we
know the Shavian realist is supposed to be.) The deeper paradox
is that the emergence of Marchbanks's conviction of his own
strength coincides with an apparent act of renunciation on his
part. "He has learnt to live without happiness" (140), says
Candida; and Marchbanks agrees: "Life is nobler than that.
Parson James: I give you my happiness with both hands: I love
you because you have filled the heart of the woman I loved"
(140). Marchbanks's willingness to deny himself romantic fulfillment should not be mistaken for self-denial in the deeper sense
of rejecting the claims of his own nature. On the contrary, it is
in his moment of fullest realization of self, not sacrifice of self,
that the young man is able to love his former antagonist. Shaw
is as convinced as ever that it is necessary for a person to assume
his manhood and independence; the difference here is that
Marchbanks's emergence into the unfettered exercise of his own
powers is equated with the acceptance of a vocation that transcends personal happiness.

As Marchbanks is about to leave the house just before the
final scene, Candida calls him back to "stay and learn" (136).
The kind of education the young man undergoes is very different
from that of most characters in Shaw's plays. Sergius Saranoff,
Captain Brassbound, and John Tanner simply find themselves
out; Marchbanks actually becomes a new person. His words at
the end, spoken with "the ring of a man's voice—no longer a
boy's" (140), announce the mature human being developing
from the earlier "snivelling little whelp" (127). Before, Marchbanks was not really a poet, but an acutely perceptive post-
adolescent who thought he was a poet. While critics have tended
to ridicule his rhapsodizings about the "tiny shallop" (111)́ or the
"archangel with purple wings" (129) as instances of Shaw's in-

ability to portray creative people, such strictures somewhat misconstrue the tone of this characterization. The earlier Marchbanks is not an unconvincing portrait of an artist, but a portrait
of an unconvincing artist. As with Smith in *Immaturity,* the
most that can be claimed is that he may be a great man in
embryo. To be sure, Marchbanks's subsequent enlightenment—
culminating in "Out, then, into the night with me!" (140)—
may itself seem grandiloquent, causing us to feel that *Candida*
is a play that has very nicely dispelled clichés about the nature
of the family only to replace them with clichés about the nature
of the poet. But however imperfectly realized, Shaw's very intention is remarkable if seen from the perspective of his previous
works. For here the attainment of maturity is depicted not in
terms of the hero's acquiring greater practical effectiveness, but
in terms of his coming to understand—and accept—his commitment to an unworldly calling.

The Devil's Disciple (1897) is an even more striking development out of earlier Shavian assumptions. How can Dick Dudgeon, the devil's disciple, at the same time be a "Puritan of the
Puritans" (*TPP* xxiv)? The answer is that it is easy with Mrs.
Dudgeon as mother:

[Dick] is brought up in a household where the Puritan religion has
died, and become, in its corruption, an excuse for his mother's master passion of hatred in all its phases of cruelty and envy. . . . In
such a home the young Puritan finds himself starved of religion,
which is the most clamorous need of his nature. With all his mother's indomitable selffulness, but with Pity instead of Hatred as his
master passion, he pities the devil; takes his side; and champions
him, like a true Covenanter, against the world. He thus becomes,
like all genuinely religious men, a reprobate and an outcast.

(xxiv)

Like the realist of the *Quintessence,* Dick is a creature of impulse,
not of duty. He concludes, simply enough, that if his mother
and her family represent God, he prefers Satan. That his anti-
religion is in fact a manifestation of religion he does not see
because his instincts have not yet broken through to the surface

of his conscious understanding. A visit to the Reverend Anthony Anderson's home opens his—and our—eyes. First, we see Dick acting very differently from Shavian apostles of survival when he remains unmoved by the pastor's effort to warn him that his life may be in danger. Next Anderson is called away, setting the stage for Dick's self-revelation. The British come to seize the pastor as a traitor, and Dick impulsively lets himself be arrested in Anderson's place, thus effectually placing his own head in a noose.

It should not be thought, however, that Dick's noble deed involves either self-abnegation or the duty espoused by his hypocritical relatives. In explaining that he can find "no manner of reason for acting as I did" (49), he affirms the primacy of impulse over external restraints. His moral act has nothing to do with what Shaw elsewhere calls the "customary formulas" (*TPP* xxvii, *n.o.t.*) for moral conduct. Nor did he act out of romantic love for Anderson's wife, Judith: "What I did last night, I did in cold blood, caring not half so much for your husband, or (*ruthlessly*) for you (*she droops, stricken*) as I do for myself. I had no motive and no interest: all I can tell you is that when it came to the point whether I would take my neck out of the noose and put another man's into it, I could not do it. I dont know why not: I see myself as a fool for my pains; but I could not and I cannot. I have been brought up standing by the law of my own nature; and I may not go against it, gallows or no gallows" (52). In short, Dick remains the self-realized person— but in previous plays one would hardly expect the man who obeys the "law of [his] own nature" to embrace martyrdom.

This is as much of a surprise to Dick as to anyone else, for he does not realize that his supposed diabolism is simply a rejection of pious cant and not of the real substance of religion. He is in fact no more "satanic" than Trefusis, a character he resembles in messianic flamboyance. Even his rebuke of Anderson—"By your leave, Minister: I do not interfere with your sermons: do not you interrupt mine" (24)—could be taken to suggest that Dick is a preacher without knowing it. His actions bear this out well. In the opening act, for instance, he assumes the role of comforter and shepherd to young Essie far more naturally than Rev. Anderson had attempted to assume a similar role with Mrs. Dudgeon. During the scene of the reading of the will, Dick's outburst against the hypocrisy of the assembled company is precisely what might have been expected from a clergyman less tactful than Anderson. When he is arrested Dick puts on the parson's coat: as he does so, he is amused because "the idea of himself as a parson tickles him" (37)—and who if not Shaw has taught us that funny things conceal hidden truths (*Back* 239)? The donning of the coat is a *true* accident, a purely chance occurrence that inadvertently penetrates to the heart of a mystery. When the British learn Dick's identity, they intend to hang him anyway—"Since you have taken the minister's place, Richard Dudgeon, you shall go through with it" (64)—and these words also are prophetic. For at the end of the play Dick *does* "go through" with it: after being rescued he becomes a preacher, in an act that is not the denial but the discovery of his nature.

On the surface, the hero of Shaw's next drama is a great man cut to the exact pattern of the pragmatism of the *Quintessence*. "Goodness," say Shaw's notes to *Caesar and Cleopatra*, "in its popular British sense of self-denial, implies that man is vicious by nature, and that supreme goodness is supreme martyrdom. Not sharing that pious opinion, I have not given countenance to it in any of my plays" (202). Caesar is the realist who can make judgments "quite independently of convention and moral generalization" (201, Notes). His secret is the assertion of will, not submission to system: the impression of greatness is produced by showing him "not as mortifying his nature by doing his duty . . . but as simply doing what he naturally wants to do" (203, Notes). When tempted by Britannus to take vengeance for the honor of Rome, he has no interest in using ideals to disguise personal viciousness: "I do not make human sacrifices to my honor" (150). He is kind to Cleopatra, but not from a sense of obligation—as she says, "His kindness is not for anything in *me:* it is in his own nature" (164). He is impervious to insult because he realizes that nothing outside himself can degrade him. Like all those whose passions come from within and are not merely re-active, he strikes others as cold and egotistical.[1]

Caesar is the archpragmatist whose lack of principle is justified by the results of his actions. His humaneness is selfish, and his selfishness humane. His cohorts may be furious because he has freed political prisoners, but Caesar knows that "every Egyptian we imprison means imprisoning two Roman soldiers to guard him" (133). Pothinus, the ambitious eunuch, tells him that Cleopatra will some day betray him: "Well, my friend," he replies, "is not this very natural?" (171). The names of his enemies are delivered to him in a bag, which he promptly pitches into the ocean—why should he condemn men who will join him themselves once they realize he will triumph (149)? (And this is exactly what happens in the case of his former enemy, the

1. In his preface to *Major Barbara* Shaw complains that phrases such as "passionate love of truth" have died out; modern playgoers think in-stead of "passional crime" and assume that "people in whom passion has a larger scope are passionless and therefore uninteresting" (218). Caesar is such a person; so is Don Juan, whom Lucifer dismisses as a "cold self-ish egotist" (*Super* 95). The point missed by the playgoer is that the "larger scope" to which Shaw refers expresses itself not as an indifference to individuals but as an extension to *all* human beings of the kindness most people reserve for only a few. When Sylvia complains to Charteris, "I dont think that you care a bit more for one woman than for another," he replies, "You mean I dont care a bit less for one woman than for another" (*Phil* 105). The adolescent maiden in *Methuselah* consoles the rejected Strephon: "I care for you much more seriously than before; though perhaps not so much for you in particular. I mean I care more for everybody" (*Back* 205). In response to Iddy's protest that he cannot marry two women, Maya explains to him that "Vashti and Maya are one: you cannot love me if you do not love Vashti" (*Simp* 50). The sympathy and charity that are expressions of a man's own nature will not be susceptible to fluctuation based on making invidious distinctions between fellow creatures: no matter how injured the egotism of the recipients of such equable affection may be, "Perfect love casteth out choice" (*Simp* 40).

murderer Lucius Septimius.) Shaw notes approvingly that when Caesar wishes to "produce an impression of complete disinterestedness and magnanimity, he has only to act with entire selfishness; and this is perhaps the only sense in which a man can be said to be *naturally* great" (202, Notes).

Yet the triumphant figure of Shaw's essay does not quite correspond to the character in the play. For while Caesar surpasses the hero of *Arms and the Man* in his skill at managing money and troops, settling prolonged disputes with an apt thought, and combining generosity with a resourceful self-regard, he is ultimately a more self-divided and circumscribed character than his lucky predecessor. If he detests books and dreaming (132), he also renounces the "tedious, brutal life of action" that makes Romans "mere doers and drudgers" (167). In praising the good talker who has "wit and imagination enough to live without continually doing something" (167), he suggests that mental qualities have value in themselves, apart from the results they produce. In the opening scene, it is the Sphinx's very immobility that appeals to him: "I conquer, and you endure; I work and wonder, you watch and wait" (101). It is as if Captain Bluntschli had suddenly become endowed with the yearnings of a Marchbanks. His response to the desert scene—"Rome is a madman's dream: this is my Reality" (102)—reverses the expected Shavian precedence of values by asserting the validity of imaginative vision against the claims of worldly life. Although an expert in the latter area, Caesar shares Dick Dudgeon's contempt for danger and foresees his own death with resignation and perhaps even mild relief. For upon his discovery that Pothinus has become the victim of Cleopatra's fit of righteous rage, his powerful outburst ("And so, to the end of history, murder shall breed murder . . . "—181) suggests a world-weariness whose bitterness spreads to tinge the fabric of the whole play. And when he further explains that the "one man" who might be found to *know* that Cleopatra did wrong in having Pothinus killed would have "either to conquer the world as I have, or be crucified by it"

(180–181), the oblique allusion to Christ suggests Caesar's awareness that a person may accurately perceive both the folly of vengeance and the perils of earthly life without necessarily being plunged thereby into the complications that attend his own chosen struggle for power. Pragmatism is not a goal to which Caesar aspires, but a given for which he must settle. *Caesar and Cleopatra* is a version of *Arms and the Man* in which the soldierly hero's salient qualities have become detached from the comic framework that insured their successful operation in the earlier and comparatively facile play.

We can see Marchbanks, Dick Dudgeon, and Caesar as the apexes of triangles whose other points are respectively Morell and Candida, Anderson and Burgoyne, Cleopatra and Rufio. Morell embodies genial affection and vigorous dedication to a goal, marred by lack of awareness concerning his true position in both home and pulpit.[2] Candida exemplifies maternal insight and household wisdom divorced from appreciation of such higher matters as her husband's socialism or her suitor's poetry. While Marchbanks is undeniably a weak personality in some respects, the contrasts to Morell's sentimentality and Candida's mundaneness underscore his comparative toughness of mind and force of imagination. It is because the young poet's insights are deeper than those of his motherly idol that some critics, most notably Nethercot (7–17), have attempted to demote Candida from the rank of realist to that of Philistine. But this is to go as far to one extreme as Marchbanks's view of her as virgin mother goes to another. Candida's concluding explanation to Morell of the real nature of their relationship is not the utterance of an easy plodder who hasn't yet reached the stage of being able to understand what ideals are, but rather of a person with a secure grasp of the realities of a situation usually obscured by romantic con-

---

2. Shaw uses the character of another curate, Lexy Mill, to prevent us from overreacting to Morell's flaws. The older man's good qualities continue to command respect when contrasted to his protegé's vapid attempt to imitate them (see especially 82, 133–134).

vention. The same applies to her refusal to be duped by the loaded language of respectable moral categories: "Suppose [Marchbanks] learns [what love is] from a bad woman, as so many men do . . . will he forgive me for . . . abandoning him to the bad women for the sake of my goodness, of my purity, as you call it?" (116). No Philistine would be able to understand this reasoning, much less supply it himself.[3] If Shaw were discussing Candida as a character in an Ibsen play, she would definitely be a realist. Yet Shaw's giving the last word to the "secret in the poet's heart" (141) in the final stage direction suggests that the same qualities that would have made Candida a realist in 1891 make her half a Philistine in 1895. It is not the meaning of the terms themselves, but rather Shaw's attitude toward them, that has changed. While still recognized and respected, the Shavian pragmatist (Candida) must now make room for that former contradiction in terms, an impractical realist (Marchbanks).

In a similar way, Shaw defines Dick Dudgeon's strengths and limitations by comparing him to Burgoyne and Anderson. On the basis of his speeches alone, Burgoyne is thoroughly Shavian in his perceptions about duty and officialdom. Some of his best re-

3. I agree with Charles Carpenter's view (109–110) that Nethercot has misconstrued a key piece of evidence: the letter (written in 1904 to James Huneker) in which Shaw refers to Candida as a "very immoral female, . . . a woman without 'character' in the conventional sense . . . straight for natural reasons, not for conventional ethical ones . . . as unscrupulous as Siegfried." While this missive reflects Shaw's annoyance at the public's sentimental adoration of his heroine, his apparent animadversions are in fact couched ambiguously. General audiences will of course interpret his remarks as a curt dismissal of Candida. Readers of the *Quintessence,* however, will recognize that the quoted phrases precisely describe qualities of the Shavian realist, who is also "immoral" according to the conventional code (*Quint* 27), "straight" through following his will instead of submitting to custom (*Quint* 31), and a precursor of the race of "heroes" (*Quint* 25) to which Siegfried belongs in the *Wagnerite.* (Note that the grounds on which Shaw "attacks" Candida closely parallel those on which he praises Julius Caesar in the Notes to *Caesar and Cleopatra* quoted on p. 100).

marks ("Martyrdom . . . is the only way in which a man can become famous without ability"—54) might well be envied by Dick himself. But Burgoyne is not concerned with embodying his convictions in action. A realist intellectually, "Gentlemanly Johnny" is content to accept the system that requires him to hang Dick as "a mere matter of political necessity" (58). He represents the reduction of moral passion to an ethos of style, becoming thereby an idealizer of the same "gentlemanly" manner he uses to convey astute observations devoid of real effect. His temperamental antithesis in the play is Anderson, the plain-spoken "man of action" who goes on to become captain of a militia unit after rescuing Dick from the gallows. At first Anderson might seem as marred by stylistic affectation as Burgoyne—certainly the speeches delivered in his role as clergyman are reminiscent of Lexy Mill at his worst. But this is not because Anderson lacks genuineness, but because this man who sold the family Bible to buy a pair of pistols has not yet discovered the role that truly expresses himself. Anderson may suspect this when he responds to Dick's fear of being preached at by saying, "Dont be alarmed, sir: I am no great preacher" (32), and proceeds to warn of practical danger. Seeing more deeply than Anderson, Dick of course realizes that it is the pastor whom the British will want to hang as an example to the rebels. But while not a man of Burgoyne's wittiness or Dick's insight, Anderson is wholly admirable within his limited range. As the central character, Dick may be seen as potentially capable of uniting Burgoyne's brilliance and Anderson's effectiveness. But *only* potentially. In the present world, the saint must be rescued by the practical man.

In the more treacherous ambiance of Shaw's next play, Rufio and Cleopatra serve as warnings of the hazards that follow when the realist's power is mastered by Philistine and idealist temperaments. While Caesar refers to Rufio as his "son" (189) and "comrade in arms" (116), the bodyguard plays jackal to his master's lion, possessing the latter's efficiency without his vision. Unlike Caesar, he is a Caesarian (124), who wants his chief to become king of Rome (118). To his complacent nature, his leader's noblest utterances are mere "heroics" (170). Cleopatra, on the other hand, illustrates the misuse of Caesar's governing skills as means for pursuing pettily selfish ends. Caesar's attempt to educate the young girl fails to raise her above her own level. Since she remains "cruel at heart" (161), her mastery of the queenly role becomes an idealist's disguise used to justify covert malice. Urged by Caesar to cast out fear (111), she succeeds in doing so only by intimidating others. Caesar's greatness is obviously not a composite of the qualities of Rufio and Cleopatra; and still less is either of the latter used (as Anderson was) to suggest some quality needful to complete the hero's virtues. Rather they both illustrate that Caesar's attributes remain constructive only if held firmly in check by an enlightened directing intelligence. When Caesar is asked "where is your right" to do an act, he replies that "it is in Rufio's scabbard" (121, n.o.t.); but Rufio himself, upon being appointed governor of Egypt at the end, significantly remarks: "I am Caesar's shield; but of what use shall I be when I am no longer on Caesar's arm?" (189). As for Cleopatra, she has Pothinus murdered the moment her tutor's back is turned. The ruffianism of the one and the viciousness of the other together dramatize the failure of Caesar's combination of force and vision to survive in his absence. As is so often the case in Shaw's works, the potential social impact of the exceptional person is thwarted because ordinary humanity cannot be ennobled from without.

Despite the difference in their ages, Marchbanks, Dick, and Caesar share some important qualities. All act resourcefully in difficult situations, defend truth over appearances, and are romantically susceptible but finally not concerned with love as their highest goal. Marchbanks leaves behind the security and warmth of the hearth; Dick tells Judith he "can see the beauty and peace of this home . . . yet . . . It's not in my nature . . . to be domesticated" (36); Caesar forgets to say goodbye to Cleopatra before he leaves Egypt. When Candida reminds Marchbanks how he "had to live without comfort or welcome or refuge: always lonely, and nearly always disliked and misunderstood" (139), she also describes Dick, an outcast from society, and to some extent even Caesar, a genius who has found "no man kindred" (101) to himself. Marchbanks longs for a "sense of the silent glory of life" (128) far away from Morell's sermons and Candida's scrubbing-brushes; Caesar seeks in the Sphinx an analogous "image of the constant and immortal part of my life, silent, full of thoughts, alone in the silver desert" (102). Each of the three men combines an inner reserve with a childlike openness to experience. When Dick at the end of his ordeal claims to have "behaved like a fool," Anderson replies, "Like a hero"; and Dick adds, "Much the same thing" (74). Formerly, Shaw would have used this interchange to satirize romantic ideals; now the same lines foreshadow his treatment of Siegfried (an authentic hero *because* he is a fool) in *The Perfect Wagnerite*. For Shaw has come to see not only that heroism is usually foolish, but also that folly can occasionally be heroic. Marchbanks, Dudgeon, and Caesar are the same basic personality portrayed at three different stages of development. In their ability to penetrate to the reality behind conventions, they resemble the "one in a thousand" Shaw praised in the first part of his work on Ibsen; but each is now allowed that yearning for a realm beyond pragmatic contingencies which had, in Shaw's earlier view, turned some of Ibsen's most extraordinary characters into repellent "idealists."

In these later plays of Shaw's first dramatic decade, time has acquired a new, teleological significance. When Marchbanks finally relinquishes the desire for personal happiness because "life is nobler than that" (140), he has broken free from his personal past into a realm of potentiality. In *The Devil's Disciple* this process is generalized: time past is seen negatively by Burgoyne ("History . . . will tell lies, as usual"—67), but time to come is seen positively by Dick ("My life for the world's future" —72). Upon being asked during the burning of the Alexandrian library if he would "destroy the past," Caesar replies, "Ay, and build the future with its ruins" (132). For Sartorius, Mrs. Warren, or Captain Bluntschli, it is hard to imagine any future except continuing survival in a static present. In *Arms and the Man* Bluntschli complacently affirmed that "it is our duty to live as long as we can" (8); in *Caesar and Cleopatra* the nearly identical sentiment—"I also mean to live as long as I can" (182)—is voiced by the cutthroat Lucius Septimius. Shaw's new breed of hero is both less concerned with survival and—it must be added—less likely to survive. Marchbanks, Dick, and Caesar describe an ascending scale of maturity and assurance, but a declining scale of personal safety. To employ the subtitles of the three plays: in the "Mystery" the adolescent realist undergoes his ordeal without harm; in the "Melodrama" the adult version is saved only by a last-minute rescue; and in the "History" the aging representative of the type departs in triumph only to suffer death by treachery. If none of these characters is concerned whether his qualities will increase his chances for survival, the reason is that all of them sense that caring more about life may involve caring less about one's own life. Taken together, the three stand midway between the securely finite competences of Shaw's former pragmatists and the larger—but more hazardous—aspirations of a "race that can understand" (*Caes* 181).

The Perfect Wagnerite

In 1898 Shaw also composed the third of his major critical essays, *The Perfect Wagnerite*, which provides significant corroboration of the development of his thought during this period.[4] The book is sometimes dismissed as a "preposterous" attempt (Wellek 428) to read Wagner's great cycle of music dramas as a socialist allegory; but the polemical passages give the appear-

4. The book was begun on 28 April 1898 and completed before 20 August; *Caesar and Cleopatra* was started on 23 April 1898 and finished on 9 December. Thus Shaw wrote the two works more or less simultaneously.

ance of having been inserted for the benefit of Shaw's fellow Fabians and are not integral to the main line of argument. Shaw spends most of his time and eloquence dealing with the inter-relationships in the Wotan-Brynhild-Siegfried triad—a subject upon which the book's political or economic "message" bears only tangentially.

We cannot really understand *The Perfect Wagnerite* until we see that it is not so much a separate work as a developmental sequel to *The Quintessence of Ibsenism*. The emphasis upon self-respect and impulse in opposition to duty founded upon externally imposed ideals clearly involves the same convictions as those espoused in the earlier work: "All the loftiest spirits of that time were burning to raise Man up, to give him self-respect, to shake him out of his habit of grovelling before the ideals created by his own imagination, of attributing the good that sprang from the ceaseless energy of the life within himself to some superior power in the clouds, and of making a fetish of self-sacrifice to justify his own cowardice" (*Wag* 190). And the resemblances are even more specific and concrete:

In The Rhine Gold, it is pretended that there are as yet no men on the earth. There are dwarfs, giants, and gods. The danger is that you will jump to the conclusion that the gods, at least, are a higher order than the human order. On the contrary, the world is waiting for Man to redeem it from the lame and cramped government of the gods. Once grasp that; and the allegory becomes simple enough. Really, of course, the dwarfs, giants, and gods are dramatizations of the three main orders of men: to wit, the instinctive, predatory, lustful, greedy people; the patient, toiling, stupid, respectful, money-worshipping people; and the intellectual, moral, talented people who devise and administer States and Churches. History shews us only one order higher than the highest of these: namely, the order of Heroes.   (189)

The reference to the dwarfs, giants, and gods as symbols of "the three main orders of men" suggests the earlier book's tripartite division into Philistines, idealists, and realists. But here one must proceed with caution, for Shaw adds the order of "Heroes," a fourth class. What relation have the four orders of the *Wagnerite* to the three orders of the *Quintessence?*

The class of dwarfs, represented by Alberic, is actually a perversion of human nature rather than an expression of it. Alberic renounces love in order to wield the Plutonic power represented by the gold of the Rhine. Ugly and stupid as he is, however, the choice is still not a natural one. "Few men," Shaw reminds us, "will make this sacrifice voluntarily" (171); and the dwarf himself is interested in forswearing love only when his own amorous inclinations have been rebuffed by the Rhine maidens, at which point there is nothing for him to do but "curse the love he can never win, and turn remorselessly to the gold" (171). Alberic thus serves as an illustration of Shaw's belief that vice is not radical in human nature—it consists of good perverted into evil.

Shaw's description of the dwarfs ("the instinctive, predatory, lustful, greedy people") does not, though it suggests the Philistines, correspond very clearly to any of the categories of the *Quintessence*. This is not surprising, for each of the three main classes in the *Quintessence* is presented as a part of *normal* human nature. Alberic, however, is a pathological case. If we thus consider the dwarfs as an extraneous class representing the Philistine temperament perverted into the service of evil, we are then left with the giants, the gods, and the Heroes. Now the correspondence becomes obvious—the giants, described as "patient, toiling, stupid, respectful, money-worshipping people," correspond to the Philistines; the gods, described as the "intellectual, moral, talented people who devise and administer States and Churches," correspond to the idealists; and the Heroes are the highest order, corresponding to the realists.

A closer comparison of the two works will show that these parallels run too deep to be dismissed as Procrustean fancy. In the earlier book we were told that the idealist, though lower than the realist, is "higher in the ascent of evolution than the Philistine" (*Quint* 30); now we are told that the god Wotan cannot forswear as did Alberic because "love, though not his highest need, is a higher than gold: otherwise he would be no god" (*Wag* 192). In the *Quintessence* it was argued that the will "cannot be fulfilled today under the conditions that secured its fulfillment yesterday" (125); in the *Wagnerite* a result of the evolution of life is that "yesterday's law [has] already fallen out with today's thought" (174). There ideals are used to give vicious actions a moral sanction (*Quint* 117); here Alberic, "in stirring up the moral fervor of Wotan, has removed his last moral scruple about becoming a thief" (*Wag* 180). The *Quintessence* argues that "the spirit or will of Man is constantly outgrowing the ideals" (121); the *Wagnerite* advocates "the redemption of man . . . by the growth of his will into perfect strength and self-confidence" (219). Ibsen advocates the "importance of being always prepared to act immorally" (*Quint* 121–122); Wagner heralds the "totally unmoral person . . . an anticipation of the 'overman' of Nietzsche" (*Wag* 200). The realist is one who "has come to have a deep respect for himself and faith in the validity of his own will" (*Quint* 31); Siegfried is the "healthy man raised to perfect confidence in his own impulses" (*Wag* 213).[5] The ideals were masks, every one of which "requires a hero to tear it off" (*Quint* 25); and now along comes "the Hero," who is nothing more than the former realist placed in a more elaborate scheme of evolutionary eschatology.

Shaw is using both Ibsen and Wagner to explore the same theme: the *Wagnerite* is really an elaborate recasting of the *Quintessence*. The underlying assumptions of the two works are largely identical; and there is no significant difference between the giants and the Philistines, between the realist and the Hero. What gives the later work its great importance for the development of Shaw's ideas, however, is the surprising change in emphasis between the equivalent classes of "idealists" and "gods."

5. In the first American edition (1899)—the British edition appeared a year earlier—Shaw had written "the perfectly healthy man raised to perfect confidence. . . ." "Perfectly" was deleted in the second British edition (1902). (For all passages cited in this chapter, the 1902 edition is a final text identical to the Standard Edition of 1932.)

Here Shaw introduces his discussion of Godhead, and its chief representative Wotan:

The mysterious thing we call life organizes itself into all living shapes, bird, beast, beetle and fish, rising to the human marvel in cunning dwarfs and in laborious muscular giants, capable, these last, of enduring toil, willing to buy love and life, not with suicidal curses and renunciations, but with patient manual drudgery in the service of higher powers. And these higher powers are called into existence by the same self-organization of life still more wonderfully into rare persons who may by comparison be called gods, creatures capable of thought, whose aims extend far beyond the satisfaction of their bodily appetites and personal affections, since they perceive that it is only by the establishment of a social order founded on common bonds of moral faith that the world can rise from mere savagery. But how is this order to be set up by Godhead in a world of stupid giants, since these thoughtless ones pursue only their narrower personal ends and can by no means understand the aims of a god? Godhead, face to face with Stupidity, must compromise.[6] Unable to enforce on the world the pure law of thought, it must resort to a mechanical law of commandments to be enforced by brute punishments and the destruction of the disobedient. And however carefully these laws are framed to represent the highest thoughts of the framers at the moment of their promulgation, before a day has elapsed that thought has grown and widened by the ceaseless evolution of life; and lo! yesterday's law already fallen out with today's thought. Yet if the high givers of that law themselves set the example of breaking it before it is a week old, they destroy all its authority with their subjects, and so break the weapon they have forged to rule them for their own good. They must therefore maintain at all costs the sanctity of the law, even when it has ceased to represent their thought; so that at last they get entangled in a network of ordinances which they no longer believe in, and yet have made so sacred by custom and so terrible by punishment, that they cannot themselves escape from them. Thus Godhead's resort to law finally costs

6. In the 1899 edition, the preceding two sentences read as follows: "But how is this order to be set up by Godhead in a world of stupid giants, since these thoughtless ones pursue only their narrower personal ends and are therefore purchasable by the gold of Alberic? Godhead, face to face with Pluto, must compromise." The revised text first appears in the 1902 edition.

it half its integrity—as if a spiritual king, to gain temporal power, had plucked out one of his eyes—and it finally begins secretly to long for the advent of some power higher than itself which will destroy its artificial empire of law, and establish a true republic of free thought. (174–175) [7]

Wotan, chief of the gods, is the one-eyed deity in question. He must compromise because his efficacy is not commensurate with his vision. Since "his power has been established in the world by and as a system of laws enforced by penalties" (192), he is trapped into becoming the slave of the system himself; for "a god who broke his own laws would betray the fact that legality and conformity are not the highest rule of conduct" (192). Such a discovery would, Shaw continues, be "fatal to his supremacy as Pontiff and Lawgiver" (192); yet to constrict his actions for the purpose of avoiding such an exposure is equally fatal to Wotan's godlike aspirations.

Valhalla, the home of the gods, has a dual function. Like the "ideals," it is both a mask to hide reality and a standard of perfection which a realist seeks to emulate. To some extent it is a symbol of Wotan's vision of what Godhead ideally would be. But it is also a spectacular showpiece, intended to associate "the legislative power with such displays of splendor and majesty" as will awe the imaginations and thus secure the respect of the many who are not intelligent enough "to comprehend the thought of the lawgiver" (175). In order to fulfill his contract under the

7. Since Shaw has been disparaged (for instance by Wellek, 428) for his supposedly "preposterous" distortion of *The Ring,* it is worth noting how closely key elements in his account correspond to Wagner's own text. The passage quoted here is an eloquent paraphrase of Wotan's long address to Brünhilde in Act II of *Die Walküre:* "My spirit aspired to power, and . . . I went and won myself the world. I thought no falsehood, yet I did falsely, carried out contracts where harm lay hid. . . . Mightless by law, my spirit is gone . . . I who by treaties was lord, by these treaties now am a slave. Yet one can manage what I don't dare, a hero, never helped by my power; who, strange to gods, is free of their grace; . . . this one can do what I fear to try, and never urged him do, though it was all of my wish" (Richard Wagner, *The Ring of the Nibelung,* trans. by Stuart Robb [New York: E. P. Dutton, 1960], 106–110).

law to the plodding giants who have built Valhalla, Wotan is placed in the agonizing position of having to pay the debt for their labor by stealing from Alberic the ring that represents material power. Thus the god outdoes the dwarf in mischief: it is one thing that malign powers exist, but that "Godhead should steal those malign powers from evil, and wield them itself, is a monstrous perversion" (181). This, however, is the "way of the world" (181), the sad state of "tangles and alliances and compromises" (183) in which Wotan must become enmeshed to achieve what Cashel Byron called "executive power."

Wotan's alliance with the law is symbolized in the poem by his marriage to Fricka; once that union occurs, "it is Fricka's mechanical force, and not his thought, that really rules the world" (196). The actual methodology of the law's operation is the province of Loki, the "dialectician-in-chief" (192) whose job it is to inculcate Wotan's warriors with "the conventional system of law and duty, supernatural religion and self-sacrificing idealism, which [the warriors] believe to be the essence of his godhood, but which is really only the machinery of the love of necessary power which is his mortal weakness" (192).[8] What is even worse is that "such systems, in spite of their moral pretensions, serve selfish and ambitious tyrants better than benevolent despots" (192). In other words, Alberic needs only to win back the ring and he will be able to play Wotan's game far more easily than Wotan himself. Thus the result of the god's initial compromise will be the advent of complete mindlessness wielding unchallengeable powers of physical coercion.

Shaw is both fascinated and distressed by Wotan's predicament. In no sense does he condemn the hapless god:

There is no such thing as Man in the world: what we have to deal with is a multitude of men, some of them great rascals, some of them great statesmen, others both, with a vast majority capable of managing their personal affairs, but not of comprehending social or-

8. The phrase "love of necessary power" (1902) originally read "ambitious love of power" (1899).

ganization, or grappling with the problems created by their association in enormous numbers. . . . Such people, like Wagner's giants, must be governed by laws; and their assent to such government must be secured by deliberately filling them with prejudices and practising on their imaginations by pageantry and artificial eminences and dignities. The government is of course established by the few who are capable of government. . . . All these capable people are thus in the position of Wotan, forced to maintain as sacred, and themselves submit to, laws which they privately know to be obsolescent makeshifts, and to affect the deepest veneration for creeds and ideals which they ridicule among themselves with cynical scepticism.
(214–215)

This is not an isolated example of such reasoning. Thirty-five years later, in his preface to *On the Rocks* Shaw was again to reveal his belief in the necessity of governing by imposture. Writing of Galileo, he argues that "it is quite credible that both his immediate judges and the Pope believed with at least half their minds that he was right about the earth and the sun" (172). Nonetheless, they "had to consider . . . whether the Christian religion, on which to the best of their belief not only the civilization of the world but its salvation depended . . . could stand the shock of the discovery that many of its tales . . . must have been written by somebody who did not know what the physical universe was really like" (172). Consequently, it was necessary to resort to imposture: "Is it any wonder that the Pope told Galileo that he really must keep his discoveries to himself, and that Galileo consented to deny them? Possibly it was the Pope who, to console him, whispered 'E pur se muove' " (172). As he grew older Shaw became more sympathetic—perhaps *too* sympathetic—to Wotan's compromise.[9]

9. For example, "Mendacity Compulsory in Kingcraft and Priestcraft" (*Far* 69–71, Pref); the discussion of Mahomet's predicament in "having to rule a body of Arab chieftains . . . who . . . could not be trusted . . . to behave as he himself would have behaved spontaneously" (*Simp* 5, Pref); and Shaw's own performance of "bogus miracles" as a vestryman (*Back* 263, Post). See also his related argument that the undeveloped moral sense of children must be nurtured by "poetic fictions" (*IWG* 363–365; *EPWW* 69–70).

The interesting point for our present purposes is that at the time of writing the *Wagnerite* Shaw should have appreciated Wotan at all. In the foregoing analysis of the *Quintessence* it was noted that although there is both a stupid idealism and a noble idealism, Shaw is not so much interested in making distinctions between the two as he is in attacking all idealism as being incompatible with the most determined pragmatism. The gods of the *Wagnerite,* as I have said, correspond to the idealists. Wotan, chief of the gods, manifests the heroic side of idealism; but far from damning him for being foolish enough to aspire to greatness instead of doggedly applying himself to survival, Shaw deals compassionately with the tragic implications of a noble nature caught in a cruel predicament.

What then *has* happened to the side of idealism represented in the *Quintessence* by Manders and Werle? This has its partisans among the gods, too. We learned in the earlier work, for instance, that idealism involved conventionality and absolutism—precisely the qualities embodied here not by Wotan but by his precedent-prone consort, Fricka. We learned too that ideals involved lies, illusions hiding the truth, and rationalism crippling the will. In this work all of these are symbolized not by Wotan but by Loki, who is both "the Lie that must, on the highest principles, hide the Truth" (198) and "the god of Intellect, Argument, Imagination, Illusion, and Reason" (176–177), whose job it is to create fearful mirages and appearances by which only the Hero will not be intimidated. There is no change in meaning between one book and the other—Fricka and Loki represent exactly those repellent qualities of idealism condemned in Shaw's reading of Ibsen. But whereas in the *Quintessence* all kinds of idealism were lumped together and attacked, in the *Wagnerite* Fricka and Loki are separated from and contrasted to Wotan. They are not an integral part of his being—he himself is in passionate revolt against them.

What has occurred is a shift in emphasis. Through the novels and the earliest plays Shaw basically undercuts idealistic pretension in favor of a practical perspective. But in slightly later plays characters such as Marchbanks, Dick Dudgeon, and Caesar seek a fuller existence than one predicated on a credo of survival. In Wotan, Shaw presents the resort to pragmatism not with the conviction that it should be embraced because it represents the best possible means of confronting the world, but rather as a tragic flaw symbolized by the "cost of that eye which is not the eye to the main chance" (*HMC* 238). It is for his grand vision, not his corrupting attempts to wield "executive power," that Wotan is praised. The gold of the Rhine represents "the Plutonic empire and the mastery of the world through its power" (178); but far from advocating its possession, Shaw warns us that "if there were no higher power in the world to work against Alberic, the end of it would be utter destruction" (173–174).

In the *Quintessence,* Shaw described "the errors of the idealists in the terms of the life they have risen above rather than in those of the life they fall short of" (119). I have previously argued that the difference between the two methods is not, as Shaw claimed, one of intelligibility but one of attitude. To evaluate the idealist basically from the point of view of the life he has risen above is to reduce him to a standard which is below him. To evaluate the same errors from the point of view of the higher life which he falls short of is to measure him by the standard to which he aspires. Judged by the ideal of the "perfect Adam," Brand is a hero though he did not achieve success; judged by the norms of the imperfect Adam, he is simply a fool for his pains. It is the difference between the perspective of the Philistine who "sneers at idealism from beneath" (118) and that of the realist/Hero who is "surveying it from the clear ether above, which can only be reached through its mists" (118–119). Though Shaw grants that many of Ibsen's idealists are heroic, it is the bad outcome of their striving, not the vision toward which they strive, which he (more than Ibsen) chooses to emphasize. In *The Perfect Wagnerite* all this is reversed. It is Wotan's aspiration that is presented: how "with his heart stirring towards higher forces than himself, [he] turns with disgust from these lower forces" (183) that have debased him.[10] Wotan is not judged from the vantage point of the dwarfs and giants but from that of a fellow-sufferer who fully appreciates his tragedy. And if the order of Heroes in the *Wagnerite* is treated perfunctorily in comparison to the class of realists who figured so prominently in the *Quintessence,* the reason is that most of the realist's virtues have now been incorporated into the god's own personality.

Thus *The Perfect Wagnerite* presents an explicit formulation of the new strand of Shaw's development suggested by the plays discussed in the first part of this chapter. By the time of this last of his major critical essays, Shaw had acquired a sense of ultimate goals whose genesis can be sensed in his growing doubts as to whether concrete solutions to the problems of civilization in fact lay just around the corner. It had been the original Fabian assumption that the enfranchisement of the working classes would in time guarantee the adoption of a socialistic society. But the newly founded Independent Labor Party had begun to drift away from Fabianism even before the great Conservative victory in the election of 1895; and practically none of the Fabian proposals had been implemented as the decade neared its end. These points have been made by a leading historian of the movement (McBriar 82–92, 286–289), who aptly notes that "the progress of Capitalism in England during the 'nineties had been far from producing the social effects predicted on the basis of the depression of the 'eighties" (83). While the divisions within Fabian ranks that were to result from the issues of imperialism (the Boer War), free trade (Chamberlain's tariff reform), internal leadership (H. G. Wells's challenge to the organization's "old gang"), and pacifism (World War I) were still to come, McBriar finds signs as early as 1896 that Shaw's own hopes were beginning

10. The words "stirring towards" (1902) originally read "turning to" (1899). Both here and in the examples previously cited, Shaw's revisions attempt to place Wotan's character in a more unambiguously favorable light.

to falter (82–83). "The Illusions of Socialism," written that year, contains both his first suggestion of disillusionment with democratic procedures (*NDW* 418) and his first effort to find a functional justification for certain kinds of idealistic illusion he had formerly tended to disparage. The fact is that Shaw's pragmatism could not outlive his optimism. It is no accident that the period of the mid- to late nineties, which marks the beginning of his disenchantment with "inevitable" short-term progress, also reveals his initial gropings toward a long-range metaphysic that would make sense of life's exigencies in some larger terms. At the heart of this metaphysic is a total view of the self that Shaw gained by grasping the relationship between Wotan in Wagner's *Ring* and Julian the Apostate in Ibsen's *Emperor and Galilean.* This theory of self-realization provides an indispensable basis for understanding the major plays of Shaw's maturity.

4 Dialectic of the Self

▄▖

Julian

In the *Quintessence* (49–59), the most thorough analysis is devoted to the longest and most pretentious of Ibsen's dramas, *Emperor and Galilean* (1864–1873).[1] This is in one sense surprising, for there is no indication that Shaw shared Ibsen's touching conviction that this starched leviathan was his masterpiece. Still, Shaw understands that the play's thematic importance outweighs its dramatic limitations, and he responds accordingly.

According to Shaw, Ibsen is attempting to come to terms intellectually with the unresolved metaphysical problems raised by *Brand* and *Peer Gynt*. Brand advocated the complete, if necessarily fanatical, sacrifice of the individual self to the divine will. Peer, in reacting against this ethic, sets up for himself the opposing "ideal of unconditional self-realization" (47). From a Shavian viewpoint, both these responses to existence fragment reality by treating partial perspectives as if they had absolute validity.

1. Some elements of this discussion of *Emperor*—which follows closely my doctoral dissertation (Harvard University, 1969)—have been anticipated by J. L. Wisenthal in *The Marriage of Contraries: Bernard Shaw's Middle Plays* (Cambridge: Harvard University Press, 1974). Wisenthal and I share an interest in the theme of reconciliation of opposites; our approaches to Shaw are similar at several points. I have referred to the more important of these overlapping readings in subsequent footnotes, but wish to make clear that my conclusions were reached independently. My main aim has been to depict the development of Shaw's total philosophic vision, rather than to trace how a particular dialectical pattern is rendered in a group of plays.

120

If the hero of *Emperor and Galilean* fails in his turn, it is the outcome of human rather than metaphysical error; for Maximus the Mystic does have an understanding of how life is to be made whole, wrong though he is to consider Julian the man to accomplish the goal.

Maximus knows that there is no going back to "the first empire" of pagan sensualism. "The second empire," Christian or self-abnegatory idealism, is already rotten at heart. "The third empire" is what he looks for: the empire of Man asserting the eternal validity of his own will. He who can see that not on Olympus, not nailed to the cross, but in himself is God: he is the man to build Brand's bridge between the flesh and the spirit, establishing this third empire in which the spirit shall not be unknown, nor the flesh starved, nor the will tortured and baffled.   (54)

It is important to see that the emphasis of the passage is upon combination and not exclusion: idealism will still exist, but not Brand's variety; egotism likewise will thrive, but not Peer's variety. Olympus and the Cross, self-sacrifice and self-realization, the human and the divine—these forces will not be locked in combat but be transcended on a higher level.

Unfortunately, Julian does not understand the subtleties of Maximus's dialectic. He is, to be sure, "prompted step by step to the stupendous conviction that he no less than the Galilean is God" (54);[2] and Shaw finds that conviction all to the good. But the Emperor's egotism causes him to seek the obliteration of opposites: "Christ appears to him, not as the prototype of himself, as Maximus would have him feel, but as a rival god over whom he must prevail at all costs" (55). In short, Julian simply becomes a megalomaniacal idealist attempting to revive paganism "by cruel enforcement of external conformity to its rites" (55). Manders might have done as much, and at the same time have been equally oblivious to what Maximus was driving at when the Mystic tried to indicate that the question is not one of *this* or *that,* but of both:

2. The words "no less than" (1913) originally read "and not" (1891).

MAXIMUS. Is it not written, "Thou shalt have none other gods but me"?

JULIAN. Yes—yes—yes.

MAXIMUS. The seer of Nazareth did not preach this god or that: he said "God is I: I am God."

JULIAN. And that is what makes the emperor powerless? The third empire? The Messiah? Not the Jews' Messiah, but the Messiah of the two empires, the spirit and the world?

MAXIMUS. The God-Emperor.

JULIAN. The Emperor-God.

MAXIMUS. Logos in Pan, Pan in Logos.   (56—Shaw's quotation)

Shaw's comment on this interchange is significant:

But it is of no use. Maximus's idea is a synthesis of relations in which not only is Christ God in exactly the same sense as that in which Julian is God, but Julian is Christ as well. The persistence of Julian's jealousy of the Galilean shews that he has not comprehended the synthesis at all, but only seized on that part of it which flatters his own egotism. And since this part is only valid as a constituent of the synthesis, and has no reality when isolated from it, it cannot by itself convince Julian. In vain does Maximus repeat his lesson in every sort of parable, and in such pregnant questions as "How do you know, Julian, that you were not in him whom you now persecute?"   (56)

Maximus is not anti-Christian, but antifactional. Julian on the other hand, despite his sublime pretensions, wishes simply to replace one absolutism with another and thus reduces the great experiment to a traditional exercise in deadly rivalry between isolated elements of the human personality.

Slowly Julian comes to realize that something is wrong and speculates as to what it is: " 'There is a mysterious power outside us, which in a great measure governs the issue of human undertakings' " (58—Shaw's quotation). But Julian's attempt now to attribute the entire difficulty to some mysterious "world-will" that has ambushed him is not accepted by Shaw:

It was something for Julian to have seen that the power which he found stronger than his individual will was itself will; but inasmuch as he conceived it, not as the whole of which his will was but a part, but as a rival will, he was not the man to found the third empire. He had felt the godhead in himself, but not in others. Being only able to say, with half conviction, "The kingdom of heaven is within ME," he had been utterly vanquished by the Galilean who had been able to say, "The kingdom of heaven is within YOU." But he was on the way to that full truth. A man cannot believe in others until he believes in himself; for the conviction of the equal worth of his fellows must be filled by the overflow of the conviction of his own worth. (58)

This passage expresses Shaw's view of the place of the self in the universe. While his belief is nothing so simple as the authoritarian idea that by doing a higher will one is automatically achieving self-realization, neither is it anything so simple as the reverse idealization that stipulates that by simply pursuing one's personal desires one is automatically fulfilling a higher will. What Shaw demands is a crucial kind of action in which the *perfectly* self-realized person is also advancing the purposes of ultimate reality. A closer look at Shaw's view of the relationship between self-realization and ethics will help show how this achievement is possible.

For Shaw the self is the root of all values. Robert Smith, the hero of *Immaturity,* found "the power to stand alone . . . worth acquiring at the expense of much sorrowful solitude" (83); Owen Jack in *Love among the Artists* knew that "a man's own self is the last person to believe in him, and is harder to cheat than the rest of the world" (149); Trefusis in *An Unsocial Socialist* asserted that a man's duty to himself is "the first and hardest of all duties" (104). Laudatory references in the novels to selfishness, self-reliance, self-sufficiency, self-regard, and self-respect are ubiquitous.[3] And from the fictional protagonists there is an unbroken progression to a long series of dramatic heroes whose combination of self-direction and confidence amazes the com-

3. See *Imm* 94, 143, 208, 223, 298; *Knot* 174, 214, 225, 270, 329; *Love* 66, 84, 122, 149, 237, 330; *Cash* 89, 125, 211; *Unsoc* 23, 52, 104, 115, 206, 248. To numerous excerpts already quoted from the *Quintessence* should be added those on Lasalle (23–24) and the parrot (39–40).

mon mortals who can only note that "one man that has a mind and knows it can always beat ten men who havnt and dont" (*Cart* 208). If we grasp the centrality of the self in Shaw's thought, it will be easy to understand why Lady Cicely shies away from marriage with Brassbound when she senses in his desire to "take service" under her (*Brass* 284–285) an obstacle to the independence he finally achieves (286); why Ann White-field is disinclined to be used as inspiration by the poet she compares to a "bird who must press its breast against a thorn to make itself sing" (*Super* 153); why the She-Ancient in *Back to Methuselah* has lost interest in art because it is a form of "striving to create perfection in things outside [herself]" (243); why Shaw repeatedly reminds us that "mankind cannot be saved from without" (*Back* xii) and rarely mentions self-sacrifice except in a tone that is satirical if not scathing.[4]

Where the self is all, experience subverts solipsism—it is by trusting one's impulses and working through them, not by living a life of self-repression, that one achieves a meaningful relationship to existence. Those who complain of Shaw's puritanical attitude toward sex and alcohol will be hard pressed to find a single passage where he urges abstention from what he disapproves of. Rather, the man who enjoys reminding his audience of Blake's dictum that "the road of excess leads to the palace of wisdom" urges the "stern asceticism of satiety" (*Super* xxii). Speaking in his own voice as well as through his characters, Shaw repeatedly advocates an experiential philosophy of life: "Never resist temptation" (*Super* 211); "Do whatever you like" (*Brass* 283); "Let life come to you" (*Simp* 42 and *passim*). To a hypothetical young lady who vows to rebel against a respectable upbringing based on self-sacrifice and duty, Shaw offers encouragement despite his awareness that her reaction will be excessive: "By all means do as you propose. Try how wicked

4. For a sampling, see *Imm* 249–250, 343; *Love* 201; *Quint* 32–34; *Wag* 236–237; *Brass* 279; *Super* xx, 22, 225 (Maxims); *Barb* 297; *Fanny* 291; *Over* 187; *True* 102.

you can be: it is precisely the same experiment as trying how good you can be. At worst you will only find out the sort of person you really are. . . . The would-be wicked ones find, when they come to the point, that the indispensable qualification for a wicked life is not freedom but wickedness" (*Art* 304, 312). When young Golding Bright pleaded incompetence in response to Shaw's exhortation that he write a book, his mentor snapped back: "That is just why I recommend you to learn. If I advised you to learn to skate, you would not reply that your balance was scarcely good enough yet. A man learns to skate by staggering about and making a fool of himself. Indeed he progresses in all things by resolutely making a fool of himself" (*CL* I, 465).

That such eager susceptibility to all things new may involve false leads and harmful consequences is a risk Shaw cheerfully accepts, arguing that "the man who has never made a mistake will make anything; and the man who has never done any harm will never do any good." This conclusion of the pamphlet called "Imprisonment" (*Crim* 229) might almost have been in the minds of Margaret Knox and Bobby Gilbey, those sheltered postadolescents of *Fanny's First Play* who deliberately break the law and go to jail as a means of expanding their experiential frame of reference. Even that riskiest of enterprises—marriage— Shaw extols as an "indispensable factor in the education of the complete man or woman" (*HMC* 223); he laments the "uncompleted experience" of the priest or nun (*And* 67, Pref). Nothing that enlarges one's capacity for life is to be regretted: in *Getting Married,* the promiscuous Mrs. George is a more fully self-realized person than the abstemious Lesbia Grantham. And for all Shaw's disapproval of amorism and aestheticism, the young inhabitants of "As Far as Thought Can Reach" (*Back,* Part V) are deprived of neither—encouraged by their elders to do as they please, the "newly born" discard art and sex only after outgrowing them. Even in the attenuated world of *Farfetched Fables* (1949), the openness is all—a schoolroom is invaded by a flying youth clothed in feathers, who has been transformed from spirit to flesh because he was curious to see what matter was like. When asked his reaction to being a body, he replies: "I do not like nor dislike. I experience" (130).

Shaw's deeply held belief in the self as the source of values was to receive its most direct and suggestive expression in the final sections of the *Methuselah* cycle:

Zoo. . . . I knew quite well what you meant by your torch handed on from generation to generation. But every time that torch is handed on, it dies down to the tiniest spark; and the man who gets it can rekindle it only by his own light.   (158)

The Newly Born. . . . I shall enjoy life for ever and ever.
The She-Ancient. If you should turn out to be a person of infinite capacity, you will no doubt find life infinitely interesting.   (212)

The He-Ancient. . . . I have seen you walking over the mountains alone. Have you not found your best friend in yourself?
Acis. What are you driving at, old one? What does all this lead to?
The He-Ancient. It leads, young man, to the truth that you can create nothing but yourself.   (241)

Such utterances suggest that what we see is what we are. All perception is "projection" having as much validity as the self behind it: "Better keep yourself clean and bright: you are the window through which you must see the world" (*Super* 216, Maxims). The premise of this tritely phrased epigram underlies a good many penetrating psychological insights, ranging from Mary Sutherland's suggestion to Adrian Herbert in *Love among the Artists* that "the change in me that you hint at is only a change in your way of looking at me" (298) to George Fox's admission to Barbara Villiers in *Good King Charles's Golden Days* that he can know of women "only what the woman in myself teaches me" (176–177). The tenet that the self is the medium through which existence is filtered has as its corollary not the raptures of self-indulgence but the rigors of self-knowledge.

It is the primacy of the self that accounts for much in Shaw's writing that his contemporaries found disturbing. The positions he takes on ethical questions are for the most part not very shocking—the twist comes when ethical imperatives are translated from the language of self-sacrifice into that of self-realization. The best known example is Shaw's lifelong objection to corporal punishment and vivisection on the grounds that they are degrading to the souls of their *doers*.[5]

If the self is the unit of value, punishment for reprehensible behavior must be *self*-reactive rather than externally imposed. The *Quintessence* makes this very clear. Shaw does not argue, for instance, against exploitative idealization of woman on the grounds of sympathy for women but rather because "men are waking up to the perception that in killing women's souls they have killed their own" (8, 2d Pref). Mrs. Solness cannot make a happy home for her husband "because her own happiness has been sacrificed to his genius" (94, *1913*). Rubeck uses Irene as a means to the end of creating his great work of art; his retribution is that he loses his artistic inspiration and mutilates his own masterpiece—"as he used her up and left her dead, so with her death the life went out of him" (115). The punishment of the liar is "not in the least that he is not believed, but that he cannot believe anyone else" (14). This last remark is a precursor

5. Like many of Shaw's views, this one has been subject to misunderstanding. Here is Hesketh Pearson on the subject: "Shaw's lack of imagination is quaintly illustrated in his remarks on human cruelty and suffering. He condemns blood sports, not because they give pain to the animal but because they give pleasure to the spectator, and his chief objection to flogging as a punishment is that it demoralizes the flogger and those who abet or witness it, not that it hurts the person who is flogged. But the average sensitive human being who is forced to watch the torture or execution of a rabbit or a man does not worry about the souls of the sportsman, the hangman, the flogger, the inquisitioner, the firing squad, the chaplain, or the onlookers; he puts himself in the place of the victim, feels some of his terror and his pain, and knows that, but for the grace of God, himself might have provided the sport of brutes" (39–40). The lack of imagination here is Pearson's. *Saint Joan* does not cause us merely to feel how terrible it would be to be burned, but also how terrible it would be to have shared the responsibility for burning. The former emotion is only an elaborately disguised self-pity; the latter, rejecting a simplistic distinction between brutes and victims, appeals to a wrongdoer's *self*-respect as the basis of reformation.

of the comment in his preface to *Misalliance* that "the penalty of the impostor is not that he is found out (he very seldom is) but that he is taken for what he pretends to be, and treated as such" (77). *Heartbreak House* supplies a case in point in the character of Boss Mangan, who acts the "tough guy" and then is hurt to discover that others assume he has no feelings. Likewise, the "punishment" of Warwick in *Saint Joan* is that he cannot undergo the anguish that finally overwhelms De Stogumber.

In the same way that the penalty for evil is self-inflicted, the motives for humanitarian acts are shown to be validly rooted in self-interest. It is not from a sense of self-abnegation that Dick Dudgeon submits to the rope or Joan to the stake: for the person who is *naturally* a saint, the act of martyrdom is not the destruction but the fulfillment of his nature.[6] The same perspective underlies Shaw's political views: he never urges anyone to become a socialist by sacrificing his own interests: on the contrary, he argues that socialism *is* in the long-range interest of all persons. His very insistence that the common man has no choice but to look out for himself until the system changes is intended to provoke the uncommon man into seeing the value of changing the system.[7] Sometimes, as in "Socialism for Millionaires," he

6. The recantation speech in *Saint Joan* (whatever reservations one may have about its strained diction) makes clear that the heroine's death is not an act of self-sacrifice. Her willingness to recant indicates that Joan has no intention of dying for a principle, but finally she *prefers* death to life on the terms offered her.

7. "Mrs Warren's defence of herself . . . is no defence at all of the vice which she organizes. It is no defence of an immoral life to say that the alternative offered by society collectively to poor women is a miserable life, starved, overworked, fetid, ailing, ugly. . . . The man who cannot see that starvation, overwork, dirt, and disease are as anti-social as prostitution—that they are the vices and crimes of a nation, and not merely its misfortunes—is (to put it as politely as possible) a hopelessly Private Person. . . . Many friendly critics . . . remonstrate sincerely, asking me what good such painful exposures [of social evils] can possibly do. . . . The good of mentioning them is that you make people so extremely uncomfortable about them that they finally stop blaming 'human nature' for them, and begin to support measures for their reform" (*Mrs W* 166, 169

makes this point indirectly through a tongue-in-cheek commiseration for the "hidden sorrows of plutocracy" arising from the problems excessive wealth poses for its possessors;[8] elsewhere, he argues straightforwardly that it is imposible for the rich to escape the evil effects of poverty (for example, *EFS* 21). His hope for a new basis of society was not derived from the naive belief that man is an angel; while Shaw preferred to leave the "fallacies of absolute morality" out of the discussion entirely, he was willing, if pushed, to regard man as "an obstinate and selfish devil, who is being slowly forced by the iron tyranny of Nature[9] to recognize that in disregarding his neighbor's happiness he is taking the surest way to sacrifice his own" (*EFS* 82).

For Shaw, "the way to Communism lies through the most resolute and uncompromising Individualism" (*Quint* 102, *1913*). In the *Quintessence* he considers the plight of Rita and Allmers at the end of *Little Eyolf:*

The solution of their problem, as far as it is solved, is, as coming from Ibsen, very remarkable. It is not, as might have been expected after his long propaganda of Individualism, that they should break up the seraglio and go out into the world until they have learnt to stand alone, and through that to accept companionship on honorable conditions only. Ibsen here explicitly insists for the first time that "we are members one of another," and that though the strongest man is he who stands alone, the man who is standing alone for his own sake solely is literally an idiot.[10] It is indeed a staring fact in

—Pref). The word "anti-social" (Standard Edition) originally read "immoral" (1905).

8. Compare "Miseries of the Vagrant Rootless Rich" (*True* 10–12, Pref). One of the "Maxims for Revolutionists" claims, "The more a man possesses over and above what he uses, the more careworn he becomes" (*Super* 219).

9. Despite his rejection of Darwinian natural selection, Shaw's view of Nature has more in common with the bleak vision of Mill and Tennyson ("red in tooth and claw") than with the raptures of the Romantic poets. He consistently sees Nature as an indifferent, tyrannical presence against which man must wage constant battle for survival. See *EFS* 27–28, 93–94; *IWG* 80–83, 319; *Rocks* 163, Pref; *EPWW* 346–347.

10. Literally: that is, etymologically. "Idiot" is derived from a Greek

history and contemporary life that nothing is so gregarious as self-ishness, and nothing so solitary as the selflessness that loathes the word Altruism because to it there are no "others": it sees and feels in every man's case the image of its own. "Inasmuch as ye have done it unto one of the least of these my brethren ye have done it unto me" is not Altruism or Othersism. It is an explicit repudiation of the patronizing notion that "the least of these" is *another* to whom you are invited to be very nice and kind: in short, it accepts entire identification of "me" with "the least of these." (101–102, *1913*)

The continuation of this passage makes clear that there is no contradiction between Shaw's passionate advocacy of "prag-matic" individualism and his equally passionate opposition to "economic" individualism (that is, laissez faire capitalism of the Manchester School variety).[11]

There is no hope in Individualism for egotism. When a man is at last brought face to face with himself by a brave Individualism, he finds himself face to face, not with an individual, but with a species, and knows that to save himself, he must save the race. He can have no life except a share in the life of the community; and if that life is unhappy and squalid, nothing that he can do to paint and paper and upholster and shut off his little corner of it can really rescue him from it. (102, *1913*)

A humanitarian is not a "do-gooder" but a person with a sense of his self-interest that is far deeper and more imaginative than that of the conventionally "selfish" person. Thus Shaw writes of Alberic not as a villian but as one "too stupid to see that his own welfare can only be compassed as part of the welfare of the world" (*Wag* 172); thus he warns us in *Man and Superman* that "in an ugly and unhappy world the richest man can purchase nothing but ugliness and unhappiness" (219, Maxims); thus he praises Christ's injunction that one should love one's neighbor as oneself (*And* 24, Pref); thus he can retort during the First World

word meaning "private person," an expression Shaw sometimes employs as a euphemism for it, as in note 7 above.

11. Also referred to as "Individualist Anarchism" (*EFS* 77) or "Un-socialism" (*EFS* 262) in numerous places in Shaw's political writings.

War to those who exulted in German losses: "they were our losses as well" (*Heart* 19, Pref). "As Far as Thought Can Reach" again makes clear that deeper love is reached by an extension of a sense of self that transcends the petty egotism of romantic attachment.

THE NEWLY BORN. Oh yes: I will be more than she could ever have been.
STREPHON. Psha! Jealous!
THE NEWLY BORN. Oh no. I have grown out of that. I love her now because she loved you, and because you love her.
THE HE-ANCIENT. That is the next stage. You are getting on very nicely, my child. (*Back* 239–240)

Thus Marchbanks came to love Morell.

Survival may be, as I previously held, the root premise of Shavian drama; but in the moment of fullest self-awareness a person realizes that his survival involves more than his own self: "man, having fought and won his . . . personal liberty, only to find himself a more abject slave than before, is turning with loathing from his egotist's dream of independence to the collective interests of society, with the welfare of which he now perceives his own happiness to be inextricably bound up" (*Unsoc* 254, Appendix). A person begins with himself, but he must not end there: the impulse must outgrow the source. This new political awareness rests solidly on new metaphysical underpinnings. "Good people" says Shaw, "follow a light that shines within and above and ahead of them" (*Back* lxx). The Romantic tradition would speak of the light within; traditional religion would place that light "above and ahead." Shaw sees the second as the outgrowth of the first, as the result of the "overflow" of the sense of one's own worth, as the achievement of a paradoxical state in which the individual will and the "world-will" become one, when man finally "ceases to be selfish" because he is "self-satisfied at last" (*Quint* 24).

To integrate this view with the theme of *Emperor and Galilean,* we might begin by reformulating Julian's problem: he lacks a strong enough sense of self to cease being an egotist. He can see the possibility of a higher relation between ego and cosmos only as a personal threat. In the words of Maximus, the "right man" to found the third empire is

"He who shall swallow up both emperor and Galilean. . . . Both shall succumb; but you shall not therefore perish. Does not the child succumb in the youth and the youth in the man: yet neither child nor youth perishes. You know I have never approved of your policy as emperor. You have tried to make the youth a child again. The empire of the flesh is fallen a prey to the empire of the spirit. But the empire of the spirit is not final, any more than the youth is. You have tried to hinder the youth from growing: from becoming a man. Oh fool, you have drawn your sword against that which is to be: against the third empire, in which the twin-natured shall reign. For him the Jews have a name. They call him Messiah, and are waiting for him."   (55–56—Shaw's quotation)

Julian of course does not understand the point of the organic metaphor: what for Maximus is an eagerly awaited act of self-realization is for him only a demand for self-transcendence. To Shaw it is obvious that a man can no more transcend himself than a quart bottle can hold a gallon. If the container does hold the larger amount, we must have been mistaken about its capacity in the first place. What others would call self-transcendence Shaw sees not as a conquest of self but as the growth of a new self, an actualization of inner potentiality. The metaphor he uses to convey this is that of *rebirth*: the cry "Ye must be born again" rings like an echo through the pages of his works as a metaphor for the self-generated higher state.[12] The death of the old self is analogous to the way the youth "succumbs" into the man, or the seed "dies" into the flower. But for the logic-bound Julian, these are only infuriating paradoxes.

In writing *Emperor and Galilean* (subtitled "A World-Historic Drama"), Ibsen had been influenced by the ideas of Hegel.

12. See *Knot* 272; *Super* 171–172, Rev Hdbk; *Mis* 4–5, Pref; *Back* 7. Note also Shaw's treatment of "resurrection" in Ibsen's *When We Dead Awaken* (*Quint* 31).

Shaw's work too is deeply rooted in an urge for dialectical synthesis. This has been suggested in my earlier contention that the
Philistine, idealist, and realist must not be regarded as mutually
exclusive and disjunct categories because the fuller understanding and efficiency of the realist will incorporate both the Philistine's sober plodding efficiency and the idealist's vision of a
higher life. But the Shavian passion for union can be seen in
many places beyond the *Quintessence*: in his regarding the ideal
human personality as androgynous rather than unisexual (Knight
—in Kaufmann, 121–123); in his fusion of a trinity of values
("three in one and one in three") in the heaven of *John Bull's
Other Island* (177); in his attempt to weld mighty opposites in
the resolution of *Major Barbara;* in his hope that Creative Evolution would have an appeal catholic enough to unite persons of
many different doctrinal persuasions (see "Modern Religion II,"
SR 60–80); in his exploration of a possible unification of East
and West in the late *Simpleton of the Unexpected Isles;* in his
insistence in a last full-length play (1947) that there will be no
better world "until law and science, politics and religion, are
all one" (*Buoy* 45).

In *Emperor and Galilean* the synthesizing of contradictory
elements expresses a relationship between free will and necessity.
Shaw begins his analysis with the statement that the reference in
that play to Cain, who "slew because he willed, willed because
he must, and must have willed to slay because he was himself"
(50), is an old-fashioned dilemma with "no very deep significance." But it is interesting that his own discussion of Julian and
Maximus parallels that dilemma if for free will versus necessity
we substitute the individual self versus ultimate reality. The will
of the individual is free because it is in his control: yet as the
agent of the higher reality the self is bound by larger forces that
transcend personal will. This problem, very much in evidence in
Emperor and Galilean, appears tantalizingly (in a passage Shaw
does not himself quote) when Julian asks the mysterious voice
how he shall establish his empire:

JULIAN. And by what way?
THE VOICE. By the way of freedom.
JULIAN. Speak clearly! What is the way of freedom?
THE VOICE. The way of necessity.
JULIAN. And by what power?
THE VOICE. By willing.
JULIAN. What shall I will?
THE VOICE. What thou must.   (V, 112–113)

The emphasis of this passage is similar to that in other Ibsen plays, where the heroes, from Brand to Borkman, utter strenuous paeans to the power of will and yet also speak as if their actions were preordained. Borkman echoes the very words of Cain: "People do not understand that I had to, because I was myself—because I was John Gabriel Borkman—myself, and not another" (XI, 266–267). So does Master Builder Solness: "I am what I am, and I cannot change my nature!" (X, 201). Or Ibsen himself in a letter to George Brandes: "In my opinion it comes to much the same thing whether, in writing of a person's character, I say 'It runs in his blood' or 'He is free—under necessity' " (V, xiv–xv).

In his analysis of *Emperor and Galilean* Shaw puts it this way: "What troubles [Maximus] is his having misled Julian by encouraging him to bring upon himself the fate of Cain and Judas. As water can be boiled by fire, man can be prompted and stimulated from without to assert his individuality; but just as no boiling can fill a half-empty well, no external stimulus can enlarge the spirit of man to the point at which he can self-beget the Emperor-God in himself by willing. At that point 'to will is to have to will' " (58). How can one reconcile the rejection of external stimuli with the belief that a person who follows his impulses is somehow bound by necessity? This is not so difficult as it first seems. Heraclitus held that "man's character is his fate." Is not the Shavian point of view similar? In *The Sanity of Art* Shaw reminds his readers that one of the purposes of idealism is to enable people to avoid feeling the powerful claims of their own natures:

"The woman tempted me," "The serpent tempted me," "I was not myself at the time," "I meant well," "My passion got the better of my reason," "It was my duty to do it," "The Bible says that we should do it," "Everybody does it," and so on. Nothing is left but the frank avowal: "I did it because I am built that way." Every man hates to say that.   (311)

Yet Shaw's characters say that very often—it is interesting that in a writer so very intellectual, motives so often boil down to Lady Cicely's "I was made so, I suppose" (*Brass* 248), William the waiter's "It's in the character, sir" (*Tell* 236), Margaret Knox's "I did it because I'm that sort of person" (*Fanny* 295), or even the Dauphin's "I am not built that way; and there is an end of it" (*Joan* 83). The theme of *The Devil's Disciple* and *Androcles and the Lion* is that a man finds his "true profession" (*Disc* 73) or "real faith" (*And* 133) in what both plays call the "hour of trial." Neither Ferrovius nor Dick Dudgeon actually changes; rather each one discovers that his real nature involves impulses that have nothing to do with conscious understanding or rational control.

When in *Androcles* Lavinia is asked why she should not pretend to sacrifice incense to Diana for the sake of form, she can only reply: "I cannot do it . . . it is physically impossible. . . . Once there was a dear little mouse that used to come out and play on my table as I was reading. I wanted to take him in my hand and caress him . . . but my hand refused: it is not in the nature of my hand to touch a mouse. Well, Captain, if I took a pinch of incense in my hand and stretched it out over the altar fire, my hand would come back. My body would be true to my faith even if you could corrupt my mind" (114). To call this "necessity" raises a problem, because that word suggests exactly those forms of external compulsion against which Shaw elsewhere inveighs so eloquently. And to be sure, the kind of impulses to which Lavinia refers may *appear* to be external and arbitrary because one can give no rational account of them. Still, the necessity Shaw has in mind is no such force, but rather the *in-*

ner necessity later described by Franklyn Barnabas in *Back to Methuselah:* "Do not mistake the mere idle fancies for the tremendous miracle-working force of Will nerved to creation by a conviction of Necessity. I tell you men capable of such willing, and realizing its necessity, will do it reluctantly, under inner compulsion, as all great efforts are made. They will hide what they are doing from themselves: they will take care not to know what they are doing" (82).

Once it is seen that one's nature can be a kind of fate without ceasing to be uniquely individual, many of Shaw's apparent contradictions can be newly interpreted and reconciled.[13] We should now be able to understand, for instance, why in one place he can argue that a creative writer "is an instrument in the grip of Creative Evolution" (*Back* 257, Post) while elsewhere defining an original work of art as one that results from "a spontaneous internal impulse" (*Quint* 11). In the plays we can see why Lady Cicely does not have even a "mad little bit of self left in me" (285) and yet can advise Brassbound, "Do whatever you like. Thats what I always do" (282); why Mrs. George in *Getting Married* can say that she has never in her life "done anything that was not ordained for me" and then insist, "Ive been myself"

13. The extent to which a person has "free will" is a question which finds Shaw usually echoing the dictum that "people come into the world ready-made" (Mrs. Byron in *Cash* 152–153). He often refers to a person as a "born" this or a "born" that; and his conviction appears to be that a man is free to realize (or not realize) his inner nature, but not to alter it significantly. Thus in a review of *The Second Mrs. Tanqueray* he takes Pinero to task for failing to understand that "a woman of that sort is already the same at three as she is at thirty-three" (*Theat* I, 47), and argues that a healthy child will grow up according to the way it is naturally "built" irrespective of the attempts of parents to modify its nature along lines they approve (*Mis* 11, Pref; *And* 94, Pref). A discussion of the question can be found in two sections ("Judge Not" and "Limits to Free Will") of the preface to *Androcles* (63–66). One might also consider the implications, for Shaw's own thought, of his statement that Lamarckian evolution reinforced the "acceptance of the congenital character of the individual as the determining factor in his destiny" (*Back* lvii).

(338); why Joan can "owe everything to the spirit of God," but then add "that was within me" (159); why the Deaconess in *Geneva* can tell the statesmen to bring their problems to Jesus while also urging that they should "look within, look within" (114); why George Fox in *Good King Charles's Golden Days* can say he hears "an Almighty Voice call 'George Fox, George Fox: rise up: testify,' " only to have King Charles reply, "Pastor: it is not given to every man as it has been to you to make a religion for himself" (178–179). Now we can see too why in discussing the saintly vocation Shaw points out that its members are both "self-elected" and "called from above": their obedience is "to the impulse of the Holy Ghost," but that impulse is "within them" (*True* 15, Pref). And, finally, it should be clear why the "third empire" of *Emperor and Galilean* moves beyond the personal self to the "world-will" while the resulting "Emperor-God" is, nonetheless, in Maximus's words, " 'self-begotten in the man who wills' " (56).

The "third empire" will be created by those whose sense of self is so strong that it overflows to unite with the ultimate forces underlying existence. Driven by deep impulse, such persons will act because they must, and yet remain free; for the higher reality has no other means of actualization than through the inner vision of the creatures who strive to apprehend its nature and achieve its ends. If Shaw finds the problem of Cain and Judas being "great freedmen under necessity" (54) to be superficial and yet argues in relation to the "third empire" that "to will is to have to will" (58), the difference is that the God of the Bible is external to Cain in a way that the "world-will" is not external to Julian. A comparison of characteristic passages from Bunyan, Ibsen, and Shaw will provide a final clarification of these ideas. The author of *The Pilgrim's Progress* was well aware that having godlike thoughts involves more than merely thinking that one has them (185); but in the seventeenth century there was at any rate a clear way to resolve any ethical dilemmas raised by conflicting claims between self and divinity:

IGNORANCE. What be good thoughts respecting ourselves?
CHRISTIAN. Such as agree with the Word of God.
IGNORANCE. When does our thoughts of ourselves agree with the Word of God?
CHRISTIAN. When we pass the same judgement upon ourselves which the Word passes. (186)

When we reach Peer Gynt's celebrated encounter with the Button Moulder, the goal of serving God remains the same; but by the mid-nineteenth century "the Word" has disappeared.

THE BUTTON MOULDER.
>   To be oneself is: to slay oneself.
>   . . . to stand forth everywhere
>   With Master's intention displayed like a signboard.

PEER.
>   But suppose a man never has come to know
>   What Master meant with him?

THE BUTTON MOULDER.
>   He must divine it.

PEER.
>   But how oft are divinings beside the mark . . .

THE BUTTON MOULDER.
>   That is certain, Peer Gynt; in default of divining
>   The cloven-hoofed gentleman finds his best hook. (IV, 252–253)

Deprived of an external standard, man must rely on his own— often perilously fallible—intuition. Shaw attempts to move from nineteenth-century skepticism to an affirmative religious position. If for Ibsen's "Master" and "divining" one substitutes "God" and "imagination," we arrive at the following from *Saint Joan:*

JOAN. I hear voices telling me what to do. They come from God.
ROBERT. They come from your imagination.
JOAN. Of course. That is how the messages of God come to us.
>   (66)

Bunyan's Christian subordinated his own will to God's; Ibsen's egotist substitutes his own will for God's. Shaw's saint has synthesized her soul with the holy spirit, dissolving the distinction between internal impulse and external force into a perfect unity.

In relation to this solution, Julian's error is that he saw the problem of his own will and the "world-will" in terms of opposition rather than fusion. To return to a crucial passage, it was something for him "to have seen that the power which he found stronger than his individual will was itself will; but inasmuch as he conceived it, not as the whole of which his will was but a part, but as a rival will, he was not the man to found the third empire" (58). That phrase "the whole of which his will was but a part" expresses the same relation Undershaft will later have in mind when he tells Cusins that what drives the armaments factory is not his own power but "a will of which I am a part" (*Barb* 327), or that Adam will invoke when the serpent tells him "the voice in the garden is your own voice" and he replies, "It is; and it is not. It is something greater than me: I am only a part of it" (*Back* 15). Though he never worked his theory of self-realization into systematic form, it is interesting that in three distinct places covering a period of thirty years, Shaw uses nearly identical wording to express his conception of the relation between the self and the universe.

Wotan

Now we are ready to carry one step farther the affinity that has already been noted between *The Quintessence of Ibsenism* and *The Perfect Wagnerite,* for Shaw's discussion of the Ring cycle bears an especially important relation to his interpretation of *Emperor and Galilean* in particular. Wotan is Julian in a more perceptive frame of mind: outgrowing the partiality that destroyed Ibsen's hero, he does come to understand the relation between his will and the "world-will." This insight develops slowly, to be sure. At first Wotan wishes to bring about the coming of the Hero by a bit of resourceful eugenics involving Siegmund and Sieglinde; but when rebuffed by Fricka because of the incestuous adultery that results, he has no choice but to condemn Siegmund: "A hero may have defied the law, and put his own will in its place; but can a god hold him guiltless, when the whole power of the gods can enforce itself only by law?" (196). One need say nothing worse of Fricka than that she is "absolutely right" (196); and Wotan thus orders that Siegmund shall be slain by Hunding—only to find his order thwarted by his daughter Brynhild. Now this is a perplexing circumstance, for Wotan had supposed Brynhild to be his "true will, his real self (as he thinks): to her he may say what he must not say to anyone, since in speaking to her he but speaks to himself" (193). What Wotan does not yet realize is that in disobeying his commands, Brynhild is nonetheless fulfilling his will. She is his *true* will, not his conscious intentions. What she thwarts is Wotan's explicit command to fulfill his obligations to Fricka under the law—obligations against which Wotan himself is in deep revolt. Brynhild is "Godhead's own very dearest soul" (198); she represents the "inner thought and will of Godhead, the aspiration from the high life to the higher that is its divine element, and only becomes separated from it when its resort to kingship and priestcraft for the sake of temporal power has made it false to itself" (196). It is immaterial whether one calls this subconscious will Wotan's character or his fate. The idea expressed in *Emperor* of one's essence being a kind of Necessity, operates here also. Wotan himself tells Alberic, " 'All things happen according to their nature; and *you* cant alter them' " (206); Wotan's very sword is named "Nothung" (Need). If Wotan's careful plans for the coming of the Hero do not work in the expected manner, it is because he only gradually discovers what his nature is.

For Shaw the key to understanding the action of *The Ring* is that "the god, since his desire is toward a higher and fuller life, must long in his inmost soul for the advent of that greater power whose first work, though this he does not see as yet, must be his own undoing" (190). Wotan is quite right in seeking the higher and nobler life. Like Maximus, Rosmer, and other heroic idealists, however, he fails to realize that the goal cannot be achieved by an external operation performed by himself: "It does not occur to him that when the Hero comes, his first exploit must be to sweep the gods and their ordinances from the path of "the heroic will" (193).[14] The Hero must destroy Alberic "without any illicit prompting from Wotan" (193). Wotan sticks the sword into a tree "so that only the might of a hero can withdraw it" (193); but Shaw comments, he is "blind to the truth that no weapon from the armory of Godhead can serve the turn of the true Human Hero" (193–194). Thus it follows naturally that when Siegfried wishes to acquire a sword he does not take the god's but forges his own weapon from the melted fragments of Nothung.

At work here is the same seemingly paradoxical dialectic that was central to Shaw's analysis of *Emperor and Galilean*. There the "third empire" required the death of the self, yet its coming was " 'self-begotten in the man who wills' " (56). Likewise here: the triumph of the Hero requires the eclipse of Wotan, yet the coming of the Hero is not possible except insofar as it is generated by Wotan himself. Godhead seeks to act "for the sake of that soul in itself which cares only to make the highest better and the best higher" (198). This ideal, like the "third empire," is an unrealized one placed in the future; yet the hope of its potential achievement depends upon "that soul in itself" which is Godhead's own essence. The higher state takes its origin from the self which wills its own death and then succumbs in order to grow, like the youth into the man, into something better. In the *Quintessence* the word used to describe this process was "rebirth." So here: our troubles will not cease until the divine impulse "passes completely away from Godhead, and is reborn as the soul of the hero" (198). Wotan must seek out Erda, the "First Mother [so that] through her womb, eternally fertile, the inner true thought that made him first a god [will be] reborn as his daughter, uncorrupted by his ambition, unfettered by his machinery of power" (193).

The superiority of Wotan to Julian lies in his ability to work

14. The words "the heroic will" (1902) originally read "his will" (1899).

with rather than against the process. In spite of his initial resistance, the god "finally begins secretly to long for the advent of some power higher than itself" (175); the truth and heroism that overthrow him are the "children of his inmost heart" (219); he is "finally acquiescing in and working for his own supersession" (219).[15] Upon learning in his last council with Erda that there can be no escape from destruction, then "from the innermost of him breaks the confession that he rejoices in his doom, and now himself exults in passing away with all his ordinances and alliances" (208). What Julian could see only as a humiliating course of self-abnegatory defeat, Wotan has willed as the evolutionary equivalent of the "third empire."

In this frame of mind Wotan goes forward to the meeting with Siegfried that forms the climax of Shaw's analysis. Here several of the motifs of the work come together. Posing as "The Wanderer," Wotan is pleased when the boy asserts his knowledge that "the broken bits of Nothung would be of no use to him unless he made a new sword out of them right over again from the beginning" (209). When Siegfried next demands to know what has happened to one of Wotan's eyes, the god "replies allegorically that the eye that is gone—the eye that his marriage with Fricka cost him—is now looking at him out of Siegfried's head" (209). A little hurt by Siegfried's arrogance and lack of respect, Wotan reveals his true identity and lifts his "world-governing spear" only to have it shattered beneath the stroke of Nothung. The metaphor of the two eyes represents the Hero's regaining the spiritual integrity so tragically divided by Wotan's original alliance with the forces of law and order. Likewise, the destruction of his spear represents his own supersession by an instrument, the descendant of Nothung, which originated with himself. Then

15. This is similar in both meaning and expression to Shaw's remark about *Candida:* "To distil the quintessential drama from pre-Raphaelitism, medieval or modern, it must be shewn at its best in conflict with the first broken, nervous, stumbling attempts to formulate its own revolt against itself as it develops into something higher" (*PP* vii). The phrase "at its best" (Standard Edition) was not in the original text (1898).

the god's anger subsides and he rejoices: "Up then . . . I cannot withhold you" (209); and as the fires of Loki roll down the mountain, Siegfried joyously walks through them: "And never a hair of his head is singed. Those frightful flames which have scared mankind for centuries from the Truth have not heat enough in them to make a child shut its eyes" (209–210)'. Or to put it another way: the illusions of moral absolutism have been dispersed by the triumph of the human will.

While the victory of Siegfried can be interpreted most readily as the forward thrust of man's progress over dead ideals, it is also possible to see Wotan, Brynhild, and Siegfried as three aspects of one psyche. Brynhild is the catalyst (will) by which the conscious mind (Wotan)' develops into new intuitive maturity (Siegfried). Thus it is no coincidence that, just prior to Siegfried's braving the flames, Wotan "disappears forever from the eye of man" (209); for once the soul of Godhead has been "reborn" as that of the Hero (198), the god himself can no longer be said to exist. In a very real sense, Wotan has *become* Siegfried.

One passage in Shaw's analysis of *The Rhine Gold* particularly helps clarify the precise meaning of Siegfried's triumph. Shaw is describing the gathering of the gods outside Wotan's castle at the end of the opera:

In the glory of this moment Wotan has a great thought. With all his aspirations to establish a reign of noble thought, of righteousness, order, and justice, he has found that day that there is no race yet in the world that quite spontaneously, naturally, and unconsciously realizes his ideal. . . . But the fertility of the First Mother is not yet exhausted. The life that came from her has ever climbed up to a higher and higher organization. From toad and serpent to dwarf, from bear and elephant to giant, from dwarf and giant to a god with thoughts, with comprehension of the world, with ideals. Why should it stop there? Why should it not rise from the god to the Hero? to the creature in whom the god's unavailing thought shall have become effective will and life, who shall make his way straight to truth and reality over the laws of Fricka and the lies of Loki with a strength that overcomes giants and a cunning that outwits dwarfs? Yes: Erda, the First Mother, must travail again, and breed him a race of heroes to deliver the world and himself from his limited powers and disgraceful bargains. This is the vision that flashes on him as he turns to the rainbow bridge and calls his wife to come and dwell with him in Valhalla, the home of the gods.   (184–185)

Here we have a projected reconciliation of separated elements. Despite his aspirations, Wotan must face the disparity between thought and deed and understand "how far short Godhead falls of the thing it conceives" (184). What he looks forward to is the being who shall create the synthesis of fact and ideal which Shaw found prefigured in Brand's vision of the perfect Adam. In his analysis of *Emperor and Galilean* Shaw had invoked Brand's "rainbow bridge" metaphor to describe the "third empire in which the spirit shall not be unknown, nor the flesh starved, nor the will tortured" (*Quint* 54). And now, by a happy coincidence, Wagner's gods march into Valhalla across another "rainbow bridge," which Shaw again employs as a symbol of the anticipated fusion of wisdom and power.

The difference between *The Quintessence of Ibsenism* and *The Perfect Wagnerite* consists in the immensely expanded frame of reference of the latter. We have moved from the community to the cosmos, from social problems to those arising from "the eternal work of thrusting the life energy of the world to higher and higher organization" (208). The *Quintessence* has much less to say about "the mysterious thing we call life" (174): its perspective is involved with the individual's relation to society. The *Wagnerite* is much more explicitly vitalistic. Bearing this in mind, we can now turn to the successor to Julian and Wotan—the Shavian Don Juan.

5 Don Juan in Heaven

Published in 1903, *Man and Superman* is the first of Shaw's efforts to bear the unmistakable stamp of a major work by a major writer. Not the least of reasons is that this drama did not appear *in vacuo,* but was the culmination of much toward which he had been working since *Immaturity.* A brief exploration of two criticisms often heard of the play—that its characterization of women is both prejudiced and superficial; and that the brilliant hell scene is not organically related to the action proper—will lead directly into matters of importance for developing themes traced in the earlier parts of this essay.

The old charge that Shaw's view of women is misogynous does not necessarily stem from mistaking the qualities with which the dramatist has endowed Ann Whitefield and Violet Robinson. But it is a sad indication of the persistence of stock responses that readers have sometimes assumed that only a misogynist would portray women as efficient and self-reliant! The point is not that Shaw dislikes women, but that he *does* like efficiency; furthermore, he knows that the Ann Whitefields and Violet Robinsons of the world can play the Tanners and Tavys off the stage every time. Octavius the poet feels that it is necessary to defend a shrewd woman (in this case his sister Violet) by pleading that she is "thoroughly womanly at heart." This defense is not appreciated by Ann, who retorts: "Why do you say that? Is it unwomanly to be thoughtful and businesslike and sensible? Do you want Violet to be an idiot . . .?" (153). Unfortunately the answer to Ann's question, for some, would seem to be a blunt "Yes." But the examples of Candida, Lady Cicely, and Ann herself suffice to establish that a woman may be practical without being unfeminine.

For contemporary readers, the complaint is less likely to be that Shaw has failed to make his heroine womanly than that he has directed her efficiency toward exclusively maternal ends. It is certainly true that the "wonderfully dutiful" (6) Ann is both hypocritical and monomaniacal when it comes to stalking a mate. Seen in historical perspective, however, this insistence upon the female's pursuit of a potential father for her children was an attempt, not to reduce women to a stereotype, but to challenge the Victorian stereotype of Woman as a pure, simple, and sexless creature. Ann Whitefield's aggressive eugenics was Shaw's retort to the fantasies of an age that had come close to denying that women were physical beings at all.[1]

While Shaw's strategy is to extol Ann for exhibiting those very qualities of unscrupulous resolve which an audience of that period would have found objectionable in a woman, his method involves more than merely taking the conventional point of view and inverting it. Of course he begins there—if the Victorians say women are ethereal and sweet, Shaw makes them worldly and hard. But in fact, Ann is by no means the one-dimensional creature she at first seems to be. To begin with, her preference for Jack over Tavy is not entirely the dictate of the Life Force, but also a result of a perfectly sound desire not to hazard being

1. "We laugh at the haughty American nation because it makes the negro clean its boots and then proves the moral and physical inferiority of the negro by the fact that he is a shoeblack; but we ourselves throw the whole drudgery of creation on one sex, and then imply that no female of any womanliness or delicacy would initiate any effort in that direction. There are no limits to male hypocrisy in this matter" (*Super* xviii–xix). Such squeamishness was not confined to reproductive functions. In the late 1890's, vestryman Shaw's advocacy of the installation of public lavatories for women greatly offended colleagues who considered it ungentlemanly to suggest that a member of the fair sex might have occasion to use such a facility.

put on a pedestal: as she tells her rejected suitor, "Getting over an unfavorable impression is ever so much easier than living up to an ideal" (152). She also understands the difference between her own methods and those of Violet, who is able to get her own way "without having to make people sentimental about her" (153). As for her hypocrisy, she is fully aware both of its existence and of its pragmatic justification: "You had better marry what you call a hypocrite, Jack. Women who are not hypocrites go about in rational dress[2] and are insulted and get into all sorts of hot water. And then their husbands get dragged in too, and live in continual dread of fresh complications. Wouldnt you prefer a wife you could depend on?" (162). If society ridicules a woman's attempt to exercise natural human instincts, then Ann will not venture openly to contradict the very system of mores her own vitality subverts. Such "hypocrisy" had long been the hallmark of Shavian heroes of either sex.

Ann's character cannot be fully understood apart from her relation to John Tanner. If Ann is much shrewder than she seems at first sight, her reluctant Romeo is much sillier. The woman could never be accused of having "views" on anything; the man is an intellectual volcano with all the right ideas; but she can get what she wants, he is entirely ineffectual. The first act is an elaborate anticlimax in which Tanner, the self-proclaimed idol-smasher, is lured into defending Violet's supposed illicit sexual relations, only to be floored by her revelation that she is secretly married and finds his unconventional opinions "abominable" (43). Similar reversals occur elsewhere—most hilariously, when near the end of the play Tanner explains that he is in the grip of the Life Force, and Ann responds: "I dont understand in the least: it sounds like the Life Guards" (161).[3] Though she hasn't

2. Founded in 1887, the Rational Dress Society campaigned against such superfluous and obligatory feminine garb as petticoats and corsets. Its members often donned trousers and waistcoats in public appearances (Laver 191–192).

3. The Life Guards are a cavalry regiment forming part of the ceremonial guard of the British monarch.

the slighest idea what he is talking about, Ann's casual rejoinders
can deflate Jack as readily as Harriet's naive remarks punctured
Trefusis in *An Unsocial Socialist.* Perhaps Ann's superiority is a
matter of greater relaxation. Many of Jack's utterances have a
strained, exaggerated quality ("Oh!!! Unfathomable deceit!"[4]
or "Abyss beneath abyss of perfidy!"—44, 61) that suggests the
underlying weakness Cashel Byron had in mind when he observed
that nothing could be well done if it was done with an effort
(*Cash* 91–92). "Youthfulness is not the effect he aims at," Shaw
tells us at his first appearance; but the problem is that Jack *is*
aiming for an effect to begin with, that his restless eye is "just
the thirty-secondth of an inch too wide open" (9). Like Boaner-
ges in *The Apple Cart,* he is veritably bursting at the seams.

Tanner is defined in terms not only of his relation to Ann but
also of his function opposite Roebuck Ramsden. One of the
play's better jokes lies in the implied equivalence between Jack
and his *bête noire.* Like many people who are continually at
odds, these two are more similar to each other than they care to
admit. Shaw remarks of Ramsden in a stage direction that
"everything depends on whether his adolescence belonged to the
sixties or to the eighties" (3). Ramsden's belonged to the sixties,
while Tanner's belonged to the eighties—that is the only difference
between them: they are both "advanced" thinkers, but with appropriately different sets of ideas (evolution versus socialism).
Both are "impressive" men who enjoy dominating in an assertive,
headstrong manner, and each will fly into a furor at the slightest
suggestion that his views are not the finally correct ones. In his
insults to the older man, Jack unwittingly underscores the similarity between them in such lines as, "You have no more manners
than I have myself" (13), or "You know perfectly well that I
am as sober and honest a citizen as yourself" (14–15). Their
"joint guardianship" over Ann is itself a kind of equation (another true accident). Even in the aggressive ineffectuality of their

4. The words "Unfathomable deceit!" (Standard Edition) are not in
the original text (1904).

physical movements, they mirror each other symmetrically—
Ramsden hurls Tanner's book into the wastebasket; soon after-
ward, Tanner dives down to pluck it out and present it to his
ward.[5]

To see why Shaw cannot allow either Ann or Tanner to
emerge as the fully realized in-depth characters some readers
would like them to be, we need only note the strategy behind
his inversion of sexual roles, making woman the pursuer and man
the catch. The emphasis on this inversion may seem strange from
the creator of Grace Tranfield in *The Philanderer*, Lesbia
Grantham in *Getting Married*, Lina Szczepanowska in *Misall-
liance*, and Eliza Doolittle in *Pygmalion*—women who kept their
distance from men who threatened their autonomy and self-
respect. But we cannot forget the allegorical element in this
particular play. In all allegory, the characters can be neither too
simple nor too complex—if they are the former, the result will be
patterned dullness; if the latter, the individual psyche will obliter-
ate the larger design. This does not mean that the allegory itself
is not complex; it means rather that its intricacy is that of a total
configuration, not of the individual character. In *Man and Super-*

5. No more than Ann is Ramsden a cardboard figure. Even Tanner is
impressed by Roebuck's handling of his spinster sister's anger toward
Violet: "There, Susan! . . . I wish you could reconcile it with your
principles to be a little more patient with this poor girl. She's very young;
and theres a time for everything." When Miss Ramsden remonstrates,
"I'm surprised at you, Roebuck," Tanner comments: "So am I, Ramsden,
most favorably" (42). This passage is a touchstone for Shaw's use of the
sudden shift in tone (Abbott 125) to reveal an unexpected side in a
character whom we have been previously invited to see in simplistic terms.
The first act of the play shows this method working with high gloss—
at one point, Violet is the girl weeping in the room upstairs, Tanner is
the fearless iconoclast, Ramsden is a pompous ass. A few minutes later,
Ramsden is a man of humane feeling, Tanner a deflated egotist, and
Violet a woman exercising complete mastery over her circumstances. Such
is Shaw's fine sense of the irrational, which tells us that people are not
going to fit preconceived expectations, that life will not be reduced to a
formula. Those who find Shaw's characterization superficial often do not
see beyond the stereotypes that are only the *starting* point for the Shavian
development of character.

man Ann and Tanner do not exist simply for themselves, but as representatives of "the artist man and the mother woman" (23–24), that is, of Shaw's view of the way males and females see their functions as different sexes. Though the play's leading couple are not one-dimensional characters, they never fully break free from these symbolic points of reference. And these points, one can hardly fail to notice, correspond quite closely to those oppositions between thought and action, idealism and pragmatism, with which all the preceding chapters have been dealing. Tanner is no fool, but is easily made a fool of; Ann may be a fool, but no one could make a fool of her. As usual, vision and capability are in separate compartments. The need then is for an efficient being who is not stupid—which brings us back to the problem of *The Perfect Wagnerite*.

To proceed to the second major area of criticism, what is the hell scene's relation to the rest of the play? In Chapter 3 I argued that Shaw's pamphlet on Wagner owes much to his earlier work on Ibsen. The same is true of *Man and Superman*: it is in relation to the *Quintessence* that an important thematic unity between the two parts of the play exists. Recalling the assault in the *Quintessence* upon abstract notions of right and wrong, its denial of the "ought," and its advocacy of respect for persons over principles, will enable us to recognize John Tanner as the perfect Ibsenite. Lines such as "It is the self-sacrificing women that sacrifice others most recklessly" (22) or "[Nothing] is strong enough to impose oughts on a passion except a stronger passion still" (35) are clear pointers. In thought if not in deed, Tanner's credentials as a pragmatist are impeccable. When Octavius complains, "It's so hard to know what to do when one wishes earnestly to do right," Tanner replies, "My dear Tavy, your pious English habit of regarding the world as a moral gymnasium built expressly to strengthen your character in, occasionally leads you to think about your own confounded principles when you should be thinking about other people's necessities" (29).

The incorporeal Don Juan goes his earthly counterpart one

better in this regard. Juan has already been described in the "Epistle Dedicatory" as one who, "though gifted enough to be exceptionally capable of distinguishing between good and evil, follows his own instincts without regard to the common statute" and who thus "finds himself in mortal conflict with existing institutions, and defends himself by fraud and force" (x). Clearly, this is the plight of the realist who follows his own will in violation of conventional standards and does not scruple to ensure his own survival. The correspondence works. The *Quintessence* attacks the use of abstract labels: Juan protests that "beauty, purity, respectability, religion, morality, art, patriotism, bravery, and the rest are nothing but words which I or anyone else can turn inside out like a glove" (125). Ideals are moral principles serving to disguise evil impulses: hell in turn is "the home of honor, duty, justice, and the rest of the seven deadly virtues. All the wickedness on earth is done in their name: where else but in hell should they have their reward?" (87). And both works insist that human institutions must be reconciled with human nature. Don Juan explains his position: "Nature, my dear lady, is what you call immoral. I blush for it; but I cannot help it. Nature is a pandar, Time a wrecker, and Death a murderer. I have always preferred to stand up to those facts and build institutions on their recognition. You prefer to propitiate the three devils by proclaiming their chastity, their thrift, and their loving kindness; and to base your institutions on these flatteries. Is it any wonder that the institutions do not work smoothly?" (121).

Like *The Perfect Wagnerite*, "Don Juan in Hell" actually goes beyond general affinities and employs the specific terminology of the *Quintessence*. We have already been informed in the introduction that the Don has a "sense of reality that disables convention" (xviii); now in the dream sequence itself we are told that heaven is the home of the "masters of reality" (99)—the realists. The *Quintessence* spoke of "the origin of ideals in unhappiness, in dissatisfaction with the real" (83); now Juan tells us that "hell is the home of the unreal [that is, the ideal] and of the seekers for happiness" (99)'. An ideal was previously defined as an illusion; now Juan assaults "imagination resolved to starve sooner than face . . . realities, piling up illusions to hide them" (101). An ideal was also a lie; and the most famous speech in the play ends, as Ohmann notes (106–107), with the line—"liars, every one of them, to the very backbone of their souls" (124–125)—after a long catalogue derived from pairing a series of idealistic adjectives with the real qualities they disguise.[6]

Hell is, however, not earth: what, then, is the difference between the idealism it represents and that attacked in the *Quintessence?* Juan enlightens us on precisely this point:

The earth is a nursery in which men and women play at being heroes and heroines, saints and sinners; but they are dragged down from their fool's paradise by their bodies: hunger and cold and thirst, age and decay and disease, death above all, make them slaves of reality: thrice a day meals must be eaten and digested: thrice a century a new generation must be engendered: ages of faith, of romance, and of science are all driven at last to have but one prayer "Make me a healthy animal." But here you escape this tyranny of the flesh; for here you are not an animal at all: you are a ghost, an appearance, an illusion, a convention, deathless, ageless: in a word, bodiless. . . . Here you call your appearance beauty, your emotions love, your sentiments heroism, your aspirations virtue, just as you did on earth; but here there are no hard facts to contradict you, no ironic contrast of your needs with your pretensions, no human comedy, nothing but a perpetual romance, a universal melodrama.
(99–100)

If heaven is the home of the "masters of reality" and earth of the "slaves of reality," hell is the realization of unreality and consequently a much worse place than earth. In the world, no matter how sordid, one at least has a fighting chance of break-

6. In an analogous argument, Wisenthal (1974; 28–30) holds that the realms of earth, hell, and heaven in the play correspond to the categories of Philistinism, idealism, and realism in the essay. But as I will show, *Man and Superman*'s embodiment of categories from the *Quintessence* is less important than its *modification* of those categories to signal a major shift in Shaw's thinking.

ing out of the idealistic trap: indeed, it is this very sordidness of real events that requires the thinking person to fight his way into the light. The world may be a bad place, but at least it gives the negative side of idealism the lie. But what of a place where there *were* no hard facts, where one could go on fooling oneself indefinitely so that no greater self-awareness was even hypothetically possible, where the tragicomic interpenetration of ideals and reality cannot occur because one can decide to have ideals without reality rather than face reality without ideals? It is that state of mind Shaw's view of hell gives us: it is merely a place where one may be an idealist with impunity.

The simplicity of this point has been obscured by the changes Shaw has rung on traditional heaven-hell associations. At first we may be confused. Don Juan, instead of chasing women and ending up in hell, is chased by them and ends up in heaven. The Devil, far from being a horrific demon (as he is in *Faust*), is a gentlemanly cynic as dapper as he is brilliant. And so forth. But though Shaw gets plenty of laughs from these reversals, the real joke is that the inversions are intentionally superficial; for Shaw's heaven *is* a place of salvation; his hell *is* a place of damnation. Satan is nothing more than the fully realized arch-idealist; Don Juan is nothing less than the hero of an explicitly eschatological drama, in which Shaw finally attempts to create a vision that will unite practical realism and heroic idealism.

This union was foreshadowed in his treatment of Julian and Wotan; yet Juan's pilgrimage is viewed in a light different from that which illuminated the defeat of his two predecessors. In his analysis of *Emperor and Galilean,* Shaw had emphasized not Julian's philosophy but his failure. The point is that Julian "was not the man to found the third empire" (58), that the "third empire was not yet, and is not yet" (58). The play, Shaw argues, should have been called "The Mistake of Maximus the Mystic" (54), who tried unsuccessfully to stimulate Julian externally to achieve the great goal.

There is a similar negativism about *The Perfect Wagnerite.*

After carrying the reader to the supposed triumph of the Hero, Shaw is faced with the somewhat embarrassing task of accounting for the rest of *The Ring*, which includes part of the final act of *Siegfried* as well as all of *Night Falls on the Gods* (210–238). Two things trouble Shaw. First, events of the late nineteenth century indicated that the triumph of humanity symbolized by the Hero had not materialized as expected—a problem Shaw would later try to resolve in *Major Barbara*, his modernized version of Wagner's *Ring* cycle. Second, Siegfried's personality has implications with which Shaw is definitely not comfortable. He approves, of course, of the representation of the unfettered will of humanity spontaneously generating wisdom and efficiency, but is so disturbed at having a "born anarchist" (200) posited as the solution of the metaphysical quest that he devotes a section of the book to a refutation of anarchism (222–223). Siegfried is "enormously strong, full of life and fun, dangerous and destructive to what he dislikes, and affectionate to what he likes; so that it is fortunate that his likes and dislikes are sane and healthy" (200). But what of the person whose likes and dislikes are *not* sane and healthy? It is one thing for a Shavian character such as Caesar to produce humane results by doing what he likes, but he is far from the "perfectly naive hero" Siegfried is supposed to be. Indeed, *Caesar and Cleopatra* (written at the same time as *The Perfect Wagnerite*) had been Shaw's attempt to portray a hero capable of functioning as *civilized* spokesman for an ethic based on instinct.

Despite his distrust of societal norms, Shaw appreciates the logic of the conservative viewpoint in matters of conduct—indeed, he often seems uneasily conscious of the difficulty of balancing two conflicting convictions: one, that human progress inevitably will "empty a good deal of respectable morality out like so much dirty water" (*Art* 288, Pref); the other, that "it is idle to demand unlimited toleration of apparently outrageous conduct on the plea that the offender" is a superior person (*Art* 289, Pref). As an essayist, Shaw writes that he knows "no harder practical question than how much selfishness one ought to stand from a gifted person . . . on the chance of his being right in the long run" (*Art* 288, Pref); as a dramatist, he allows the Inquisitor in *Saint Joan* to argue a vigorously conceived case against toleration (127–129). For all his advocacy of the qualities of instinct and will personified in *The Ring* by Siegfried, Shaw's caution forces him back from a wholehearted endorsement of a blond beast with overtones of primitivism. The noble savage was not his idea of a philosopher-king. Thus while Shaw is eloquent on the subject of the reconciling effects Siegfried is *supposed* to produce, Wotan really interests him more than the Hero who was to supplant him. In a review of *Die Walküre* Shaw had written earlier that "it is trouble that moves us to sympathy, and not the explanation of the trouble" (*HMC* 239) and declared himself "one of those elect souls who are deeply moved by Wotan" (*HMC* 238). Likewise in the *Wagnerite* itself, he describes how "a single drama in which Wotan does not appear, and of which Siegfried is the hero, expanded itself into a great fourfold drama of which Wotan is the hero" (217). The idealist's tragedy turned out to be more compelling than the realist's triumph.

Man and Superman is the first play in which Shaw's belief in the possibility of an *effective* idealism is presented with real conviction. We sense it early, in Tanner's description of the aims of the "artist man" (23–24); but even more striking in the context of Shaw's previous thought is Juan's rebuttal of Satan's famous "force of Death" speech (102–104). Lucifer's tirade need not be quoted: suffice it to remind the reader that it ends with a very Shavian peroration about "justice, duty, patriotism, and all the other isms by which even those who are clever enough to be humanely disposed are persuaded to become the most destructive of all the destroyers" (104). Juan's surprising reply, "Pshaw: all this is old," is followed by an even more surprising explanation. Juan argues that men are cowardly rather than evil, and then goes on to say:

You can make any of these cowards brave by simply putting an idea into his head. . . . Men never really overcome fear until they imagine they are fighting to further a universal purpose—fighting for an idea, as they call it. Why was the Crusader braver than the pirate? Because he fought, not for himself, but for the Cross. What force was it that met him with a valor as reckless as his own? The force of men who fought, not for themselves, but for Islam. . . . Every idea for which Man will die will be a Catholic idea. When the Spaniard learns at last that he is no better than the Saracen, and his prophet no better than Mahomet, he will arise, more Catholic than ever, and die on a barricade across the filthy slum he starves in, for universal liberty and equality.   (105–106)

To anyone familiar with only the early Shaw, this would seem like a very peculiar line for Juan to be taking. The term "idea" in this speech corresponds to an heroic ideal in *The Quintessence of Ibsenism*—a "universal purpose" or goal exemplified by the Cross, Islam, liberty, equality, and so forth. My initial discussion of the *Quintessence* revealed that there are two basic kinds of idealism (the reactionary and the progressive) and that Shaw in 1891 was less interested in distinguishing between them than in rejecting both in favor of a pragmatic approach. Moreover, my preliminary discussion of *Man and Superman* has shown how Shaw strengthened his critique of the negative side of idealism by equating a refusal to outgrow it with a state of damnation. But in the passage just quoted, it becomes apparent that Shaw's critical view of the positive side of idealism, far from being similarly intensified, has been completely altered. For now he follows the lead of the *Wagnerite* in stressing the *difference* between heroic and conventional ideals, with Don Juan being as eager to defend the former as to condemn the latter. Thus when the Devil, responding to Juan's praise of man's willingness to die for a "Catholic idea," retorts that people "will never be at a loss for an excuse for killing one another" (106), Juan does not embrace this seemingly Shavian observation, but explains that he is "not now defending the illusory forms the great ideas take" (106). Rather, he is defending the view that man, "who in his own selfish affairs is a coward to the backbone, will fight for an idea

like a hero" (106). In short, we now have a moral distinction
between heroic ideals ("great ideas") and the conventional ones
("illusory forms") that comprise the catalogue of condemnations
at the end of Satan's "force of Death" speech. The difference
between the two lies in the attitude of the person holding the
ideal: the names are the same.[7]

Related to Shaw's new view of idealism are his evolving conceptions of the function of consciousness and the search for
happiness. In the *Quintessence* Shaw wrote that man, by daring
more and more to face facts, gradually "raises himself from mere
consciousness to knowledge" (25). The implication of this phrase
—that consciousness per se is not the highest goal—becomes more
explicit in the *Wagnerite;* there Shaw observes that Siegfried
"unconsciously" discloses the "secret of heroism" (234), and
that Wotan wants a hero because there is "no race yet in the
world that quite spontaneously, naturally, and unconsciously
realizes his ideal" (184). In the "Revolutionist's Handbook" ap-
pended to *Man and Superman,* we are assured that a higher
being will have "superiority in the unconscious self" (174); and
the accompanying maxims assert that "the unconscious self is the
real genius. Your breathing goes wrong the moment your conscious self meddles with it" (220). The idea that "consciousness
means preoccupation and obstruction" (*Back* xxiii, Pref) runs
through Shaw's later works too; one of his long-livers in *Methusaleh* echoes the wording of the *Quintessence* by telling the
Elderly Gentleman that "consciousness of a fact is not knowledge
of it" (154). Shaw sees consciousness as corresponding to the

7. This point is expressed in a passage from Shaw's late play, *The
Simpleton of the Unexpected Isles* (60–61): "KANCHIN. We shall
make you Empress of the Isles. JANGA. Prola the first. VASHTI. Hom-
age, Prola. MAYA. Love, Prola. KANCHIN. Obedience, Prola. JANGA.
Absolute rule, Prola. PROLA. All your burdens on me. Lazy idle children. KANCHIN. Hurrah! All burdens on Prola. JANGA. The burden
of thought. VASHTI. The burden of knowledge. MAYA. The burden of
righteousness. VASHTI. The burden of justice. MAYA. The burden of
mercy. PROLA. Cease, cease: these are not burdens to me: they are the
air I breathe."

state of rationalism in mental evolution and idealism in moral evolution. The goal of such evolution, however, is not a merely self-conscious being, but one who is "completely unilludedly [*sic*] self-conscious." In striving to create brains, life seeks "an organ by which it can attain not only self-consciousness, but self-understanding" (*Super* 109).

The antirationalistic stance announced in the *Quintessence* (17–22) and developed further in the *Wagnerite* through the figure of Loki, who represented "Logic and Imagination without living Will (Brain without Heart . . .)" (188), culminates in *Man and Superman*. The "maxims" tell us that "the man who listens to Reason is lost: Reason enslaves all whose minds are not strong enough to master her" (221); and in "Don Juan in Hell" itself the theme finds its crowning expression in Juan's description of his initiation into physical love. Face to face with woman, Juan's morals, conscience, chivalry, pity, self-regard, and perceptions urge him to resist: "My judgment was not to be corrupted: my brain still said No on every issue" (114). But though he takes woman "without chloroform" he does take her (113); and that is the "revelation" that there is more to life than rational considerations. "Up to that moment I had never lost the sense of being my own master; never consciously taken a single step until my reason had examined and approved it. I had come to believe that I was a purely rational creature: a thinker!" (113). But now Juan has learned that mind, in its totality, involves more than logic can explain.

The pursuit of happiness fares no better than the worship of reason. We already know from the *Quintessence* about "the origin of ideals in unhappiness, in dissatisfaction with the real" (83)—in short, by idealism we attempt to convince ourselves that we are happy when we are not. In the *Wagnerite*, Wotan teaches Siegmund "the only power a god can teach, the power of doing without happiness" (193). By the time we reach *Man and Superman*, this has become an *idée fixe*, whether in the maxim that tells us "Folly is the direct pursuit of Happiness and Beauty"

(219); in Tanner's assertion in the body of the play that "a lifetime of happiness . . . would be hell on earth" (13); or in the numerous tirades in the hell scene against the "tedious, vulgar pursuit of happiness" (100) and the artist's "happiness hunting and woman idealizing" (113). "The truly damned," Juan insists, "are those who are happy in hell" (87)—idealists who have passed beyond the point where they are disturbed by their own self-deception.

The importance of these attacks is that they reveal the maturation of Shaw's concern with *ultimate* values. For both rationalism and the pursuit of happiness are seen as manifestations of an obsession with personal and meanly selfish ends. This may be hard to see at first, for Juan's rejection of rationalism leads directly to the rejection of "prudence, careful selection, virtue, honor, chastity" (114)—that is, of inhibitory ideals. But far from being plunged thereby into a slough of demoralizing pleasure, Juan's horizons are widened to confront the universal. His unreasonable susceptibility to romance has taught him "how useless it is to attempt to impose conditions on the irresistible force of Life" (114)—that force whose upward movement is frustrated by the reactionary side of idealism. For in the very act of framing his excuse to the lady "Life seized [Juan] and threw [him] into her arms as a sailor throws a scrap of fish into the mouth of a seabird" (114).

The Don's repudiation of "happiness hunting" follows directly from his discovery of the limits of self-sufficiency. Not that Shaw harbors any prudish grudge against felicity: Juan's point is rather that "in the pursuit of my own pleasure, my own health, my own fortune, I have never known happiness" (123–124). After his experience with women, he was not happier, but wiser (114). At the end of the play Ann has not achieved happiness but success, "the price for which the strong sell their happiness" (165–166). In this context, the renunciation of repressive ideals, far from being an attempt to find happiness, is a renunciation of the demand for personal happiness which leads men to resort to such ideals in the first place. Following one's instincts is not license; it is learning to live without any contentment except that which is a by-product of furthering life's universal purpose.[8]

Man and Superman shares with *The Perfect Wagnerite* this vitalistic emphasis—the play's references to "Life's continual effort . . . to achieve higher and higher organization" (107–108), or "the forms into which [Life] has organized itself" (119) echo the wording of passages already quoted from the *Wagnerite*. Yet an analogous and even more significant relation between "Don Juan in Hell" and Shaw's treatment of *Emperor and Galilean* in the *Quintessence* is likely to be overlooked because a shift in terminology has taken place. Shaw no longer speaks of the "third empire" or the "world-will," but rather of the Superman and the Life Force. This last term has produced much discussion of the influence of Bergson that might more profitably have been devoted to the influence of Hegel (as mediated through Ibsen).[9] For what has happened is that the pattern

8. "You will find that your passions, if you really and honestly let them all loose impartially, will discipline you with a severity which your conventional friends, abandoning themselves to the mechanical routine of fashion, could not stand for a day" (*Art* 304).

9. Since a book published as recently as 1969 holds that "Life Force" is "almost surely a translation of Bergson's *élan vital*" (Carpenter 222), it is worth noting that: (1) *Man and Superman* was published in 1903, *Creative Evolution* in 1907. (2) The play's "Epistle Dedicatory," which eagerly acknowledges intellectual affinities with at least a dozen famous men, does not mention Bergson. (3) Shaw's first published reference to Bergson is in a footnote (p. 34) added in 1912 to *The Quintessence of Ibsenism*. (4) In a letter dated 12 October 1912, Shaw tells Augustin Hamon, who wished to translate "Life Force" as "La Force de Vie," that it would be pointless to attempt to ignore Bergson's term; and that *had he known* the expression "*élan vital*" when writing *Man and Superman*, he would have said "Life Impulse" instead of "Life Force." (5) In a speech delivered in 1919, Shaw claims the term as his own in the course of explaining his view of a motive power behind the universe: "The Chairman [of the meeting] quoted my expression and called it the 'life-force.' Bergson, the French philosopher, has called it the vital impulse, the *élan vital*" (*RS* 77). (See also *SSS* 78). Shaw's creed of "Creative Evolution" owes nothing to Bergson except its name. (The letter to

Shaw discovered in *Emperor and Galilean* becomes the prototype for the resolution of "Don Juan in Hell"—only now the
argument has come to be expressed in a new nomenclature.

Shaw attempts to reconcile his belief that every person exists
for his own use with the opposite conviction that true personal
fulfillment lies in the service of the Life Force. The solution is a
Hegelian synthesis. As Ibsen said, "He is free—under necessity."
As Juan says:

Just as Life, after ages of struggle, evolved that wonderful bodily organ the eye, so that the living organism could see where it was going and what was coming to help or threaten it, and thus avoid a
thousand dangers that formerly slew it, so it is evolving today a
mind's eye that shall see, not the physical world, but the purpose of
Life, and thereby enable the individual to work for that purpose instead of thwarting and baffling it by setting up shortsighted personal
aims as at present.   (110)

The basis for the synthesis that transcends antinomies is that the
Life Force has no means for becoming conscious of itself other
than the human mind. Man both serves the higher will and is
himself part of it. Life creates the "mind's eye," which in turn
sees "the purpose of life." As Juan says, "Life was driving at
brains" (109). Why? Because "my brain is the organ by which
Nature strives to understand itself" (127). Man serves the force
that creates, but he also creates the force he serves.

In short, Life is not external to living creatures. In the "Revolutionist's Handbook" it is not surprising that a more explicit
statement of this point is worded in religious terms: "[Man]
will presently see that his discarded formula that Man is the
Temple of the Holy Ghost happens to be precisely true, and that
it is only through his own brain and hand that this Holy Ghost,
formerly the most nebulous person in the Trinity, and now become its sole survivor as it has always been its real Unity, can
help him in any way" (173–174). The idea appears in sub-

Hamon referred to above will be published in his third installment of
Dan H. Laurence's edition of Shaw's *Collected Letters*).

stantially the same form in several pieces written after *Man and Superman,* from the preface (1905)' to *The Irrational Knot,* in which Shaw speaks of the Life Force as "a stupid instinctive force that has to work and become conscious of itself by means of human brains" (xix), to the postscript (1944) to *Back to Methuselah,* in which we are told of the "Life Force . . . struggling towards its goal of godhead by incarnating itself in creatures with knowledge and power enough to control nature and circumstances" (263). Though the term Life Force is not used, it is the assumption that underlies statements such as the following from the preface to *Androcles:* "It took a century and a half of evolutionary preachers, from Buffon and Goethe to Butler and Bergson, to convince us that we and our father are one; that as the kingdom of heaven is within us we need not go about looking for it and crying Lo here! and Lo there!; that God is . . . a spirit; that it is through this spirit that we evolve towards greater abundance of life; that we are the lamps in which the light of the world burns: that, in short, we are gods though we die like men"(61). Though Shaw felt his view of life was both "sound biology and psychology" (*And* 61, Pref), he did not insist that man would prevail. He claimed only that if man cannot save himself, it is idle to think that anything else can save him. We shall return to this key point in the final chapter.

These statements by Shaw carry forward the premise of "Don Juan in Hell" that man's purpose is to serve nature (alias the Life Force, the Holy Ghost—Shaw accepts other designations), but that nature has no other means of mastering itself than the agency of the human creature who is thus far its highest embodiment. An essay only recently published, "The Infancy of God,"[10] provides the clearest statement of the relation between internal and external forces:

10. Unearthed by Warren Sylvester Smith in *Shaw on Religion* (1967). The editor's suggestion that this undated piece belongs to the 1920's is very unlikely—part of it was included by Charlotte Shaw in *Selected Passages from the Works of Bernard Shaw* (1912). Compare Smith 133 with C. Shaw 224.

When a hungry and penniless man stands between his good and his bad angel in front of a baker's shop, the good angel cannot seize and drag him away, nor can the bad angel thrust the loaf into his hands. The victory of honesty or the consummation of a theft must be effected by the man; and his choice will depend a good deal on the sort of man he is. Not only is he an indispensable agent; not only is he the vehicle of the force that moves him; but he is also the vehicle of the force that chooses. He is, in the old phrase, the temple of the Holy Ghost. He has, in another old phrase, the divine spark within him.   (141)

This passage brings together several ideas with which we have been dealing: the emphasis upon action resulting from internal impulses; the belief in the importance of one's own nature, which acts as a kind of fate; the conviction that the whole question is a religious one. But the main point of the quotation is contained in the phrase about man being "not only . . . the vehicle of the force that moves him; but . . . also the vehicle of the force that chooses." The force that moves is beyond himself; but its originating impulse comes from within himself: the higher will cannot exist without his own will, which, if he is truly inspired, becomes part of it.

Yet if he is not thus inspired, man's own will can drive life down rather than raise it up; for the Life Force shares the limitations of the creatures who incarnate it. In a passage immediately following the one just quoted, Shaw explains: "Now, to the extent that a man is the temple of the Holy Ghost . . . , he is necessarily also the limitation of the Holy Ghost. Not even the Holy Ghost can lift ten pounds with a baby's arm or ten tons with a man's. . . . The sword will snap in the hand of God at just the point at which it will snap in a testing machine; and all the swords of God bend and snap at one point and another, or cut the wrong throats at the bidding of the ape or tiger from whom they are evolved" (141). Such a view disposes of the criticism proffered by Irvine (246) and others that Shaw's ethical philosophy consists of telling people that in doing what they please they are automatically embodying divinity.[11] It is the simplism of this very assumption that led Shaw earlier to reject the utopian anarchism of Siegfried.

The configuration of the argument developed thus far will become clearer if Shaw's new metaphysic of the Life Force is rephrased in the terminology that played so important a part in his previous work. Shaw virtually supplies such a translation himself in his later speeches on religion. "Behind the universe," he tells audiences, there is "an intelligent and driving force of which we ourselves are a part" (*RS* 17). Though possessing consciousness, this cosmic energy is a "bodiless, impotent force having no executive power of its own . . . to carry out its will in the world" (*RS* 18). That is to say, the "powerless will or force . . . has implanted into our minds the ideal of God" (*RS* 35); religious human beings are "the instruments through which that ideal is trying to make itself a reality" (*RS* 35); this realization will manifest itself as "a world of organisms who have achieved . . . God" (*RS* 35). Words such as "executive power," "will," "world," "effective," "ideal," "reality"—the mainstays of Shaw's earlier pragmatic ethic—are here placed securely within the framework of his new vital metaphysic. The noble but in-

---

11. Compare Nietzsche's expression of a related point in *Twilight of the Idols:* "Self-interest is worth as much as the person who has it: it can be worth a great deal, and it can be unworthy and contemptible. Every individual may be scrutinized to see whether he represents the ascending or the descending line of life. Having made that decision, one has a canon for the worth of his self-interest. If he represents the ascending line, then his worth is indeed extraordinary—and for the sake of life as a whole, which takes a step farther through him, the care for his preservation and for the creation of the best conditions for him may even be extreme. The single one, the 'individual,' as hitherto understood by the people and the philosophers alike, is an error after all: he is nothing by himself, no atom, no 'link in the chain,' nothing merely inherited from former times; he is the whole single line of humanity up to himself. If he represents the descending development . . . then he has small worth, and the minimum of decency requires that he take away as little as possible from those who have turned out well. He is merely their parasite" (1954; 533–534).

efficient idealism criticized in *The Quintessence of Ibsenism* has been translated into an aspiring but erring Life Force; the effective idealism advocated in *The Perfect Wagnerite* has come to be called God (compare "Godhead" in the earlier work); and the realist's will, whose former object was to ensure the organism's survival in a hostile world, now functions as a catalyst that will enable the Life Force to *become* God as the goal of the evolutionary process.

The person who is moved by the Life Force, and who in turn acts upon it, is the successor, in *Man and Superman,* to the earlier characters—Julian and Wotan—who are simultaneously free and bound by necessity. From one point of view Juan's decision to enter heaven is simple fate. As Lucifer says, heaven "suits some people. . . . It is a question of temperament. . . . It takes all sorts to make a universe" (97). A page later he tells us that the "great gulf fixed" between heaven and hell is "the difference between the angelic and the diabolic temperament. What more impassable gulf could you have?" (97). The statue informs Ana that she should not go to heaven "without being naturally qualified for it" (98)—that is, qualified by her *nature.* But for Don Juan no more than for Wotan is the fate in question an external force. Necessity is simply a name for one's deepest impulses. And Juan's inner self-awareness, unlike that of his predecessor Julian, *does* become highly developed enough to overflow and become a concern for the race. His experience of love "introduced me for the first time to myself, and, through myself, to the world" (114). His act of leaving for heaven, marking his submission to the greater purpose, is also his moment of most complete individuality: when Ana tries to follow him, he can only explain: "I can find my own way to heaven, Ana; not yours" (129).[12] If the task he has thus taken upon himself is "the law of [his] life"—which suggests a force beyond himself—

12. The word "not" (Standard Edition) originally read "but I cannot find" (1904).

it is nonetheless "the working *within* [him] of that force" (123 —italics mine). The two are inseparable.

The experience of Juan's conversion was foreshadowed in a crucial event in the life of his counterpart, the young Jack Tanner. The adolescent's "birth . . . of moral passion" (34) involved the same seemingly paradoxical interpenetration of self and higher reality. What occurred, according to Jack, was a "sense of my new individuality" (36), which in turn caused him for the first time to feel "a sense of duty to others." Now on the face of it these statements might seem contradictory: how can individuality lead to a sense of duty? But the point is that to the premoral child "veracity" and "honor" were merely "goody-goody expressions in the mouths" of others; now they have become "compelling principles in myself" (34). Abstract ideals have developed into concrete realities—only breaking free from externally imposed "habits and superstitions" (35) makes genuine moral awareness possible. And this change, far from being the surrender of self, involves the development of a more powerful sense of self than had previously existed. "I had become a new person" (36), says Jack, thus tying the entire process to the crucial issue of rebirth discussed in the preceding chapter. A synthesis called maturity results when what is beyond becomes inseparable from what is within.

The entire point of this synthesis is often missed because readers tend to seize only upon one side of it or the other and so escape its real implications. Conventionally oriented readers, and they are the more common, dismiss Shaw as a renegade anarchist who worships the personal ego. Stephen Winsten may be taken as an example of this approach. He presumes to tell us that Shaw "went wrong . . . in his morality" (153) because he had no sense of aspiration beyond himself. There is no need by now to refute this allegation. A more difficult problem is presented by "absurdist" critics who cannot bring themselves to forgive Shaw for believing that life has a purpose. These more sophisticated interpreters make the opposite complaint, that Shaw has no understanding of individuals except as pawns of universal forces. Many passages from Shaw could be quoted in apparent support of this view: in "The Revolutionist's Handbook" he writes that "the purpose of the race" is sufficient to "shatter the opposition of individual instincts" (183); in the body of the play Tanner makes statements such as "We do the world's will, not our own" (160); in the hell scene Juan repeatedly inveighs against all merely personal aims. Most famous of all is the often quoted testament in the "Epistle Dedicatory" to the play: "This is the true joy in life, the being used for a purpose recognized by yourself as a mighty one; . . . the being a force of Nature instead of a feverish selfish little clod of ailments and grievances complaining that the world will not devote itself to making you happy" (xxxi). Juan's many similar utterances provoke Lucifer's parting shot, which begins: "I prefer to be my own master and not the tool of any blundering universal force" (128).

Though Lucifer's criticism is perceptive as far as it goes, the problem is that it does not go nearly far enough. What Señor Satan ignores is that the Life Force has no abstract or external reality, but acquires meaning only insofar as its work is carried forward concretely and internally by the human mind, which is thus far its highest incarnation. To the devil, Juan's view represents humanity as lost in a mighty maze of walks without a plan. Thus there is sweet irony in Juan's countercharge that most men are not really doing Lucifer's will, but rather "drifting with [his] want of will, instead of doing their own" (124). In pursuing his own pleasures and happiness, Lucifer is essentially will-less. He cannot conceive of mind as an active agent or grasp that Shaw-Juan's "joy of life" (xxxi) involves a good deal more than the Satanic "power of enjoyment" (128).

What, finally, is the end Juan seeks in heaven? His answer is clear enough:

Are we agreed that Life is a force which has made innumerable experiments in organizing itself . . . to build up that raw force into higher and higher individuals, the ideal individual being omnipotent, infallible, and withal completely, unilludedly self-conscious: in short, a god?   (109)

I sing, not arms and the hero, but the philosophic man: he who seeks in contemplation to discover the inner will of the world, in invention to discover the means of fulfilling that will, and in action to do that will by the so-discovered means.   (110–111)

I tell you that as long as I can conceive something better than myself I cannot be easy unless I am striving to bring it into existence or clearing the way for it. That is the law of my life. That is the working within me of Life's incessant aspiration to higher organization, wider, deeper, intenser self-consciousness, and clearer self-understanding.   (123)

The ideal individual will not only be "unilludedly self-conscious," but also "omnipotent." The "philosophic man" not only seeks to discover "the inner will of the world," but also "in action to do that will." Juan wants not only "to conceive something better" than himself, but also to "bring it into existence." It is this union between thought and action in the ideal individual which is expressed in the play by the symbol of the Superman; and I should hasten to add that it is the meaning, not the word itself, that is important.[13] In *Emperor and Galilean* the "third empire" creating "Brand's bridge between the flesh and the spirit" is to be founded by the man " 'who shall swallow up both emperor and Galilean' " (*Quint* 55). In 1912 Shaw appends a footnote to those words: "Or, as we should now say, the Superman." In *The Perfect Wagnerite,* Siegfried, the man who will unite wisdom and power to redeem a Godhead that "falls [short] of the thing it conceives" (184), is described as "an anticipation of the 'overman' of Nietzsche" (200). But it is in "Don Juan in Hell" that the expression "Superman" first appears—not in any of Juan's own speeches, but (as Nethercot observes—282)˙ in an epilogue-like exchange between Satan and the statue *after* the Don has departed for the celestial regions. Shaw's later publicizing of the

13. The argument in the remainder of this paragraph is similar to Wisenthal's (1974), 51.

term may have been the most disastrous strategic blunder of his life, for it created the impression that he was popularizing Nietzsche when he had instead only found a name for a concept that had been developing in his own work for more than twenty years. The Superman is the symbol for the union of deed and ideal, power and wisdom, flesh and spirit.

This discussion of the relation of ideas in *Man and Superman* to the rest of Shaw's writings necessarily abstracts the play's meaning from its dramatic context and thus falls short of assessing its impact as a work of art. In "Don Juan in Hell" the dramatic focus is on the opposition between Lucifer and Juan; and that conflict, which gives the play its continuing power, is considerably broader in significance than the question of the specific merits of the Life Force as a philosophical concept. Indeed, had Don Juan been depicted as, say, an intelligent Roman Catholic, and Lucifer as an existentialist, the central issue would be unchanged. That issue lies in the confrontation between the man who commits himself to working for what he believes to be life's larger purpose and the man who, seeing skeptically and perhaps rightly, concludes that there is no cause to think that existence has meaning and hence that any effort expended on its behalf is futile. Despite his preference for the former position, Shaw endows Lucifer with powers of intellect and eloquence equal to those of Juan himself. The reader need only remember the great "force of Death" speech as well as Lucifer's devastating words after Juan has left the stage, "Beware of the pursuit of the Superhuman: it leads to an indiscriminate contempt for the Human" (129), to realize how much more tentative and problematic the play is than the preceding pages have been able to convey. Indeed, the reader who prefers existential absurdism to dated vitalism is free to regard Lucifer as the realist and Juan as the unreal dreamer—an interpretation which the play can sustain.

The absurdist may further argue that even Shaw's conditional resolution of the opposition of the worldly and the spiritual is invalid because it takes place in the hell scene, which occurs inside the hero's mind, far from the exigencies of being. Juan can go off to heaven; John Tanner, however, must return from dreamland to the world, where his noble ideals are made short work of by circumstances and Ann. Seen from this angle, the religious quest is a failure; and the play reinforces the tragic implications Shaw found in *Emperor and Galilean* and *The Ring*.

But it depends. The reader who sees the fundamental thrust of the play as comic will view Juan as the hero and the hell scene as the triumphant realization of hopes adumbrated in the other three acts. On the other hand, the reader who sees the conflict as fundamentally tragic and irreconcilable will view Satan as the hero and the first, second, and last acts as an ironic commentary upon a hell scene reduced to absurdity by the material surrounding it. The first reader says: "Don Juan's choice of heaven is what is really important, not the mundane comedy." The second says: "Come now: just look what happens to all that big talk about the Life Force when its advocate has to return to real life."

Granted that the issue can be seen both ways, I wonder if the second interpretation does not take too seriously Tanner's rather histrionic surrender to his destiny. Jack sees the "artist man" and the "mother woman" as locked in eternal combat; but are they? Shaw rejoices in the man who is a "force of Nature" (xxxi), but is not Ann an agent of nature's purpose? If Don Juan wants to be an instrument of the Life Force, is it not the Life Force that finally throws him into Ann's arms? He wants to create something more than human: very well, is it not Ana who calls out after "a father for the Superman" (131)? If Tanner rejects the pursuit of happiness, does not Ann also point out that marriage "will not be all happiness for me. Perhaps death" (163)? And is it not precisely at that moment that the truth finally dawns and he groans, "Oh, that clutch holds and hurts. What have you grasped in me? Is there a father's heart here as well as a mother's?"—his one moment of real self-discovery in the play? Tanner himself is too rashly polemical to see that Ann's instinctive vitality and his own intellectual vitality are different aspects of the same phenomenon. His inflated ego does not even permit him to recognize that he is as enamored of Ann as she is of him—his compulsive flight from her is the hoary ruse of the flirt who expects to be chased. The real conflict is not, as Tanner thinks, between "the artist man and the mother woman" (24) but rather between the "Life Force" of Juan and the "force of Death" of Satan. Juan himself attempts to dismiss the implications of this opposition by claiming that the Life Force "is not so stupid as the forces of Death and Degeneration. Besides, these are in its pay all the time" (108). For him (and for Shaw on the level of explicit formulation), the failure of personal aspiration and the apparent existence of evil are only the result of the cosmic energy's unsuccessful experiments. But Satan robs us of the certainty of an eventual happy ending—he suggests that a cherished commitment to a hypothetical larger purpose may be a waste of life, that an individual's failure, far from being a mere false step in an inevitable journey up the evolutionary ladder, may itself be of ultimate significance. *Man and Superman* aspires toward synthesis and remains a comedy; but the subversive utterances of Satan (expressing Shaw's inner self-doubts) remind us that the drama may not, after all, be taking place in a universe where tragedy is impossible.

PART THREE

6　John Bull's Other Island

In a program note circulated to the press in 1915, Shaw refers to "a group of three plays of exceptional weight and magnitude on which the reputation of the author as a serious dramatist was first established, and still mainly rests" (*ST* 118).[1] The first, *Man and Superman,* was completed in 1903; the second, *John Bull's Other Island,* in 1904; and the third, *Major Barbara,* in 1905. Suggesting that only the inordinate length of *Man and Superman* prevented issuing them in a single volume, Crompton quotes a letter to Trebitsch (1919) in which Shaw proposes the title "Comedies of Religion and Science" for a comprehensive German edition of his "big three" (75, 237). The dramatist's invitation to audiences to discover in these works some larger interrelatedness seems unpromising at first; for *Man and Superman* deals with the war of the sexes, *John Bull's Other Island* with Anglo-Irish relations, and *Major Barbara* with the Salvation Army and munitions. But in a discussion of Shaw it is always important to distinguish subject matter from theme, and if one moves beyond what these works are *about* to the basic oppositions from which their dramatic force is generated, it becomes evident that they are so closely connected, and the progression from one to the next is so pointedly articulated, that they

1. This passage has also been cited by Frederick P. W. McDowell in "Politics, Comedy, Character, and Dialectic: The Shavian World of *John Bull's Other Island*" (*PMLA*, LXXXII [1967], 542–553), an article to which my own treatment of the play is indebted at several points (specifically noted).

deserve to be regarded as a trilogy. More closely united than the trios that made up his previous collections (*Plays Unpleasant, Plays Pleasant,* and *Three Plays for Puritans*), together these dramas constitute a massive triptych. Progressing from his earlier studies of individuals and their relation to society, Shaw in this group of plays attempts to engage the larger forces that move men, nations, and the cosmos.

On the topical level *John Bull's Other Island* is a comic exposure of the way members of different nations mythologize one another. The play as much as the trenchant preface attacks "those two hollowest of fictions, the Irish and English 'races' " (18). Englishman Tom Broadbent's conception of what an Irishman is like is so artificial that he can be easily fooled by an impostor who goes through the gestures of the conventional stage version of the type. Broadbent sees the Irish as good-natured, charming, whimsical, melancholy, humorous, and ineffectual—in short, as the opposite of the sensible, earnest, practical Englishman whom Ireland supposedly needs to straighten out her problems. He is so sure of his common sense that he can accompany his marriage proposal to a girl (several minutes after meeting her) by the assurance that his Englishness guarantees him to be "not a man to act hastily or romantically" (112). In fact, of course, Broadbent is what his Irish partner, Larry Doyle, calls a "romantic duffer" (81), whose susceptibility to the stock ideals of politics and romance might lead one to conclude that "no Englishman has any common sense, or ever had, or ever will have" (87). Since Larry possesses a critical intelligence that is very far from romantic in Broadbent's sense, the play comes to depict what Shaw in his preface refers to as "the actual distinction between the idolatrous Englishman and the fact-facing Irishman" (18). The conventional picture of the romantic Irishman and the practical Englishman becomes reversed: "The Englishman is wholly at the mercy of his imagination, having no sense of reality to check it. The Irishman, with a far subtler and more fastidious imagination, has one eye always on things as they are" (18, Pref).

Although this inversion of types is just what we would expect from Shaw, it does not at all follow that the Irishman is therefore practical and the Englishman ineffectual. Broadbent, fool that he is, is magnificently efficient; Doyle, insightful as he is, is sublimely helpless. Thus the opposition between English and Irish becomes a metaphor for a contrast between capacity for action and the lack of it; as Larry explains to Nora Reilly after Broadbent has made the proposal she had awaited for eighteen years from Doyle himself, "I'm an Irishman, and he's an Englishman. He wants you; and he grabs you. *I* want you; and I quarrel and have to go on wanting you" (166). Ireland becomes the symbol of this state of psychic impotence: in speaking of his youth, Larry explains that he had "only two ideas at that time: first, to learn to do something; and then to get out of Ireland and have a chance of doing it" (91). It is only Broadbent who "in English earnest" (111) can go *to* Ireland to do things. But how can one explain why the behavior of each man is so at variance with his nature?

Part of the answer is to be found in Larry's long speech to Tom in Act I, which begins as an outburst on the effects of the Irish climate:

Oh, the dreaming! the dreaming! the torturing, heart-scalding, never satisfying dreaming, dreaming, dreaming, dreaming! (*Savagely*) No debauchery that ever coarsened or brutalized an Englishman can take the worth and usefulness out of him like that dreaming. An Irishman's imagination never lets him alone, never convinces him, never satisfies him; but it makes him that he cant face reality nor deal with it nor handle it nor conquer it: he can only sneer at them that do. . . . It saves thinking. It saves working. It saves everything except imagination, imagination, imagination; and imagination's such a torture that you cant bear it without whisky. . . . And all the time you laugh! laugh! laugh! eternal derision, eternal envy, eternal folly, eternal fouling and staining and degrading, until, when you come at last to a country where men take a question seriously and give a serious answer to it, you deride them for having no sense of humor, and plume yourself on your own worthlessness as if it made you better than them. (84–85)

Shaw once wrote that there are two kinds of imagination, one involving the ability to imagine things as they are not, and the other the ability to imagine things as they are (*Mis* 103, Pref).[2] A rather patrician version of the typical Irishman, Larry clearly has the second kind: far from being a conventional idealist who cleaves to illusions, he is a progressive realist who faces the truth. Yet a paradox arises because the very strength of Larry's grasp of facts has driven him into derisive cynicism as a refuge from frustration. So while he sees what really is, he cannot act in the real environment; whereas Broadbent, in a mental state of idolatry, can. Shaw has inverted the usual stereotypes only to reveal that they turn out to be true on a deeper level—the point becomes not that the Englishman is helpless and the Irishman is practical, but that the Irishman's impracticality, although very real, is the result of his very clarity of vision; and the Englishman's efficiency, also very real, depends upon an energy not impeded by obstacles it has not the intelligence to discern. The resulting division between efficiency and insight thus becomes the equivalent, in political terms, of the rivalry between the "artist man and the mother woman" (24) in *Man and Superman,* but with this striking difference: in the earlier play one can see the possibility of transcending the opposition; here the division itself is of final significance.

The thematic similarity between the two plays also finds expression in a symbolic similarity. The core of *Man and Superman* is the hell scene, around which Shaw weaves a treatment of the saved versus the damned state of mind. The metaphor of heaven versus hell is also employed in *John Bull's Other*

---

2. Note also Napoleon in the "Tragedy of an Elderly Gentleman": "I have the only imagination worth having: the power of imagining things as they are, even when I cannot see them" (*Back* 173).

Island, mainly through a third major character in the play. This is "Mr" Keegan, a priest defrocked for "madness" supposedly brought upon him by a dying Hindu whom he confessed. The second act opens with a conversation between Keegan and a grasshopper on the subject of heaven, earth, and hell (96). After the unfortunate incident between Broadbent and the pig, Keegan further elaborates upon the relation between the world and hell (151); and the play's final scene brings the three principal characters together for a discussion that culminates in Keegan's famous definition of "heaven" (177). The use of the contrast between English and Irish to signify an opposition between the pragmatic and the ineffectual in the realm of *action* is explicitly formulated by Broadbent, who holds that "there are only two qualities in the world: efficiency and inefficiency, and only two sorts of people: the efficient and the inefficient. It dont matter whether theyre English or Irish" (170). The subsequent extension of the political opposition into the realm of the spirit is Keegan's contribution: "My country is not Ireland nor England, but the whole mighty realm of my Church. For me there are but two countries: heaven and hell; but two conditions of men: salvation and damnation" (175). In order to see how the heaven-hell symbolism is placed in a new perspective by this second play of Shaw's eschatological trilogy, it will be necessary to discuss more completely the three major characters.

As vociferous as Jack Tanner, Tom Broadbent is an idealist of a much lower order who takes his stand "on the solid ground of principle and public duty" (149). His noblest utterances do not transcend the realm of abstract platitude: "I am a lover of liberty" (75), or "Every civilized man must regard murder with abhorrence" (75). He has a standard set of villains—ranging from Tories to Jews—and a standard set of panaceas—boiling down to the "principles of the Liberal party" (132)—for the sum total of human ills. His speeches inevitably verge on declamation in the interests of Peace, Reform, Home Rule, and Humanity, all of which are espoused in a manner that is as impassioned as it is rehearsed. He has no sense of the fatuity of his remarks—as when he misses the point of Keegan's story of the dying Hindu and praises the account as a tribute to the "liberty of conscience enjoyed by the subjects of our Indian Empire" (151). Broadbent begins as a likable enough character, but his concluding plan to steal the peasants' land by lending them more money than their property is worth and then reclaiming the mortgages indicates the extent to which his initial Pickwickian geniality has acquired some disturbing Falstaffian overtones.

We already know from *The Quintessence of Ibsenism* that idealism involves a substitution, rooted in a need to escape self-knowledge, of the abstract for the concrete. Broadbent always sacrifices the personal and concrete to the political and abstract: he greets Larry's outburst on "dreaming" (quoted above) with the words, "Never despair, Larry. . . . Home Rule will work wonders under English guidance" (85). His offer of marriage to Nora while drunk (so he thinks) raises the "delicate moral question" of whether or not he was "drunk enough not to be morally responsible" (121), and he disapproves of the laconic realism of Larry's suggestion that he get to know the girl better before deciding. Unlike his friend, Doyle understands that there is no such thing as "Ireland" in the abstract: he is returning not "to visit the Irish nation, but to visit my father and Aunt Judy and Nora Reilly and Father Dempsey and the rest of them" (86). Broadbent does not understand that a genuine concern for others is the "overflow" of one's own self-interest and cannot be a substitute for it: "I dont say that an Englishman has not other duties. He has a duty to Finland and a duty to Macedonia. But what sane man can deny that an Englishman's first duty is is his duty to Ireland?" (75) One should not disparage Shaw's achievement here by arguing that the character is perceived from the outside, for the whole point is that the man *has* no inner life; whatever capacity for consciousness he might once have possessed has been objectified in terms of abstract "causes," the advocacy of which stems more from ideological compulsion than humane concern. The difference between Broadbent on the one hand and Doyle and Keegan on the other is the difference between a temperament that sees the trials and evils of life encouraged "only when the Tories are in office" (152) and one that sees them as rooted in human nature.

Thus far the picture of Tom Broadbent is exactly what one would expect from what we already know of Shaw's view of reactionary idealism and its relation to self-realization. As usual, however, Shaw becomes really interesting at exactly that point at which what we expect ceases to apply. Broadbent is in fact not so simple. Even Larry himself is puzzled that his friend seems to be an idiot and a genius at once (89). Broadbent is shrewd enough to sense, for instance, that Larry's reluctance to return home has more to do with the awkwardness of a reunion with Nora Reilly than with reservations about the Irish character (89). When he himself later meets Nora at the Round Tower, Tom refuses to take advantage of her anger over Doyle's absence and tells her honestly that Larry has been delayed by an auto breakdown (112). Broadbent's later courtship of Nora reveals that he can say many sensible things, such as "First love is only a little foolishness and a lot of curiosity" (162), or "What really flatters a man is that you think him worth flattering" (165). Nor is he worried about making a fool of himself. Larry may perceive reality more clearly when he warns Broadbent not to take Haffigan's pig for a ride in the car as part of his campaign to run for an Irish seat in Parliament, but he has to admit that Tom wears his folly lightly and to good effect: "He'll never know theyre laughing at him; and while theyre laughing he'll win the seat" (148). When the car goes out of control and the pig is mangled (much to the amusement of the onlookers), Broadbent laments that "a valuable and innocent animal has lost its life" (146); and Larry senses the real feeling showing through these rhetorical rags when he asks Aunt Judy, "Suppose you had a vote! which would you rather give it to? the man that told the story of Haffigan's pig Barney Doran's way or Broadbent's way?" (148). There seems little doubt what the verdict of Rosscullen's electorate will be.

Just as Broadbent's lack of consciousness has its advantages, so Larry's compulsive turning inward has its liabilities. He can tell immediately that Haffigan is a fraud, understands perfectly that changing the name of a practice does not change the realities of human nature, knows that the beneficiaries of land reform will become the new exploiters by adopting the attitudes of their former landlords, senses that the adventure with the pig will be an absurd mishap, and perceives that Broadbent wants Nora not only as a wife but as a politically useful commodity who will canvass local votes and ensure his election. But he can't talk Broadbent out of the trip to Ireland, won't get into Parliament himself on the basis of his insights, doesn't prevent the escapade with the pig, and loses the girl. Although Broadbent's proposal to Nora is partly a first-rate "stroke of electioneering" (165), it also springs from an impulsive sympathy which is very far from the cruel detachment with which Larry treats her at their first private talk after an eighteen-year separation. Broadbent's cigar-waving attempt to find "poetry in everything" is patronizing to Keegan, but it is no worse than Larry's need to reject the ex-priest's utterances as "drivel" (176) because they threaten to penetrate the defensive cynicism behind which his sensitivity is hidden. Larry may understand the nature of personal relationships better than Broadbent, but this does not in the least mean that he is more successful at establishing such relationships. On the contrary (as Broadbent observes), "life's too earthly for him: he doesn't really care for anything or anybody" (163)—while the openly affectionate Tom feels that it is "an absolute necessity of my nature that I should have somebody to hug occasionally" (163). Larry senses the lack within himself—ironically, the only person for whom he can admit a personal fondness is Broadbent himself (157).

Keegan might at first be taken for the saint who has moved beyond the realm of intellectuality in which Larry is caught up.

He considers pigs and grasshoppers his brothers and has no bitterness toward the Church that defrocked him. Wide traveling
during his youth has enabled him to understand that what a
man discovers in external reality is a projection of his own self
—the wonders he sought in great cities were all awaiting him
when he returned to Ireland: "They had been there all the time;
but my eyes had never been opened to them. I did not know
what my own house was like, because I had never been outside
it" (101). His madness is the vision of the inspired prophet
whose "way of joking is to tell the truth. It's the funniest joke
in the world" (101). But this symbolic madness is not only an
instrument of insight; it is also one of escape—he is constantly
calling people's attention to it—"You see I'm quite cracked;
but never mind: I'm harmless" (100); "You must also allow
for the fact that I am mad" (150)—as if to invite them to dismiss
what he says. In fact, Keegan's "insanity" is as self-protective as
Larry's cynicism in that it saves him the frustration and anguish
he would have to undergo were he to demand to be taken
seriously. It is interesting that the inhabitants of Rosscullen by
and large don't seem to consider him mad at all (100, 153).

Neither Larry nor Keegan can be accused of not appreciating
Broadbent's executive capacity. Shaw himself goes so far as to urge
that Broadbent's "power of taking himself seriously . . . was the
first condition of economy and concentration of force, sustained
purpose, and rational conduct" (14, Pref), and that "the virtues
of Broadbent are not less real because they are the virtues of the
money that coal and iron have produced" (15, Pref). Keegan
is willing to grant that Broadbent has "some excuse for believing
that if there be any future, it will be yours; for our faith seems
dead, and our hearts cold and cowed" (170)—and says he may
even vote for him. Doyle goes even farther, admitting to Broadbent that "in the main it is by living with you and working in
double harness with you that I have learnt to live in a real
world and not in an imaginary one" (87). If Broadbent's view is
that "something *must* be done" (174), Keegan's is that "when

we cease to do, we cease to live" (174)'; and Larry does not falter in the support of "those who can" (129). Why, then, do the three characters seem hopelessly divided?

Larry and Keegan do not share Broadbent's contention that "the world belongs to the efficient" (173) because they see his efficiency as only one of a desired conflux of attributes, while Tom treats it as an end in itself. In *Man and Superman* the aim of evolution was a being who would unite wisdom and power, flesh and spirit. Larry and Keegan share Juan's passion for an inclusive totality of vision. The more secular of the two, Larry, is an internationalist who believes that "frontiers are hindrances and flags confounded nuisances" (88). Since he sees his job as a civil engineer as being "to join countries, not to separate them," he views the state of damnation as one of isolation, and Rosscullen as "that hell of littleness": "My father wants to make St George's Channel a frontier and hoist a green flag on College Green; and I want to bring Galway within 3 hours of Colchester and 24 of New York. I want Ireland to be the brains and imagination of a big Commonwealth, not a Robinson Crusoe island" (88). Larry's secular internationalism finds its spiritual counterpart in Keegan, whose universal Church also transcends particular countries (175). Keegan's "I am a Catholic" (175) echoes Don Juan's "every idea for which Man will die will be a Catholic idea" (105). Like Juan, he has a vision of heaven as a mighty synthesis of forces: "In my dreams it is a country where the State is the Church and the Church the people: three in one and one in three. It is a commonwealth in which work is play and play is life: three in one and one in three. It is a temple in which the priest is the worshipper and the worshipper the worshipped: three in one and one in three. It is a godhead in which all life is human and all humanity divine: three in one and one in three. It is, in short, the dream of a madman" (177). Unfortunately, Broadbent manifests a psychic compartmentalization fatal to the spirit of synthesis. As Doyle puts it, "I never stop wondering at the blessed old head of yours with all its ideas in

watertight compartments . . . warranted impervious to anything it doesnt suit you to understand" (87). Keegan in turn
has noticed "a saying in the Scripture which runs . . . Let not
the right side of your brain know what the left side doeth. I
learnt at Oxford that this is the secret of the Englishman's
strange power of making the best of both worlds" (150). Of
course Broadbent will make the best of both worlds in action by
understanding neither in thought.

Thus the impulse toward union is overwhelmed by a dominant
spirit of polarization. Keegan sees such division of forces as the
state of damnation: "Standing here between you the Englishman, so clever in your foolishness, and this Irishman, so foolish
in his cleverness, I cannot in my ignorance be sure which of you
is the more deeply damned" (175). And Keegan also makes clear
that the split involves all three characters: "Mr Broadbent
spends his life inefficiently admiring the thoughts of great men,
and efficiently serving the cupidity of base money hunters. We
spend *our* lives efficiently sneering at him and doing nothing.
Which of us has any right to reproach the other?" (174). Larry
Doyle states the predicament of separate compartments at the
beginning of the play: "Live in contact with dreams and you
will get something of their charm: live in contact with facts and
you will get something of their brutality. I wish I could find a
country to live in where the facts were not brutal and the dreams
not unreal" (92). But there is no "rainbow bridge" to actualize
the dream.

The problem may be paraphrased from a point already made
in Shaw's analysis of *Emperor and Galilean*—that an element
of a synthesis is only "valid as a constituent of the synthesis, and
has no reality when isolated from it" (*Quint* 56). As a component of a vision, Broadbent's efficiency is indispensable; divorced
from vision, it is asinine:

KEEGAN. . . . The ass, sir, is the most efficient of beasts, matter-of-
fact, hardy, friendly when you treat him as a fellow-creature,
stubborn when you abuse him, ridiculous only in love, which sets

him braying, and in politics, which move him to roll about in the public road and raise a dust about nothing. Can you deny these qualities and habits in yourself, sir?

BROADBENT (*goodhumoredly*) Well, yes, I'm afraid I do, you know.

KEEGAN. Then perhaps you will confess to the ass's one fault. . . . That he wastes all his virtues—his efficiency, you call it—in doing the will of his greedy masters instead of doing the will of Heaven that is in himself. He is efficient in the service of Mammon, mighty in mischief, skilful in ruin, heroic in destruction. But he comes to browse here without knowing that the soil his hoof touches is holy ground.   (172)

Without such knowledge Broadbent's energies are only those of an "efficient devil" (172).

It is possible at this point to see how *John Bull's Other Island* developed from *Man and Superman*. The dream-vision, "Don Juan in Hell," was Shaw's attempted resolution of the psychic quest that had begun with *Immaturity*. But the resolution remained tentative because of doubt that the heavenly state could be translated from the mental realm into the real world to which the hero must return upon awakening. Now in *John Bull's Other Island* Shaw takes the hypothetical consummation of the preceding play and tests it in actuality. Can the synthesis of wisdom and power be achieved if we move from incorporeality and no place to Broadbent's forty-two-inch waist and the drab verisimilitude of Rosscullen? When the attempt is made thus to incarnate the vision, the result is a striking change in the function of the heaven-hell symbolism.

The first sign of this change occurs in Keegan's conversation with the grasshopper at the opening of Act II:

THE MAN. . . . But tell me this, Misther Unworldly Wiseman: why does the sight of heaven wring your heart an mine as the sight of holy wather wrings the heart o the divil? What wickedness have you done to bring that curse on you? Here! where are you jumpin to? Wheres your manners to go skyrocketin like that out o the box in the middle of your confession (*he threatens it with his stick*)?

THE GRASSHOPPER (*penitently*) X.

THE MAN (*lowering his stick*) I accept your apology; but dont do it again. And now tell me one thing before I let you go home to bed. Which would you say this country was: hell or purgatory?

THE GRASSHOPPER. X.

THE MAN. Hell! Faith I'm afraid youre right. I wondher what you and me did when we were alive to get sent here.   (96)

This suggested equivalence of earth and hell is later developed when Keegan explains how the Hindu he confessed revealed to him "the mystery of this world":

This world, sir, is very clearly a place of torment and penance, a place where the fool flourishes and the good and wise are hated and persecuted, a place where men and women torture one another in the name of love; where children are scourged and enslaved in the name of parental duty and education; where the weak in body are poisoned and mutilated in the name of healing, and the weak in character are put to the horrible torture of imprisonment, not for hours but for years, in the name of justice. It is a place where the hardest toil is a welcome refuge from the horror and tedium of plea-sure, and where charity and good works are done only for hire to ransom the souls of the spoiler and the sybarite. Now, sir, there is only one place of horror and torment known to my religion; and that place is hell. Therefore it is plain to me that this earth of ours must be hell, and that we are all here, as the Indian revealed to me —perhaps he was sent to reveal it to me—to expiate crimes commit-ted by us in a former existence.   (151–152)

To which Aunt Judy replies: "Heaven save us."

In "Don Juan in Hell" the state of damnation was defined in terms of the individual's progressive immunity to recognizing the self-deception in which his illusions are rooted. Hell is the state of mind where one can be an idealist with impunity; salvation, in contrast, can be achieved by the man who abandons the desire for happiness and devotes himself to advancing the pur-pose of life in a spirit of self-knowledge. It is a matter of the angelic versus the diabolic *temperament* (97)—Juan needs only to choose heaven in order to go there, because the will is firmly in command of the self. But Shaw's next play gives a sense of the will being trapped *within* the self—as Keegan says to the grasshopper, "If you could jump as far as a kangaroo you couldnt jump away from your own heart and its punishment. You can only look at Heaven from here: you cant reach it" (95–96). Formerly, the state of salvation depended entirely on the accuracy of one's perception of reality. Juan steers to heaven because he sees life's purpose; Lucifer drifts in hell because he thinks life has none. But in *John Bull's Other Island* the person who sees truly is just as apt to be "drifting" as he who does not —perhaps even more so. Although he may have the "angelic temperament," Keegan cannot "choose" heaven because his self is imprisoned in an environment that transforms his "dream of a madman" from the vision of an inspired prophet into the chimera of a cracked head. This environment, the world, had no such desolating omnipresence in *Man and Superman* because Juan's vision was somewhat isolated from its complications. Whatever the inadequacies of the hero's effort to implement the synthesis in society, the projected union of wisdom and power at least had value as a formulated goal that might be potentially capable of realization. But in *John Bull's Other Island* the mind is no longer its own place: the depths of Keegan's nature will not allow him to feel at home in the same world that Broadbent finds "quite good enough" (170). If it is true, as Keegan argues, that the world is hell, and if Broadbent in turn finds joy on earth to be possible, then the state of mind of the master of efficiency may be gauged from Don Juan's withering assertion, "The truly damned are those who are happy in hell" (87).

The implied tragedy of the play is thus one of paradox: why should understanding the nature of reality impede efficiency? Should it not rather vastly increase it? It is as if Shaw had recalled Don Juan's question, "Does a ship sail to its destination no better than a log drifts nowhither?" (128) and, after some thought, concluded: "Yes." The division between the worldly and the spiritual is especially infuriating because it is quite insusceptible to amelioration by political means. But a tone of fury is very far from the resignation of the concluding scene of the play, in which each of the three main characters drifts farther away from the other two into self-enclosed darkness. One is not surprised that Broadbent and Keegan talk through rather than to each other:

BROADBENT. . . . Well, look at your magnificent river there, going to waste.

KEEGAN (*closing his eyes*) "Silent, O Moyle, be the roar of thy waters."

BROADBENT. You know, the roar of a motor boat is quite pretty.

KEEGAN. Provided it does not drown the Angelus.

BROADBENT (*reassuringly*) Oh no: it wont do that: not the least danger.

You know, a church bell can make a devil of a noise when it likes.

(168)

One might look to Larry and Keegan as offering more hope of contact because they share much in common—both like to wander alone, have traveled widely to see the world, are proud to be Catholics, and are sometimes thought "mad" by others (McDowell 552n). Indeed, Larry's comment that "in Ireland the people is the Church and the Church the people" (130) states in embryonic form what will become the core of Keegan's definition of heaven. But when Keegan says he pities Ireland, the ensuing interchange borders on altercation: there can be no accommodation between Doyle's derisive view of Ireland and Keegan's vision of the country as a potential heaven (175). Larry the intellectual must repress his own visionary longings; he represents that state of development where consciousness has become so keen as to be crippling, and he knows it. He grows livid when Keegan calls Broadbent an ass (172) because he knows practicality is a better alternative than high-minded inertia. There is no point in giving land to the new class of peasant landlords: "They are too small, too poor, too ignorant, too simple-minded to hold it against us: you might as well give a dukedom to a crossing sweeper" (169). Larry's use of the word "us" is accurate —as McDowell notes (551), he owns stock in the syndicate himself.

Yet the same intellectuality that prevents Larry from surrendering to the sublimities of Keegan's mysticism makes him equally unwilling to accede to the simplicities of Broadbent's pragmatism. I have already suggested that his very dismissal of Keegan's utterances as "sentimental" has an obsessive quality about it, as if he must do this in order to escape the hurt involved in facing the truth of what the priest says. And barriers to communication exist not only between Keegan and Broadbent and between Keegan and Larry, but between Larry and Broadbent as well. Witness the following interchange concerning the fate of one of the small landowners soon to be dispossessed:

LARRY. Oh, we'll employ him in some capacity or other, and probably pay him more than he makes for himself now.

BROADBENT (*dubiously*) Do you think so? No no: Haffigan's too old. It really doesnt pay now to take on men over forty even for unskilled labor, which I suppose is all Haffigan would be good for. No: Haffigan had better go to America, or into the Union, poor old chap! He's worked out, you know: you can see it.

KEEGAN. Poor lost soul, so cunningly fenced in with invisible bars.

LARRY. Haffigan doesnt matter much. He'll die presently.

BROADBENT (*shocked*) Oh come, Larry! Dont be unfeeling. It's hard on Haffigan. It's always hard on the inefficient. (170)

Here Larry miscalculates the extent of Broadbent's callousness, just as Broadbent misses the element of sarcasm in his friend's remark about the imminence of Haffigan's demise. I say *element* of sarcasm because Larry is divided against himself—he agrees in part that "Haffigan doesnt matter." Thus the movement of the last scene is one in which each of these characters grows more isolated from the rest while at the same time the personality of each seems more and more defined by his relation to the other two. What results is a kind of unhealthy interdependence that offers little hope of this trio ever becoming "three in one and one in three."[3] And without the synthesis of forces, their

---

3. Shaw's organization of the action around three principal characters is analogous to the method of dramas such as *The Devil's Disciple*. In the earlier case, however, two of the three (Anderson and Burgoyne) served mainly as foils to a central figure (Dick Dudgeon); here Broad-

personalities threaten to become reductive stereotypes—Broadbent's efficiency is only opportunism, Larry's intellectuality is captiousness, and Keegan's spirituality is "dreaming." In his discussion of *Emperor and Galilean* Shaw had said that the "third empire" would be a "synthesis of relations in which not only is Christ God in exactly the same sense as that in which Julian is God, but Julian is Christ as well" (56). If for the Trinity of Julian-Christ-God we substitute the triad of Broadbent-Larry-Keegan, all expectation vanishes because the characters of the real persons involved subvert the personified abstractions of the paradigm. Or, to put it differently, the integrity of Juan's vision in *Man and Superman* is exploded by the dualism of the world of *John's Bull's Other Island*. The result is that Ireland, instead of looking forward to a future under efficient leadership (as Broadbent predicts), may have "no future at all" (170). The latter is Keegan's view: "For four wicked centuries the world has dreamed this foolish dream of efficiency; and the end is not yet. But the end will come" (174). The end may no longer be a consummation, but a catastrophe; no longer Caesar's "race that can understand" (181), but extinction. For the first time in Shaw's work, the apocalyptic note is struck.

Viewed as a series of discussions organized around a common theme and bearing down with cumulative weight upon the final scene, *John Bull's Other Island* is a major work whose poignancy is beautifully realized. The Irish atmosphere is depicted with a charm that is very far from the fey pretentiousness of the works of the Irish literary revival; the characters gradually acquire a symbolic dimension without losing their reality as individuals, and Shaw's poetic tone does not become forced here as in other plays where he tries self-consciously to create it. Moreover, Keegan's conviction that "every dream is a prophecy: every jest is

---

bent, Doyle, and Keegan are equal in importance. Moreover, the individual members of this tripartite group are more distinctly representative of broad human qualities than their counterparts in *Candida* or *Caesar and Cleopatra*.

an earnest in the womb of Time" (176) perfectly expresses the concluding mood of resignation impinged upon by frail hope.

The slender prospect that mere dream might be transformed into vision depends on the central character, Larry Doyle, the alienated intellectual whom McDowell (552) sees as a potential mediator of the positions of Broadbent and Keegan, just as in Shaw's next play some have seen another intellectual, Professor Cusins, as the possible reconciler of differences between Undershaft and Barbara. It is true that Larry has illusions of his own— his pan-nationalism, for instance, expresses itself in a condescension ("Youre all children: the big world that I belong to has gone past you and left you"—129) that fails to note that events in the "big world" are little more than elaborately disguised equivalents of the small behavior of the Haffigans and Dorans of Rosscullen. Nonetheless, Larry (like Cusins) has a realistic awareness of his condition, coupled with a strong sense that it is more important for a man to find something he can respect and do it than to pride himself on how little respect he has for the things he is not doing. While it may lack *Major Barbara*'s crackling brilliance, *John Bull's Other Island* makes a deeper impression because the tenuousness of Larry's final position seems a more accurate reflection of reality than the dubious triumph of Cusins.

7 Major Barbara

■▬▬▬▬▬▬▬▬▬▬▬▬▬▬▬▬▬▬▬▬▬▬▬▬▬▬▬▬▬▬▬▬▬▬▬▬▬▬■

Preliminary Obstacles

Conceptually Shaw's most ambitious play, *Major Barbara* (1905) is also the one least capable of being understood in isolation from his overall development. This drama poses enormous critical difficulties, nearly all of which concern the central character, Andrew Undershaft. Though in my opinion *Major Barbara* is finally not a successful work, it deserves and will repay the most careful study. Lesser writers might well envy Shaw the distinction of having produced a failure on this level.

There are some initial difficulties that must be cleared away. First, one must understand Shaw's technique of treating the play as a kind of game between himself and his audience; second, one must avoid some common misconstructions concerning the relation between Shaw and purported sources such as Nietzsche's *Beyond Good and Evil;* finally, it is important to see that any *literal* interpretation will be distorted. Misunderstanding in almost every instance comes down to confusion on one of the above points.

Many have felt that *Major Barbara* suffers from its author's propensity to carry paradoxical wit to cynical extremes. Why was it necessary for Shaw to trace the well-being of Undershaft's employees to the manufacture of destructive armaments; would not an automobile factory have done as well? A number of readers have followed Chesterton (185) in interpreting Barbara's "conversion" to her father's views as the expression of Shaw's rejection of the religious impulse. But does either of these conclusions really follow? Eager to grant his opposition the strongest possible case, Shaw uses weapons of destruction as an example of material power open to the *most* telling challenge and criticism. If he can make his point stick regarding bombs, it will automatically be true of automobiles—whereas the reverse would not be the case. As for religion, the play says nothing whatever concerning spiritual impulses per se. Barbara is neither a recluse nor an ascetic; as a member of the Salvation Army she has already committed herself to a variety of spiritual life that aims to have an impact upon persons in society. Given this commitment, Shaw argues that the premises Barbara uses to realize it are unsound because she has ignored an important factor. But no conclusion may be made concerning monks, nuns, or other religious; in any case, it would be naive to suggest that the creator of Don Juan, Keegan, and the later "Ancients" had no sympathy for the contemplative life.

These few instances emphasize the extent to which the reader of *Major Barbara* must constantly take an active role. The play is a battle of wits in which the dramatist and his audience attempt to outmaneuver each other and in the process become increasingly involved in an expanding range of ambiguity that makes it difficult to grasp the meaning hidden (to crib a phrase Shaw used in another connection) at "the center of the intellectual whirlpool" (*Back* lxxxv). But one need not accept Francis Fergusson's conclusion that the "witty dialectics" (193) are purely theatrical and that Shaw cares nothing for his play's correspondence to truth.

The relation of the play to possible sources provides us with an embarrassment of riches—comparisons with Euripides, Plato, Blake, and Nietzsche (to mention a few) can be illuminating provided we understand that Shaw utilizes these writers exactly insofar as it serves his own purposes. To take one example, there are many parallels between *Major Barbara* and *Beyond Good and Evil;* yet the Shavian ethical position surely cannot be equated with Nietzsche's "transvaluation of values." The famous sequence where Undershaft tries in vain to find Stephen a suitable occupation illustrates the point:

UNDERSHAFT. . . . Well, come! is there *anything* you know or care for?

STEPHEN (*rising and looking at him steadily*) I know the difference between right and wrong.

UNDERSHAFT (*hugely tickled*) You dont say so! What! no capacity for business, no knowledge of law, no sympathy with art, no pretension to philosophy; only a simple knowledge of the secret that has puzzled all the philosophers, baffled all the lawyers, muddled all the men of business, and ruined most of the artists: the secret of right and wrong. Why, man, youre a genius, a master of masters, a god! At twentyfour, too!   (311)

Though both eloquent and pointed, this was not written by a Nietzschean, but by a moralist who *does* see the world in terms of good and evil. The Shavian critique of morality is basically a plea that we be rather more discriminating (in realizing that poverty is a "crime," for example) than people usually are in making ethical judgments. To point out that the passage is inadequate as an explication of Nietzsche is hardly a valid criticism of the play. Shaw's ethical dualism is a source of dramatic strength: it is precisely because he considers Barbara's aspirations morally higher than Bodger's that the Salvation Army's dependency upon the resources of a distiller is so fraught with poignancy. Despite the apparent paradox of a merchant of death being offered as a positive moral force, a brief examination will reveal that the ethical perspective of *Major Barbara* is the same as that of *The Quintessence of Ibsenism,* where Shavian relativism also was equivalent to a pluralism of means employed within a framework of humane ends.

According to the *Quintessence,* an "ideal" is an illusion that has been abstracted into an ethical principle. In opposition to the resulting system of "morality" predicated upon how things "ought" to be, Shavian comedy reveals an ironic contrast be-

tween this artificially contrived state and the real world.[1] Thus
it comes as no surprise to find Undershaft chiding Cusins:
"Ought! ought! ought! ought! ought! Are you going to spend
your life saying ought, like the rest of our moralists?" (331). His
exhortations to his daughter insist only that ethics be concrete:
"You have made for yourself something that you call a morality
or a religion or what not. It doesnt fit the facts. Well, scrap it.
Scrap it and get one that does" (328). However regrettable the
"incarnation of morality" whose conscience is clear and duty
done when it has "called everybody names" (333), the Shavian
antithesis is not a conscienceless refusal to make judgments but
rather an insistence that things be called "by their *proper* names"
(287—italics mine). In the second edition of the *Quintessence*
Shaw had insisted that "conduct must justify itself by its effect
upon life and not by its conformity to any rule" (125). The
morality of *Major Barbara* is the same. When Bill Walker refuses to give his name to Barbara, she puts him down as "the
man who—struck—poor little Jenny Hill—in the mouth" (275):
he *is* his action. Undershaft is the personification of the relativist
whose belief that "there is only one true morality for every man;
but every man has not the same true morality" (262) is only the
secular equivalent of Barbara's "Our father . . . fulfils himself
in many ways" (274). Indeed, if we can understand that Barbara
and Undershaft are really saying the same thing in different
fashions, we are less apt to be confused by the outcome of the
play.

The third difficulty in understanding the drama concerns the
danger of literalism, against which Shaw warned in the last
paragraph of his preface: "Major Barbara, is, I hope, both true
and inspired; but whoever says that it all happened, and that

1. Much of the play's fun comes from the comic juxtaposition of abstractions with their real equivalents: "Hatred is the coward's revenge
for being intimidated" (334); or Undershaft's response to Stephen's conviction that "character" governs England: "Whose character? Yours or
mine?" (313).

faith in it and understanding of it consist in believing that it is a record of an actual occurrence, is, to speak according to Scripture, a fool and a liar" (241). But it is not necessary to bring the preface to the rescue of the play, the improbability of whose story itself is emphasized by sudden shifts in the manner of treatment. As Abbott remarks (121), the first act is high comedy, the second is a piece of low-life realism, and the third is sheer utopian fantasy. This mix of styles has the purpose of preventing the reader from orienting himself to the play on a realistic level, of forcing him instead to distance himself from the entire action and make sense of it in some larger terms.

The latter function is also served by the dialogue:

UNDERSHAFT. May I ask have you ever saved a maker of cannons?
BARBARA. No. Will you let me try?
UNDERSHAFT. Well, I will make a bargain with you. If I go to see you tomorrow in your Salvation Shelter, will you come the day after to see me in my cannon works?
BARBARA. Take care. It may end in your giving up the cannons for the sake of the Salvation Army.
UNDERSHAFT. Are you sure it will not end in your giving up the Salvation Army for the sake of the cannons?
BARBARA. I will take my chance of that.
UNDERSHAFT. And I will take my chance of the other. (*They shake hands on it.*) Where is your shelter?
BARBARA. In West Ham. At the sign of the cross. Ask anybody in Canning Town. Where are your works?
UNDERSHAFT. In Perivale St Andrews. At the sign of the sword. Ask anybody in Europe. (262–263)

Note here the extreme stylization, deliberately calling attention to the artifice of the dialogue. The formal sequence of balance and antithesis in which the characters echo symmetrically each other's phrases functions to remove the play from the realm of literal reality; the very idea of the exchange of visits (the hinge of the plot) suggests a fantasy world, a kind of "just suppose it were possible" situation only a shade removed from "once upon a time." In this atmosphere, everything must be understood figuratively. For instance, when Cusins, the professor of Greek who joined the Army to worship Barbara, ends by saying that he "wants to give the common man weapons against the intellectual man" (337), one critic takes this as a declaration of an intention to give Undershaft's guns to Rummy Mitchens and Snobby Price (the "common people" who appear in the play) and concludes on that basis that the moral of the work is ridiculous (Woodbridge 67–68). But it would make as much sense to take Barbara's objection to Bodger's whiskey as proof that the drama was intended as a temperance tract. One must move beyond guns and Bibles to the symbolic oppositions they represent in this Shavian parable.

The Shavian Hero

Shaw described *Major Barbara* as the last of a "group of three plays." In the first of them, *Man and Superman,* he had dramatized his conception of a union of the practical and the nobly idealistic. Whether a person is mentally in "heaven" or in "hell" depends on whether he is active or indifferent in relation to the goal of creating the Superman. But this development from the pragmatic posture of the earlier plays could be only temporary because it is articulated in the realm of the dream-vision and collapses with Tanner's return to normal life in society. In *John Bull's Other Island* Shaw attempts to make a direct translation of the vision from the realm of the spirit to that of actuality, only to find that a deep dualism divides the "heaven" of the dream from the "hell" of a world in which the desired synthesis of forces is not possible. In *Major Barbara* Shaw attempts to address the problem raised at the end of the preceding play and determine *why* the synthesis had not been possible. The opposition of divergent forces represented by Ann/Tanner and Broadbent/Keegan here becomes more sharply drawn in the contrast between Barbara and Undershaft, that is, between Christ and cannons. Having thus polarized the conflict between wisdom and power in the most extreme terms possible, Shaw ventures a resolution in this climax of his eschatological trilogy.

Like its forerunners, *Major Barbara* employs a symbolism opposing heaven and hell, salvation and damnation.[2] Here Barbara, the representative of spiritual aspiration, is a member of the "Salvation Army"; Undershaft, the wielder of material power, is "the Prince of Darkness" (305). Barbara goes "right up into the skies" (340); her father's trombone sounds like "the laughter of the damned" (305). Barbara tells ruffian Bill Walker that he's "going to heaven" (282); but the nature of Undershaft's occupation suggests to the imbecilic Lomax that "getting into heaven" is not exactly his line (261). Yet almost immediately an apparent paradox arises: although Undershaft is "infernal" (286), "Mephistopheles" (290), and a "cunning tempter" (334), he is also "Father Undershaft" (284), "St Andrew Undershaft" (209, Pref), and "a confirmed mystic" (279). Although his armaments factory is the "Works Department of Hell" (314), it is also a lovely town that "only needs a cathedral to be a heavenly city instead of a hellish one" (318). Indeed, Barbara's expectation that Perivale St. Andrews will be "a sort of pit [full of] lost creatures with blackened faces" (314) would have served more accurately as a description of her own Salvation Army shelter. In *Man and Superman* the inversion of the usual connotations of heaven and hell is initially misleading because Shaw's hell really is a place of damnation and his heaven one of salvation. In *Major Barbara* the paradox is misleading because it is not a paradox—the inversions disguise a dynamic relationship that Shaw believes only our conventional prejudice prevents us from perceiving. Unlike Broadbent, Doyle, and Keegan (who remain essentially static in relation to one another), Barbara, Cusins, and Undershaft participate in an exploratory process of growth.

Andrew Undershaft is the culminating figure in a long line of

2. This point has been similarly documented by Wisenthal (1974), 85.

Shavian heroes (beginning with Sartorius) who see their salvation in terms of survival. As he puts it, "I had rather be a thief than a pauper. I had rather be a murderer than a slave. I dont want to be either; but if you force the alternative on me, then, by Heaven, I'll choose the braver and more moral one" (331). Like Mrs. Warren before him, Undershaft refuses to accept the premises of a ruling class that attempts to rationalize exploitation by using idealistic morality to convince the exploited that their miserable state is blessed. He is the realist who, perceiving the hidden truth that "poverty is a crime," rejects the ethic of self-sacrifice, asserts the validity of his own will, and manufactures cannons with the motto "UNASHAMED." In doing so, he fulfills a family tradition: he is the seventh in a line of Undershafts who, like the Antonines, adopted their successors.

Undershaft combines the practicality of Cashel Byron with the self-conscious articulateness of Jack Tanner. But whereas Tanner only thinks he is a strong man, Undershaft really is a strong man, who does not need to flail about in order to create an impression of importance. Eloquent as he is, the cannon magnate's real strength is not revealed in his long speeches but in his short ones—no man ever got more mileage out of a "No," "Thank you," "Just so," or "I shall be delighted." In verbal sparring, he is the master of devastating brevity:

CUSINS. Well, I can only say that if you think you will get [Barbara] away from the Salvation Army by talking to her as you have been talking to me, you dont know Barbara.
UNDERSHAFT. My friend: I never ask for what I can buy.
CUSINS (*in a white fury*) Do I understand you to imply that you can buy Barbara?
UNDERSHAFT. No; but I can buy the Salvation Army.   (288)

While this character represents the practical sense pushed to a frightening logical extreme, Shaw is not making an atavistic return to earlier heroes in his dramas of survival. If Undershaft seems devilish where his forerunners were shrewd, he will at any rate turn out to be a devil with a difference.

His daughter Barbara, in turn, is a minister with a difference; for like her father, she is a moral realist. Never does she really practice the expiatory religion of the Salvation Army, which encourages people to pretend to terrible sins they never committed in order to emphasize the miracle of being "saved" by Jesus. In this context, it is typical that a ruffian named Bill Walker, after striking Army worker Jenny Hill, should try to "atone" for his act by paying a fine in the form of a donation to the Army and, when this is rejected, by attempting to get himself beaten up by a professional boxer named Todger Fairmile. Barbara's refusal to encourage him in such expiatory rites removes external salvation from Bill at precisely the moment he most wants to be punished. Though her terminology is conventional (she is full of words like soul, devil, and God), no less than her father does Barbara place moral responsibility within the conscience of the individual. As Shaw puts it in the preface, she does not want Bill to pay for his villainy, but to cease being a villain (225). She wants an internal change based upon Bill's own sense of self-esteem, not an external alteration based on subservience to an abstraction. The ruffian disintegrates under this unusual approach. "Awm as good as her!" (274) he snivels helplessly. And if Bill only believed it, he would be.

Shaw admits in his preface that in real life Barbara might have succeeded in enabling Bill to redeem himself. But the salvation of our suffering Everyman in this Shavian morality play is cut short by the appearance of Goods, in the form of Undershaft's matching gift. Lord Saxmundham, formerly Bodger the whiskey distiller, offers to contribute five thousand pounds to the Army, provided that an equivalent sum be supplied by other donors. Not one to let an opportunity like this pass by, Undershaft proceeds to write a check the Army cannot afford to refuse. Cynically concluding that *his* contribution was rejected because it was too small, Bill now turns on Barbara with the famous taunt: "Wot prawce selvytion nah?" (296). Barbara might be asking herself the same question—unable to accept that what's good for

Bill is somehow not good for Bodger, she quits the Army. But she does not immediately see that Undershaft may have acted, not to destroy her aspirations, but to bring home to her consciousness the fact that it is impossible to save Bill while society is organized in the present fashion. The spiritual inertia into which Undershaft has plunged his daughter turns out to be no more irrevocable than the physical "deep sleep" (*Wag* 198) into which Wotan cast Brynhild at the end of *The Valkyrie*. The rest of the play deals with Barbara's creative confrontation of her own disillusionment and her attempt to discover "some truth or other behind all this frightful irony" (316).

Perhaps Barbara would have been less distraught had she been present earlier when Undershaft explained the nature of his "religion" to Cusins.

UNDERSHAFT. . . . There are two things necessary to salvation. . . . The two things are . . . money and gunpowder.
CUSINS. . . . Excuse me: is there any place in your religion for honor, justice, truth, love, mercy, and so forth?
UNDERSHAFT. Yes: they are the graces and luxuries of a rich, strong, and safe life.
CUSINS. That is your religion?
UNDERSHAFT. Yes.   (283-284)

Here Undershaft's opening line concerning "two things necessary to salvation" seems very definite indeed. But the dialogue that follows qualifies the idea by suggesting that "money and gunpowder" are not a denial of traditional religious values (honor, truth, love, and so forth) but something that makes adherence to them possible. Without enough money and gunpowder "one cannot afford" virtues; but the possession of money and gunpowder alone will not automatically provide them.[3] The implication of the passage is that material power is a "necessary" but not sufficient cause of salvation in the gospel according to St.

3. Compare the preface to *The Irrational Knot*, written in the same year as *Major Barbara*: "Conscience is a luxury, and should be indulged in only when the vital needs of life have been abundantly satisfied" (xiv–xv).

Andrew. Playing his "game" masterfully, Shaw tempts the careless reader to mistake his surface strategy for his underlying meaning.

The final act contains a similar interchange between Barbara and her father concerning the "souls" of his workmen:

UNDERSHAFT. I save their souls just as I saved yours.

BARBARA (*revolted*) *You* saved my soul! What do you mean?

UNDERSHAFT. I fed you and clothed you and housed you. I took care that you should have money enough to live handsomely—more than enough; so that you could be wasteful, careless, generous. That saved your soul from the seven deadly sins.

BARBARA (*bewildered*) The seven deadly sins!

UNDERSHAFT. Yes, the deadly seven. (*Counting on his fingers*) Food, clothing, firing, rent, taxes, respectability and children. Nothing can lift those seven millstones from Man's neck but money; and the spirit cannot soar until the millstones are lifted. I lifted them from your spirit. I enabled Barbara to become Major Barbara; and I saved her from the crime of poverty. . . . It is cheap work converting starving men with a Bible in one hand and a slice of bread in the other. . . . Try your hand on *my* men: their souls are hungry because their bodies are full.   (329–330)

In response to Barbara's demand to know what he *means* by the apparently outrageous claim to have "saved" her soul, Undershaft explains that his material support rescued her *from* "the seven deadly sins" (the counterparts of Juan's "seven deadly virtues" in *Man and Superman*—87). Undershaft's gift of freedom from certain external obstacles has a purely negative function: only Barbara could decide what she had been freed *for*. The point is not, as Chesterton thought, that the religious element is defeated, but that "the spirit cannot soar until the millstones are lifted." Undershaft knows that material sustenance is the precondition—*not* the guarantee—of spiritual aspiration: what would be the point of telling Barbara to try her hand on his workers (330) if he seriously meant his earlier boast, "I save their souls," to mean that he has already secured their salvation in a *positive* sense? His point is rather that the workers' "souls are hungry because their bodies are full"—which can hardly seem an ignoble sentiment to the girl who had said in the previous act, "I cant talk religion to a man with bodily hunger in his eyes" (290).

Thus the play's treatment of the question of the proper use of power is a subtle one. It does not claim that if a person has power he will automatically have wisdom, but rather that if a person does not have power no wisdom he does have will be of any use. Integrity and courage by themselves are not enough: for as Cashel Byron had argued long before, "If you havent executive power as well, your courage will only lead you to stand up to be beaten by men that have both courage and executive power; and what good does that do you?" (89). The moral purity Cusins thirsts for is not feasible; as Barbara tells him, "Turning our backs on Bodger and Undershaft is turning our backs on life" (338). Whoever wishes to separate himself from the "wicked side" of things merely guarantees his own impotence before the Bodgers of the world. The Shavian view holds that *all* money is tainted; those who do not have material sustenance want to get it and those who do have it want to keep it: the resulting struggle of wills is only disguised by conventional idealistic abstractions. Shaw attacks the notion (which he sees as a perversion of Christianity) that humane and intelligent persons are obliged to be nicely passive and self-effacing, thereby assuring the triumph of the very evil they are above confronting. The side of life traditionally considered devilish must be controlled before it can be abolished. The attempt to gain such control has its dangers, of course, but the risks must be taken: "You cannot have power for good without having power for evil" (337).

The explanation of this burgeoning militancy in Shaw's art can be sought in his developing political consciousness in real life. Not that *Major Barbara* marks any overt shift in convictions; the play is in some ways a predictable Shavian document. Trenchant descriptions of the effects of poverty make the point that the enlightened wealthy can have no real interest in perpetuating it (329); the action itself exposes philanthropy as a ruse enabling the unenlightened wealthy to soothe their consciences in the very act of strengthening their privileged positions. But the tone in which Shaw presents these familiar ideas suggests that his patience with the Fabian policy of watchful waiting is now wearing thin. Just two years earlier, "John Tanner" offered a critique of the price paid for respectability by the Fabians, who had come to be well spoken of "not because the English have the smallest intention of studying or adopting the Fabian policy, but because they believe that the Fabians, by eliminating the element of intimidation from the Socialist agitation, have drawn the teeth of insurgent poverty and saved the existing order from the only method of attack it really fears" (*Super* 190, Rev Hdbk). While the use of a persona enabled Shaw deftly to sidestep the suggestion that these sentiments were his own, the gist of "Tanner's" argument must have struck root in his mind by the time he comes in *Major Barbara* to upbraid the poor for being more often complacent than insurgent. Like the Fabian Society, the Salvation Army opts to pursue its goals by working *through* the existing social system, and thus "draws the teeth" (*Barb* 288) of the very class that might otherwise revolt against the oppression that the Army serves to palliate. Moreover, the Fabian essayist who once urged people to "Vote! Vote!! Vote!!!" (Henderson 241) and held that "when Democracy fails, there is no antidote for intolerance save the spread of better sense" (*EFS* 94) now creates a leading character who exults in the claim that the "pious mob fills up ballot papers and imagines it is governing its masters; but the ballot paper that really governs is the paper that has a bullet wrapped up in it" (331). Of course, Undershaft (like Tanner) cannot be taken as identical to Shaw, whose own pronouncements on democracy have not *yet* come to emulate his hero's inflammatory rhetoric. Still, Undershaft's utterances cannot be explained away as a mere standpoint being exploited for theatrical effect; for by the end of the play his exhortations have apparently wrought a significant change in Barbara and Cusins. Indeed, after agreeing to terms with "Machiavelli" (299), the

Professor moves to within an inch of advocating the kind of insurrectionary class war (337) that ten years previously Shaw had dismissed as romantic nonsense. But what precisely is the young couple's succession to the leadership of the armaments firm supposed to indicate?

To give audiences a clue for following his play's intricate and baffling turns of meaning, Shaw portrays *Major Barbara*'s various conceptual strands dramatically through the developing interrelationships of the three principal characters, who begin by formally representing an opposition between ideas and gradually come to suggest a dynamism that will unite them. We can begin to sense how this process works by examning an important passage at the climax of the third act:

UNDERSHAFT. . . . Dont come here lusting for power, young man.
CUSINS. If power were my aim I should not come here for it. You have no power.
UNDERSHAFT. None of my own, certainly.
CUSINS. I have more power than you, more will. You do not drive this place: it drives you. And what drives this place?
UNDERSHAFT (*enigmatically*) A will of which I am a part.
BARBARA (*startled*) Father! Do you know what you are saying; or are you laying a snare for my soul?   (327)

To the student of Shaw this passage is both crucial and inevitable. As far back as his analysis of Ibsen's *Emperor and Galilean,* we saw Shaw's concern with a synthesis of the individual self and the "world-will." In *Man and Superman* this relation was explained in terms of the operation of the Life Force, which the individual serves but which itself exists only insofar as the human mind creates it. Is Undershaft speaking of himself in terms analogous to those previously applied to Maximus, Wotan, and Don Juan? Undershaft is the slave of a cosmic force—he does not drive the factory, it drives him. Yet he is an active agent, for he is part of the will that drives the place that drives him. Cusins is appropriately baffled, but Barbara's startled reaction suggests she understands quite well what her father has implied. Giving up momentarily on the "morality-mongering" (327) Cusins, Undershaft asks his daughter to tell the Professor "what power really means."

BARBARA (*hypnotized*) Before I joined the Salvation Army, I was in my own power; and the consequence was that I never knew what to do with myself. When I joined it, I had not time enough for all the things I had to do.

UNDERSHAFT (*approvingly*) Just so. And why was that, do you suppose?

BARBARA. Yesterday I should have said, because I was in the power of God. (*She resumes her self-possession, withdrawing her hands from his with a power equal to his own.*) But you came and shewed me that I was in the power of Bodger and Undershaft. . . . I was safe with an infinite wisdom watching me, an army marching to Salvation with me; and in a moment, at the stroke of your pen in a cheque book, I stood alone; and the heavens were empty. (327–328)

Barbara has reason to be startled by Undershaft's words, for her own speech corresponds almost diagrammatically to his in its conception of the relation between the individual and the cosmos. Barbara is echoing a point already made by Don Juan: that there is nothing so will-less as the drifting of the willful, and nothing so potent as the service of a force that advances from the efforts of those who realize rather than sacrifice themselves. "God" is created by our doing "the work he had to create us to do because it cannot be done except by living men and women" (339). The result is that paradoxical state in which free will and necessity become merged. This is why Barbara can be "in the power of God" (327), while Cusins can claim she is "original in her religion" (286). This is why Undershaft can admit that he has no power while nonetheless believing that he was "a dangerous man" until he had his will (330). His factory, a larger force to which he belongs, is the "Undershaft inheritance" (321); Barbara's inspiration, which comes from "within herself" (286), is also the "Undershaft inheritance." No wonder Barbara fears that a snare is being set for her soul and that her father is diabolically wording his speech in terms he knows will tempt her.[4] For while they have almost identical conceptions of the relation between individual and universal wills, Barbara fears that the self may become synthesized with diabolic as well as divine forces: "Oh, how gladly would I take a better [religion] to my soul! But you offer me a worse one" (328). What is the reconciliation that can bring "infinite wisdom" to the empty heavens in this most difficult of Shaw's dramas of ideas?

It may help to clarify matters here to take up again the analogy between Undershaft and Wotan in *The Perfect Wagnerite*.[5] Just as the god's bargain with Fricka to secure efficiency led him to become hedged by unforeseen "tangles and alliances and compromises" (*Wag* 183), so Undershaft's resort to instruments of destruction to ensure his survival has involved an inevitable narrowing of potential. Undershaft did not *want* to have to choose between being a slave and being a murderer (331) any more than Mrs. Warren wanted to choose between prostitution and

4. In an article (cited in note 5) anticipating his book, Wisenthal argues that "Undershaft's phrase, 'a will of which I am a part,' is deliberately ambiguous: he means the will of society, but wants Barbara to think that he means the will of God. . . . In a cancelled draft of this passage his reply to Cusins's question ('What drives this place?') is, 'Society, my friend, especially the most rascally part of society'" (1972; 61). While the phrase in question may (as Wisenthal holds) have been Shaw's means for suggesting a more craftily worded attempt at trickery, the ambiguity could instead have been designed to depict a genuine awareness on Undershaft's part that the issue of "what drives this place?" admits of more than one possibly valid answer. In the latter case, Shaw's alteration indicates no mere refinement in Undershaft's strategy of deception, but a change in the dramatist's very conception of his hero's significance. (In general, I lean toward a more positive construction of Undershaft's motives than Wisenthal would allow.)

5. Some elements of my discussion of the relation between *Major Barbara* and Wagner's *Ring* have been anticipated by J. L. Wisenthal, "The Underside of Undershaft: A Wagnerian Motif in *Major Barbara*" (*Shaw Review*, XV, 2 [1972], 56–64). While leaving my original text unaltered, I have referred in these notes to instances where our views diverge.

poverty. While Shaw insists that these characters have made the right decision under the circumstances, the whole force of his social critique depends on bringing home to the consciences of his audience that such choices are made at great personal cost. For all his ebullience, Undershaft is trapped in his trade: the system by which each of his well-fed workers "keeps the man just below him in his place" (315) is a neat model of a repressive power structure; and the implements manufactured in the factory reinforce the worst tendencies of the very society its owner so eloquently condemns! Thus in some ways Cusins is correct in describing the old man as the slave of "the most rascally part of society, the money hunters, the pleasure hunters, the military promotion hunters" (327). Undershaft's response—"Not necessarily"—is extraordinarily tentative, considering its source; furthermore, it is followed by the surprising intimation that the possibility of the Professor's accusation turning out to be wrong no longer depends upon Undershaft himself, but upon Barbara and Cusins instead. Could he have been more serious than we thought when he asked his daughter, "Have you ever saved a maker of cannons?" (262)?

That Undershaft was justified in choosing the cannons does not mean that for Shaw they represent a final good. If he looked at the cannon business as an end, Undershaft would be exactly the kind of big bad capitalist that Marxist critics have thought him (West 121–141). The factory has no moral significance whatever in itself—at one stage of human evolution the command of material power is a vital prerequisite to any further development. That Undershaft cannot personally pursue this development is only natural: even Wotan struck the sword into the stone only to learn that "no weapon from the armory of Godhead can serve the turn of the true Human Hero" (*Wag* 193–194). Undershaft's hope of not being the "slave" of rascals is entirely dependent (as he proceeds to explain) upon good people not preferring "preaching and shirking to buying my weapons and fighting the rascals" (327). But if his auditors lack the "courage and conviction" (327) to rise to the challenge, then his creed has reached an impasse; at that point he can only say "dont blame me" (327), but he cannot carry the matter further because no one man can embody within himself the entire evolutionary process. Shaw clearly believes that Undershaft must be replaced by something higher; perhaps Undershaft thinks so too. Could it not be with an awareness of being the instrument of that higher force that he persuades Barbara and Cusins to take his own power and use it to supersede him?

Undershaft never states directly that such is his purpose, because his perception of it is more intuitive than intellectual. On the level of explicit formulation, his aims are somewhat different; he wants to pass on his torch to his daughter. She "shall make my converts and preach my gospel" (287). What Undershaft thinks he thinks corresponds to Wotan's belief that *his* daughter, Brynhild, will obey his command to slay Siegmund and thus fulfill his obligations to Fricka. But Wotan discovers that his real will does not correspond to his intentions—secretly he *wants* Brynhild to disobey him. Similarly, though Undershaft may promulgate his armorer's faith to sell cannons to all causes and crimes (326), he can no more tell Cusins what to do with the cannons than Wotan could tell Siegfried what to do with Nothung. Cusins makes essentially this point in asserting his independence ("I shall sell cannons to whom I please and refuse them to whom I please"—327); and the millionaire's response ("From the moment when you become Andrew Undershaft, you will never do as you please again"—327) means that the Professor will be in the grip of the Life Force, *not* that he will be under the thumbs of the very "rascals" Undershaft proceeds to urge him to fight. Moreover, Barbara's conviction that it is among the "snobbish, uppish creatures" of Perivale St. Andrews that "salvation is really wanted" (339) indicates that she is not accepting the cannons on her father's terms, either. The fact that the aging entrepreneur adopts as his heirs two persons who he senses will be no slavish disciples suggests that there is more in Undershaft's mind than a logic based on pragmatic self-interest can explain.

It was Maximus the Mystic who first propounded the paradox that the "third empire" would require the death of the self and yet would be " 'self-begotten in the man who wills' " (*Quint* 56). Though Wotan gradually learned that the first task of the Hero would be to "sweep the gods and their ordinances" from his path (193), Siegfried would never have been conceived had not Godhead begun "secretly to long for the advent of some higher power than itself" (175). Like Wotan, Undershaft can be seen as "finally acquiescing in and working for his own supersession" (*Wag* 219). While the culmination he desires is clearly beyond his own achievement, he is nonetheless the active agent who generates the union of wisdom and power, not as in the dream-vision of Don Juan, but in the real world. Barbara and Cusins must achieve it themselves, free from Undershaft's influence, just as Siegfried must actualize his will "without any illicit prompting from Wotan" (193); yet it is the chief of the gods and the dealer in destruction who catalyze the change. Undershaft's crucial query, "Dare you make war on war? Here are the means [that is, the cannons]" (334), is that pivotal act in which the assertion of his own will becomes one with the will beyond his own. Critics have attacked the famous question he puts to Cusins since it seems to contradict everything Undershaft has affirmed before (Ozy 23). If we grant that he is sincere, Undershaft's action logically makes no sense. Yet the kind of sense an evolutionary leap makes must be perceived in relation, not to the order that already exists, but to the higher one it aspires to create. In terms of the conventional life he has risen above, Undershaft's endeavor is either diabolical (a ploy to entice Cusins to disaster) or self-destructive; in terms of the new life he falls short of, the same endeavor is that self-generated aspiration to a state beyond the self which has been the hallmark of the Shavian hero from the beginning. The question "Dare you make war on war?" marks the instant in which Undershaft creates the force he serves: it corresponds exactly to those moments when Don Juan determines to enter heaven, when Wotan hails the coming of the Hero whom he had sought to destroy, when Julian (had he possessed the courage and insight) would have embraced Christ.

The nature of the process Undershaft stimulates and undergoes can be seen in microcosm in the series of "Maxims" which the first six Andrew Undershafts wrote up in their shops (326). Each of the even-numbered maxims offers an unmitigated pragmatism without reference to values. Number two, for instance, "All have the right to fight: none have the right to judge," amounts to saying "might makes right."[6] On the other hand, maxims one, three, and five connect the philosophy of power to an ultimate goal: God, heaven, and peace respectively (such as "To Man the weapon: to Heaven and victory"). The history of the Undershafts has witnessed an oscillation between blunt pragmatism and an attempt to suggest a possible relation between such pragmatism and some moral purpose. But the final maxim, number seven—"UNASHAMED"—is ambiguous. It could simply be a curt dismissal of objections often raised against the pragmatic orientation and would therefore be classified with the even-numbered group. It could also be taken as the end result of all the others thus far—as if after those swings of the pendulum that Satan saw as part of an infinite comedy of illusion (*Super* 126), the ground has at last been cleared for a change that will radically alter the opposition by transcending it. The seventh maxim is, significantly, that of the present Andrew Undershaft. He is not the culmination of the synthesis, but the instrument that makes it possible. To paraphrase Barbara: he may be the devil, but God speaks through him sometimes (316).

When Undershaft originally proposed the exchange of visits,

6. Strictly speaking, Maxim Four does not exist, since the Andrew Undershaft in question "had no literary turn" and consequently "did not write up anything." But the man's actions ("he sold cannons to Napoleon under the nose of George the Third") firmly place him in the pragmatic group.

Barbara cautioned that the experiment might end in his "giving up the cannons for the sake of the Salvation Army" (263). He replied in turn that it might end in Barbara's "giving up the Salvation Army for the sake of the cannons" (263). Readers have of course taken Undershaft's prediction as a signal of what will later come true, but it would be fairer to note that both prophecies are fulfilled. Barbara and Cusins "give up" the Salvation Army by accepting the cannon factory, and Undershaft gives up his cannons by placing the power they represent at the service of the religious impulse. "Giving up" here means what "succumbing" meant when Maximus explained to Julian: " 'Does not the child succumb in the youth and the youth in the man: yet neither child nor youth perishes' " (*Quint* 55). The respective "professions" of Barbara and Undershaft will now develop in meaningful relation to each other instead of in isolation.[7] If Shaw did not entitle the play "Andrew Undershaft's Profession," it was because the work involved more than Major Barbara's "conversion."[8]

In *Emperor and Galilean,* Maximus lamented that " 'the empire of the flesh [pagan sensualism] is fallen a prey to the empire of the spirit [Christian asceticism]' " (*Quint* 55–56). At the end of the second act of *Major Barbara,* this situation has been reversed: the empire of the spirit (Barbara's work for the Salvation Army) has fallen prey to the empire of the flesh (Undershaft's weapons as symbols of materialism). The final act of the

7. Compare Shaw's enthusiastic quoting of a letter from a priest who had read *Saint Joan:* " 'In your play,' he writes, 'I see the dramatic presentation of the conflict of the Regal, sacerdotal, and Prophetical powers, in which Joan was crushed. To me it is not the victory of any one of them over the others that will bring peace and the Reign of the Saints in the Kingdom of God, but their fruitful interaction in a costly but noble state of tension.' The Pope himself could not put it better; nor can I" (*Joan* 36, Pref).

8. The word "conversion" is always used sarcastically in the play: for example, Cusins's "We convert everything to good here" (299) or Shirley's warning to Bill about Todger Fairmile: "He'll convert your head into a mashed potato" (277).

drama attempts to depict the possibility of a creative merging of forces. Nothing is relinquished: Cusins will take over the "death and devastation factory" (313), into which, however, he brings "capital" of his own ("the subtlest thought, the loftiest poetry yet attained by humanity"—325). If we see Shaw attempting here to go beyond the dilemma with which *John Bull's Other Island* concluded by returning to re-examine the ideas he had developed in writing about *Emperor and Galilean* and *The Ring,* then the precise function of the role of Andrew Undershaft becomes clear. Maximus's impulse toward " 'the third empire, in which the twin-natured shall reign' " (*Quint* 56) becomes the paradigm for later Shavian patterns of salvation. In each of these works Shaw employs a trinity of characters to illustrate the allegorical scheme (Julian–Maximus–Christ; Brynhild–Wotan–Siegfried; Broadbent–Doyle–Keegan; Barbara–Undershaft–Cusins). Where the work deals with a (tragic) separation of forces, the first member of the triad (Julian, Broadbent) manifests an opacity that leads to a visionary second member's (Maximus, Doyle) entrapment in what remains a permanent opposition between the first and third. Where the work outlines a (comic) fusion of forces, however, as in *The Perfect Wagnerite* and *Major Barbara,* an initial opposition between the first and second characters (Brynhild–Wotan, Barbara–Undershaft) is transcended by a pivotal act of the second that produces a synthesis-figure (Siegfried, Cusins) in whom all antinomies are to be reconciled.[9] Looking at several works at once, one could say, broadly speaking, that Undershaft is to Broadbent as Wotan is to Julian. The "damned" characters, Broadbent and Julian, mistake the unfamiliar element of the synthesis as a "rival will" which they must overcome; the "saved" characters, Undershaft and Wotan, are heroic because they have the grace to work *with* the process instead of fighting it. The "truth and heroism" that finally over-

9. It is Cusins's function as end-product of the drama's action that has misled some critics into taking him for the hero of the play. The same criterion would make Fortinbras the hero of *Hamlet.*

throw Wotan turn out to be "children of his inmost heart" (*Wag* 219); so the couple who succeed to the Undershaft inheritance are likewise *his* children—the one his real daughter, the other the son he adopts as his spiritual heir. The result is that Undershaft goes under without being overcome; he is reborn as the spirit represented by Cusins, who becomes Andrew Undershaft VIII.

The resemblance of the temperament of Undershaft to that of Wotan is more than an analogue. In a chapter added to *The Perfect Wagnerite* shortly after *Major Barbara* was written, Shaw attempted to explain more clearly why Siegfried, the great synthesis-figure, had disappointed expectations:

The dominant sort of modern employer is not to be displaced and dismissed so lightly as Alberic in The Ring. Wotan is hardly less dependent on him than Fafnir: the War-Lord visits his works, acclaims them in stirring speeches, and imprisons his enemies; whilst Loki does his political jobs in Parliament, making wars and commercial treaties for him at command. And he owns and controls a new god, called The Press, which manufactures public opinion on his side, and organizes the persecution and suppression of Siegfried.
The end cannot come until Siegfried learns Alberic's trade and shoulders Alberic's burden. Not having as yet done so, he is still completely mastered by Alberic. (*Wag* 242—italics mine)[10]

In Shaw's view, Wagner had paid too little attention to the power represented by Alberic. A prospect mentioned in passing in the

10. The entire passage is from the chapter ("Why He Changed His Mind") written in 1907 for a German translation of the book, which first appeared in English in the "expanded" second edition (New York: Brentano's, 1909). In that version, the first paragraph read: " . . . the dominant sort of modern employer is not to be displaced and dismissed so lightly as Alberic in The Ring. They are really the masters of the whole situation. Wotan is hardly less dependent on him than Fafnir: the War-Lord visits his works, acclaims them in stirring speeches, and imprisons his enemies; whilst Loki makes commercial treaties for them and subjects all his diplomacy to their approval." The Standard Edition text had already been adopted in the third edition (Leipzig: Tauchnitz, 1913). Wisenthal (1972; 56) erroneously cites the 1913 volume as the first appearance (in English) of the new chapter.

late nineteenth-century essay (that the greedy dwarf might get the ring back and "out-Valhalla Valhalla, if not buy it over as a going concern"—192) had become an early twentieth-century fact. The description of Alberic's control bears a striking similarity to Undershaft's address to Stephen when the latter accuses his father of insulting the government of his country:

The government of your country! *I* am the government of your country: I, and Lazarus. Do you suppose that you and half a dozen amateurs like you, sitting in a row in that foolish gabble shop, can govern Undershaft and Lazarus? No, my friend: you will do what pays us. You will make war when it suits us, and keep peace when it doesnt. You will find out that trade requires certain measures when we have decided on those measures. When I want anything to keep my dividends up, you will discover that my want is a national need. When other people want something to keep my dividends down, you will call out the police and military. And in return you shall have the support and applause of my newspapers, and the delight of imagining that you are a great statesman.   (312)

The point-by-point resemblance between the two speeches is less remarkable than the relevance to *Major Barbara* of the concluding idea in the addition to the *Wagnerite*. "Siegfried shouldering Alberic's burden" comes as close as four words can to describing what Undershaft attempts to bring about in this play. The dream of the union of wisdom and efficiency cannot be realized unless the Hero controls the forces of evil. Undershaft is determined that Cusins shall learn the lesson that "Alberic's work . . . is necessary work," and that to be above doing it is to be annihilated by it: the power of the shell "can destroy the higher powers just as a tiger can destroy a man: therefore Man must master that power first" (337). Far from being a glorification of material power, this is a warning against its dangers.

The connection between *The Ring* and *Major Barbara* can hardly be coincidental. In *The Rhine Gold,* Alberic's smithy "resounds with the clinking anvils of the dwarfs toiling miserably to heap up treasure for their master" (*Wag* 179); Undershaft's works, where employees are (in Barbara's words) "all standing on their little rights and dignities" (339) is the equivalent force under a more enlightened directing intelligence. Siegfried does not know who his parents are and laughs at the pedantries of Mime; the Undershaft tradition holds that the business must be left to a foundling who has no education. *Siegfried* is the third of a group of operas just as *Major Barbara* is (according to Shaw himself) the third of a group of plays. *The Rhine Gold,* the first part of *The Ring,* ends with a vision of perfection in the mind of Wotan; *Man and Superman,* the first work in Shaw's eschatological trilogy, supplies an equivalent "great thought" in the vision of Don Juan. In *The Valkyrie* Wotan's attempt to implement his vision leads to complications that conclude in a deadlock in which the god, on a hill of fire, "with a breaking heart, takes leave of Brynhild" (198); *John Bull's Other Island,* an attempt to explore the implementation of Juan's ideal in a real world, ends with the principal characters (on a hillside during sunset) pitifully divided from each other. *Siegfried* depicts, through the instrumentality of Wotan, the triumph of Siegfried, a "perfectly naive hero" (*Wag* 215), in a universe from which Alberic has conveniently disappeared; *Major Barbara* depicts, through the instrumentality of Undershaft, the ascendancy of Cusins, an intellectual of the humanist tradition, in a universe determined to master Alberic.[11] Having analyzed the causes of Siegfried's political failure, the dramatist attempts to provide a modern equivalent who will succeed and enable the race to achieve salvation. *Major Barbara* is Shaw's attempt to rewrite *Siegfried* in terms valid for the twentieth century.

11. But compare Wisenthal (1972): "Cusins, who has declared his intention to reject the Armorer's Faith, and who is different from Undershaft in almost every respect, could be such a man [as Siegfried], and on the stage the part should be acted so as to bring out his inner strength and his determination" (63). This is true enough, yet Cusins is as different from Siegfried as he is from Undershaft. The point is that Shaw is attempting to improve upon—not merely to parallel—Wagner's hero.

The Bridge and the Abyss

Criticisms of *Major Barbara* fall into three main categories. The first and most influential is Eric Bentley's conclusion (1957; 166–167) that the synthesis represented by Cusins occurred to Shaw too late to be integrated into the rest of the play; the second is the objection that Shaw's treatment of Undershaft is overly clever and intellectually incoherent; the third is the common charge (somewhat related to the first) that the ending is unsuccessful. The first two of these issues can be answered convincingly; that the last cannot be suggests the key to the play's failure.

At what point did the idea of synthesis occur to Shaw? When Lady Britomart announces in the first scene that Andrew Undershaft is going to pay the family a visit, Barbara is the only person who is not disturbed by the prospect. After the invited but not very welcome guest arrives, Lady Brit's embarrassment about Barbara's work for the Salvation Army provokes a significant interchange:

LADY BRITOMART. It is not my doing, Andrew. Barbara is old enough to take her own way. She has no father to advise her.
BARBARA. Oh yes she has. There are no orphans in the Salvation Army.
UNDERSHAFT. Your father there has a great many children and plenty of experience, eh?
BARBARA (*looking at him with quick interest and nodding*) Just so. How did *you* come to understand that?

. . . . .

UNDERSHAFT. . . . I am rather interested in the Salvation Army. Its motto might be my own: Blood and Fire.
LOMAX (*shocked*) But not your sort of blood and fire, you know.
UNDERSHAFT. My sort of blood cleanses: my sort of fire purifies.
BARBARA. So do ours. Come down tomorrow to my shelter—the West Ham shelter—and see what we're doing. (260)

The conflict is not, as we should expect, between Barbara and her father; Barbara *and* Undershaft are aligned against Lady Brit and Lomax. Barbara is surprised at the understanding from an unexpected quarter, and she can hardly be displeased that her father is not ready to concede that the Army's blood and fire is not "his sort." When Lady Brit rebukes Barbara for talking as if religion were a pleasant subject, Undershaft replies that he does not find it an unpleasant one; on the contrary, "it is the only one that capable people really care for" (263). In addition, both father and daughter agree that the human race cannot be divided neatly into good men and scoundrels (262). The conventional associations attached to their respective "professions" makes Undershaft and Barbara *seem* to be in opposition when their outlooks are essentially similar. Barbara senses this only vaguely, remarking in the next act to Peter Shirley: "You wouldnt think he was my father, would you?" (279). But readers are entitled to reply: yes, we would.

The same unlooked-for interrelatedness can be discovered between Undershaft and Cusins, beginning with their first meeting:

LADY BRITOMART. This is Stephen.
UNDERSHAFT. Happy to make your acquaintance, Mr Stephen. Then (*going to Cusins*) *you* must be my son. (*Taking Cusins' hands in his*) How are you, my young friend? (*To Lady Britomart*) He is very like you, my love.
CUSINS. You flatter me, Mr Undershaft. My name is Cusins: engaged to Barbara. (*Very explicitly*) That is Major Barbara Undershaft, of the Salvation Army. That is Sarah, your second daughter. This is Stephen Undershaft, your son.
UNDERSHAFT. My dear Stephen, I beg your pardon . . . Mr Cusins: I am much indebted to you for explaining so precisely.
(258)

What seems here like irrelevant vaudeville is actually an adroit piece of symbolic farce. Undershaft's mistake in taking Cusins for his "son" foreshadows the relation the Professor will bear to him at the end of the play. In addition, Cusins proceeds to dispel the confusion concerning the mixed-up introductions with an ease and self-command that does not go unnoticed by the maker of cannons. No less than Barbara and Undershaft do Cusins and

Undershaft find themselves understanding each other in the
midst of strangers:

UNDERSHAFT. . . . There is only one true morality for every man;
   but every man has not the same true morality.
LOMAX (*overtaxed*) Would you mind saying that again? I didnt
   quite follow it.
CUSINS. It's quite simple. As Euripides says, one man's meat is an-
   other man's poison morally as well as physically.
UNDERSHAFT. Precisely.
LOMAX. Oh, that! Yes, yes, yes. True. True.   (262)

Lomax, Sarah, and Stephen are the nonentities in the midst of
whom Barbara, Cusins, and Undershaft already form a vital
triad.

In the second act, Undershaft and Cusins are left together for
a few minutes at the shelter. Though Undershaft scores heavily
against the sentiments proffered in the Professor's translations
from Euripides, Cusins survives the onslaught by virtue of the
same urbanity and detachment so characteristic of his future
father-in-law. Moreover, his insistence that nothing can stop him
from marrying Barbara reveals a determination that Undershaft
approves of and that he cannot in any case vanquish:

UNDERSHAFT. You mean that you will stick at nothing: not even
   the conversion of the Salvation Army to the worship of Dionysos.
CUSINS. The business of the Salvation Army is to save, not to wran-
   gle about the name of the pathfinder. Dionysos or another: what
   does it matter?
UNDERSHAFT (*rising and approaching him*) Professor Cusins: you
   are a young man after my own heart.
CUSINS. Mr Undershaft: you are, as far as I am able to gather, a
   most infernal old rascal; but you appeal very strongly to my sense
   of ironic humor.
Undershaft mutely offers his hand. They shake.   (286)

Undershaft has met his match—in both senses of that phrase.

But the match to result will engage Barbara as well. The determination that has been noted in both men should remind us
that Barbara too has "a propensity to have her own way and or-

der people about" (253). If Cusins's dislike of wrangling about the name of the pathfinder strikes a responsive chord in Undershaft, it would also strike one in this young woman, who believes that the sooner men "stop calling one another names, the better" (262). All three have a touch of fine fanaticism which can be quick at the expense of others' feelings: Undershaft's dismissal of his daughter's "tinpot tragedy" (328), Cusins's sarcasm in reference to her "broken heart" (299), Barbara's honest delight at Bill Walker's fate at the hands of Todger Fairmile (292). Furthermore, all three have that urge for inclusiveness that marks Shaw's most positive characters: Undershaft is not one to keep morals and business "in water-tight compartments" (261), Cusins is a collector of religions who finds that he can "believe them all" (283), and Barbara incorporates "Dionysos and all the others" in herself (322). And there is yet another resemblance: Undershaft's philosophy of money and gunpowder, "command of life and command of death," is (he admits) mad (287); Cusins is mad as a hatter because a sane man cannot translate Euripides (287); and as for Barbara:

UNDERSHAFT (*seizing him by the shoulder*) Can a sane woman make a man of a waster or a woman of a worm?
CUSINS (*reeling before the storm*) Father Colossus—Mammoth Millionaire—
UNDERSHAFT (*pressing him*) Are there two mad people or three in this Salvation shelter today?
CUSINS. You mean Barbara is as mad as we are?
UNDERSHAFT (*pushing him lightly off and resuming his equanimity suddenly and completely*) Pooh, Professor! let us call things by their proper names. I am a millionaire; you are a poet; Barbara is a savior of souls. What have we three to do with the common mob of slaves and idolaters? (287)

Father Keegan too was "mad"—are Undershaft, Barbara, and Cusins to become the "three in one and one in three" that will turn his dream into a fact? Cusins here is the figure of potential resolution because he can see from both points of view; his sympathies are clearly with Barbara, yet he can appreciate Undershaft's materialistic premise. If the sense of powerful fusion with Cusins as the central character is not maintained in the final pages of the play, it can hardly be because the idea came to Shaw as an afterthought. It is not the preparation, but the execution, that presents the difficulty.

The second principal charge against *Major Barbara*—that Undershaft is a frivolously conceived or intellectually confused personage—usually reflects minimal engagement with the text of the play. Yet this objection does have a valid component: if Undershaft is indeed the catalyst of upward evolutionary change, why *do* audiences have such mixed feelings toward this most highly developed version of the paradigmatic Shavian hero? Even attentive readers leave the play puzzled as to whether or not the dramatist himself considers Undershaft an admirable character. The answer lies in Shaw's awareness that individualism has its perils as well as its glories. In previous chapters we have noted his perception that conventions may be violated from bad motives as well as good ones. The mystical Mrs. Knox in *Fanny's First Play* counsels that if you have inner blessedness, "the spirit will set you free to do what you want and guide you to do right"; if on the other hand inner blessedness is lacking, you had "best be respectable and stick to the ways that are marked out . . . for youve nothing else to keep you straight" (305). To be sure, a man with "no power in him to keep him steady" is well advised to "cling to the powers outside him" (307); but how is a man to *know* whether he has such powers in him or not except by the exercise of fallible judgment? It is no simple matter to distinguish the genuine avatar who unites his will with the divine voice, from the imitator who (perhaps unwittingly) substitutes his own will for it. Shaw's later plays offer several sham supermen (Cain, Napoleon, the dictators in *Geneva*) who cannot activate an evolutionary leap because they fall into Peer Gynt's error of refusing to recognize that the "world-will," Life Force, or divine voice is outside as well as inside them (*Quint* 45). The brutish Cain in *Back to Methuselah* is correct when he claims that the great man "makes the Voice respect him," but wrong when he proceeds to destroy the difficult balance between inner and outer forces by insisting that such a man finally "dictates what the Voice shall say" (*Back* 26). How to differentiate the authentic prophet who rises above the law from the enthusiast or scamp who falls below it was a problem still torturing Shaw when he included a debate between Jesus and Pilate as part of the preface to *On the Rocks* (1933):

PILATE. . . . Your truth, as you call it, can be nothing but the thoughts for which you have found words which will take effect in deeds if I set you loose to scatter your words broadcast among the people. Your own people who bring you to me tell me that your thoughts are abominable and your words blasphemous. . . . How am I to distinguish between the blasphemies of my soldiers reported to me by my centurions and your blasphemies reported to me by your High Priest?
JESUS. Woe betide you and the world if you do not distinguish!
(181)

While Christ's rejoinder is striking, it does not so much refute Pilate as draw attention to the extreme difficulty of the question he has raised. For to distinguish wrongly may mean not only to call a Christ a criminal, but also to call a criminal a Christ.

The difficulty of discriminating precisely accounts for Shaw's own ambivalence toward his hero. Undershaft is the ostensible bad man of whom it takes a Cusins to say, "Suppose he is a great man, after all!" (334). Very well, but suppose he isn't? Shaw approaches the issue with a combination of faith and doubt arising from his awareness that the urge for what is commonly called self-transcendence is both man's noblest impulse and the source of nearly all that is most despicable in human nature. Undershaft's implicit rationale, which amounts to something like "I am pursuing raw power as an important step in an evolutionary process," could conceivably turn out to be only a more subtly rationalized self-deception than that of the patriot who thinks his country pursues such power to preserve freedom for mankind. And while few are likely so to misconstrue Shaw's meaning as to confuse Undershaft with a patriot, there is no way to prove that he is not merely aping the paradigmatic process as a means of trapping Cusins and Barbara into devoting their energies to preaching his gospel and thus destroying themselves. If Undershaft is clearly being sarcastic when he tells Mrs. Baines that he is giving the Salvation Army five thousand pounds to hasten his own "commerical ruin" (298), then might he not also be sarcastic when he asks Cusins, "Dare you make war on war? Here are the means"? And is it possible that Cusins, who saw the irony behind appearances in Mrs. Baines's case, misses it in his own because now *his* vanity is flattered by the idea of being able to use power for a supposedly higher cause?

The occasional delight Undershaft takes in brutality—such as in the "oceans of blood" speech (298) or the "good news from Manchuria" incident (318–319)—serves to keep before the audience the possibility of a genuine malevolence in his character.[12] "The way of life lies through the factory of death," says Cusins (339); but what if this sentiment should turn out to underscore a paradox instead of a synthesis? No matter how much one may admire his acumen and strength, the conviction that Undershaft is "St Andrew" rather than the "Prince of Darkness" ultimately is one of faith. The skeptical are entitled to reverse the emphasis of Barbara's assessment by concluding that God speaks through him sometimes, but he *may* be a devil.

The resulting ambiguity increases the fascination of the char-

12. A point lost in the more explicit movie version, in which Shaw simplified his meaning for dissemination to a mass audience. Upon being ushered through Undershaft's factory, Cusins shouts that he is witnessing "the raw material of destruction." The old man replies: "Or *construction*. How about railway lines?" Next the Professor identifies a huge white pile as "nitrates to make explosives." Undershaft corrects him again: "Or sulphates to fertilize your fields. . . . If you prefer the explosive way, that's your affair, not mine" (Costello 104–105). While such additions are valuable in bringing to the surface a positive side of Undershaft that remained implicit in the original play, the growth in clarity involves a loss in power. For all his mildly preternatural air, Robert Morley in the film seems more like Santa Claus than Mephistopheles.

acter by blurring his relation to the drama's schematic frame-work. Indeed, *Major Barbara* ceases to convince at exactly the point where Shaw loses the ability to play *against* his own the-matic conception. The problem of the unsatisfactory ending—the third major charge against the play—arises from the author's emotional resistance to recognizing the full implications of his material. The character of Cusins is the nub of the problem. Af-ter striking favorable terms regarding salary, Cusins assures Bar-bara that his soul does not yet belong to Undershaft because "the real tug of war is still to come. What about the moral question?" (326). Yet much of what follows seems disturbingly irrelevant to the moral question:

CUSINS. May I not love even my father-in-law?
UNDERSHAFT. Who wants your love, man? By what right do you take the liberty of offering it to me? I will have your due heed and respect, or I will kill you. But your love! Damn your imperti-nence!
CUSINS (*grinning*) I may not be able to control my affections, Mac. (333–334)

The amusement value of such exchanges obscures their weak-ness in helping us to see how the Professor is being won on that "holier ground" (305) he had earlier claimed as his territory. What real convictions Cusins has for accepting the offer appear only in the final epilogue-like scene between himself and Barbara (336–339). Here some of his more vatic utterances ("I want to make power for the world"—336) and especially his culminating out-burst ("Dare I make war on war? I dare. I must. I will"—337) would have been more effective as irony than epiphany. As it is, one does not quite know whether it is Shaw or Cusins who is be-ing foolish. The result is a real problem of tone. If Undershaft remains dramatically powerful because his thematic function is subordinated to his character, then Cusins evaporates because his character is sacrificed to bolster the thematic union he is sup-posed to embody. At that point, the play becomes a polemic. Only satire could have saved the day.

It is important to see how much was at stake for Shaw in writing this play. Having already examined the conclusions of *Man and Superman* through the dark filter of *John Bull's Other Island*, the dramatist now attempts in *Major Barbara* to clarify exactly where the vision of Don Juan went wrong. In this undertaking it must have occurred to him that Juan had been altogether too glib when he responded to Satan's indictment of humanity with the rejoinder, "Pshaw! All this is old." Lucifer's "force of Death" speech had been filled with allusions to Maxim guns, torpedo boats, bullets, explosive shells, poison gas—to the very paraphernalia of destruction commanded by Andrew Undershaft in *Major Barbara*. The death force disregarded by Juan now dominates the stage as the hero of the play; and if Barbara is unable to dismiss her father's arguments as Don Juan had dismissed Satan's, the reason is that Shaw himself has come to understand that the quest for salvation cannot be reduced to the luxury of *choosing* between heaven and hell. The example of Father Keegan would be fresh in his memory to suggest that Juan's "heavenly temperament" is no ticket to heaven, because it cannot master the half of life that is inimical to it. The "wicked side" cannot be ignored; the only hope of realizing Juan's synthesis is to incorporate the death force *within* the Life Force. Shaw's attempt to rise to this challenge made the writing of *Major Barbara* the most daring act of his artistic career; unfortunately, the desirability of the kind of synthesis the play attempts is easier to demonstrate than is its possibility. When the wise seek power, are they immune to its corrupting influences? What if the elements in conflict contain within themselves the source, not of union, but of mutual cancellation? If the oppositions with which the play deals are fundamental rather than apparent, then to urge their reconciliation is to impose a comic solution on materials that are essentially tragic.

Despite some good lines, the last few pages of *Major Barbara* comprise one of those rare scenes in which Shaw's powers of expression seem to fail him. The insistence upon affirmation leads to a forced sentimentality (Barbara cooing about her "dear little Dolly boy"—339) as well as some regrettable rhapsodizing based on Biblical phrases.[13] What is worse, language is used to sidestep substance. It is one thing to imply, as is done throughout the play, that one side of life cannot be separated from another—but Barbara's "life is all one" resorts to cliché to muddle the meaning of that thought. It is one matter to insist that power can be spiritual as well as material; but Cusins's "all power is spiritual" (336) is only a paraphrase of Carlyle's disastrous aphorism "All force is moral." Surely this swelling rhetoric is strained—for all his determination in this play to confront the infernal dimension of human nature, Shaw seems reluctant to give the devil his due without also assuring us that the Prince of Darkness can be made to behave like a gentleman.

Shaw himself was never satisfied with the final act. Writing to actress Eleanor Robson, he lamented: "But oh! Eleanor, between ourselves, the play, especially in the last act, is a mere ghost; at least so it seems to me. . . . It was a fearful job: I did what I never have had to do before, threw the last act away and wrote it again. Brainwork comes natural to me; but this time I knew I was working—and now nobody understands" (Belmont 50–51). Further revisions made in later editions evidence his continued effort at improvement; but most of these changes were insufficient and mechanical.[14] There could be no solution to an

13. The passage about "the unveiling of an eternal light in the valley of the shadow" is quoted approvingly by Berst, who holds that "the poet in Shaw reaches beyond the philosopher" (174). It seems rather a case of the pseudo-poet in Shaw straining to hide the defects of the philosopher.

14. For a revealing account of the revisions Shaw made while writing the drama, see Sidney Albert, " 'In More Ways Than One': *Major Barbara*'s Debt to Gilbert Murray," *Educational Theatre Journal*, 20 (May 1968), 123–140. For a discussion of changes made after the first edition had been published, see Bernard F. Dukore, "Toward an Interpretation of *Major Barbara*," *Shaw Review*, VI, 2 (1963), 62–70. The first of these pieces reveals Shaw's effort to answer criticisms made by Gilbert Murray (the model for Cusins); the second argues that later revisions were designed to play down the attractiveness of Undershaft's character.

insoluble problem. All during his career Shaw had been exploring the theme of the union between the practical and the spiritual, fact and ideal, wisdom and power, employing in his quest the controlling metaphors of heaven and hell, salvation and damnation. The first half of his life was capped with *Man and Superman,* a great play in which he solved the problem intellectually; it was followed by *John Bull's Other Island,* in which he saw the eagerly awaited consummation destroyed by the nature of the world. Finally, in *Major Barbara* he made a culminating effort to achieve the synthesis by confronting for the first time the need for efficiency to be founded on the control of power at the most elemental level. But his drive for affirmation was so overwhelming that he was not willing to face his own growing sense that the "abyss of moral horror" (324) admits of no transcendence, that the breach between heaven and earth is absolute, that the resulting separation is the human condition. So he presented a fantasy as real—which is to say, he idealized his theme. It was Shaw's misfortune to have sensed that his view of life was tragic at precisely the moment when he was temperamentally least capable of facing tragedy.

8 Heartbreak House

^^^

In the Russian Manner?

When Shaw concluded in *Major Barbara* that one must "either share the world's guilt or go to another planet" (219, Pref), he had come to a temporary halt in his spiritual odyssey. He continued to write a play per year on the average: *The Doctor's Dilemma* in 1906, *Getting Married* in 1908, *The Shewing Up of Blanco Posnet* in 1909, *Misalliance* in 1910, *Fanny's First Play* in 1911, *Androcles* and *Pygmalion* in 1912. Taken as a group, these works suggest contraction of energy rather than a decline in ability—they are *divertimenti* manifesting the old verve and skill at work within a restricted compass.[1] But during the next several years Shaw completed only one full-length play. Written during the Great War but published only after it was over (1919),[2] *Heartbreak House* returns to the vast thematic canvas of *Man and Superman*, *John Bull's Other Island*, and *Major*

1. I am moving over the terrain rather quickly here; for *Getting Married, Misalliance,* and *Androcles* could be related easily to the controlling ideas of this study. But having already made the case for the organic unity of Shaw's work, I see little point in proceeding to submerge my argument beneath a flood of superfluous documentation. Moreover, omitting the intervening plays has the advantage of allowing the crucial relationship between *Heartbreak House* and *Major Barbara* to emerge most sharply.

2. The traditional view of the drama's composition is that it was begun in 1913 and finished in 1916. In his *Journey to Heartbreak,* however, Stanley Weintraub has shown that the entire play was actually written in 1916–1917.

Barbara. Just as Shaw had seen Wagner's *Ring* as a set of three operas to which had been added a disharmonious final member, so in writing *Heartbreak House* he transformed his own eschatological trilogy into an immense (if unforeseen) tetralogy. In writing *Heartbreak House,* Shaw thoroughly mined its most ambitious predecessors for promising material.[3]

If *Heartbreak House* is indeed related to its author's previous works, why has the play so seldom been examined from the perspective they provide? The reason may be that Shaw himself confused the issue in his preface by choosing instead to emphasize his indebtedness to Chekhov. Subtitled "A Fantasia on English Themes in the Russian Manner," *Heartbreak House* resembles *The Cherry Orchard* in several ways. Both plays use a myriad of details to intimate the larger disorder of a highly sophisticated society in the process of decline. In Chekhov's piece, people miss trains, trip over suitcases, fall asleep, and burst into tears. In Shaw's, there is no knocker on the door of the house whose bell doesn't ring; Captain Shotover, the dwelling's patriarch, dozes off at inopportune moments; Hesione Hushabye, his daughter and casual hostess of the establishment, invites guests to spend the weekend but forgets to receive them. Predictably, tears flow freely to provide hilarious pathos. Both dramatists employ farcical effects (Yephikodoff's boots squeak; Hector Hushabye does calisthenics), use "absent" characters who subtly affect the action (Madame Ranevskaya's lover in Paris; Hastings Utterword, the imperialist "numskull"), and depict amorous involvement as an attempt to escape from lack of inner self-direction. Just as *The Cherry Orchard* uses repetition (such as Gayev's imaginary pool game) to suggest people's underlying compulsions, so in *Heartbreak House* the reiterated threat of several characters to leave the house only underscores the obsessiveness

3. Cyrus Hoy's "Shaw's Tragicomic Irony: From 'Man and Superman' to 'Heartbreak House' " (*Virginia Quarterly Review*, 47 [1971], 57–78), presents an interesting parallel reading of *Heartbreak House* in relation to *Man and Superman, John Bull's Other Island,* and *Major Barbara.*

of their inability to depart. Finally, both plays are plotless in the conventional sense. The main physical event in *The Cherry Orchard* (Lopakhin's purchase of the Ranevskaya estate) occurs offstage. As for *Heartbreak House*, it is a play where little occurs except the end of civilization.

Despite these resemblances, using *The Cherry Orchard* as a lens through which to see *Heartbreak House* can be quite misleading. Viewed as an attempt to re-create Chekhovian techniques, Shaw's play is open to criticism for lapses in tone, lack of organic unity, intrusive use of farce, and characterization of persons in terms of abstract ideas instead of inner psychology. For Stark Young, *Heartbreak House* is "a sort of literary Hyde Park soapbox dialectic" for the theatre (in Kronenberger, 234–235). For J. L. Styan, it is "a ragbag of a play" (128). The "burglar scene" has been especially castigated for its irrelevance, even by a critic as sympathetic as Eric Bentley (1957; 138). But the justification for the play's jarring elements lies in the effectiveness with which they transmit the unsettling vision Shaw is attempting to project. We would do well to remember at the start that Shaw's slapstick farce usually "intrudes" for a purpose, functioning to direct attention suddenly to larger symbolic patterns near the heart of a play's meaning:

MRS HUSHABYE (*introducing*) Mr Mazzini Dunn, Lady Ut—oh, I forgot: youve met. (*Indicating Ellie*) Miss Dunn.
MAZZINI (*walking across the room to take Ellie's hand, and beaming at his own naughty irony*) I have met Miss Dunn also. She is my daughter. (*He draws her arm through his caressingly*).
MRS HUSHABYE. Of course: how stupid! Mr Utterword, my sister's —er—
RANDALL (*shaking hands agreeably*) Her brother-in-law, Mr Dunn. How do you do?
MRS HUSHABYE. This is my husband.
HECTOR. We have met, dear. Dont introduce us any more. . . .
MAZZINI (*sententiously*) How little it tells us, after all! The great question is, not who we are, but what we are.
CAPTAIN SHOTOVER. Ha! What are you?

MAZZINI (*taken aback*) What am I?
CAPTAIN SHOTOVER. A thief, a pirate, and a murderer.   (69)

Whereas the mixed-up introductions in the opening act of *Major Barbara* (see above, p. 219) made the point that Cusins was Undershaft's spiritual son, the similar technique of *Heartbreak House* suggests that nobody knows who anyone is. The first act is full of instances of mistaken identity—Shotover thinks that Ellie is the daughter of Billie Dunn the pirate instead of Mazzini Dunn the poet; Ariadne Utterword is recognized neither by Hesione (her sister) nor by Captain Shotover (her father); Randall Utterword is mistaken for his brother Hastings; "Marcus Darnley," Ellie's romantic crush, is really Hector Hushabye.

This comic confusion is heightened by the act's nearly sixty exits and entrances—Shotover alone has close to twenty. Fragmentation inevitably occurs as a character suddenly finds himself alone with a person he doesn't know, and the two must then improvise conversation as each responds to the role the other's dress and mannerisms seem to suggest. The act is full of tag phrases that define such roles: Shotover is "a wild-looking old gentleman" (43), Mazzini a "soldier of freedom" (87), Ariadne a "woman of the world" (72), Mangan a "Napoleon of industry and disgustingly rich" (53), Randall a "man about town, well dressed, fifty" (66). But since the relation between a man and his role is at best oblique and sometimes utterly deceptive, a person no sooner begins to gain some insight into someone else than a conversation is interrupted by a permutation which leaves each of them to begin all over again in the midst of new strangers. The result is total disorientation. The house is no ordinary estate, but a place where the normal rules of the social game do not apply, where the usual subterfuges disappear at unexpected moments, where intimacies are blurted out before strangers and truth breaks into things almost by accident.

The much maligned "burglar scene" is a kernel into which many of the play's distinct themes have been compressed. The scene's function in the play's religious framework will be more appropriately discussed later, but some preliminary observations may be offered here. Most obviously, the inability of even the burglar to "act naturally in this house" (the malefactor immediately demands that he be turned over to the police) underscores the peculiar effect of the setting on the assembled company. Somewhat more elaborately handled is the suggestion that the intruder's "criminal" occupation is only an inversion of the normal activities engaged in by the respectable characters on stage: the reflection that "there is more than one burglar in England" (107) points up a resemblance between the thief and the businessman Mangan, to be developed further when "the two burglars" are killed at the end of the play (142). That the intruder turns out to be Dunn the desperado indicates an equivalence with Mazzini, perhaps implying that the pirate's crass immorality and the freedom fighter's impotent sensibility are but the mirror images of each other. (Hence the significance of Billie's reaction to his namesake's attempt to shoot him—"Shooting *yourself*, in a manner of speaking" (105); and of Shotover's persistent "mistaking" of the two Dunns for the same man.) Moreover, the technique of breaking into houses to find valuables, and then making noise deliberately to get caught, is analogous in method (though different in aim) to what is being done less consciously by the inhabitants of Heartbreak House, all of whom seem driven to reveal more of themselves than is either safe or necessary—as if, without quite admitting it, they long to be caught in the act, exposed, and judged. In addition, the discovery that Billie is the former husband of housekeeper Guinness completes the circle of amorous involvements and leaves Lady Utterword as the only character outside it, thus setting up her tirade against her own emotional sterility a few moments later (108–109). Finally, the burglar's arrival, heralded by the pistol shot, breaks the isolation of the house and comes to anticipate the more spectacular puncturing of quietude brought by the bombs at the end: Hesione's lament, "Well, we have had a very exciting evening. Everything will be an anticlimax after it"

(107), turns out, like most plausible remarks in this play, to be misleading.

As for Shaw's characterization, it will of course seem abstract if measured against Chekhov's impressionistic registering of details that gradually open out to reveal a sense of a person's inner life. Yet just as "you cannot have Aesop's Fables unless the animals talk," so Shavian drama would be impossible if characters were not endowed with "powers of self-consciousness and self-expression which they would not possess in real life" (*SSS* 99). While such heightened powers of articulation and self-analysis tend to push their possessors in the direction of becoming personified ideas, this result is not inappropriate for the kind of modern morality play we shall soon find *Heartbreak House* to be. Furthermore, in Shaw's resourceful handling, personal encounters are rarely allowed to decline into a mere dialectical game of clashing concepts. Although Bentley has aptly suggested that the characters can be seen in symbolic terms (Hesione is love, Randall is pride, Ariadne is empire, Mangan is business) he also notes—with equal pertinence—that "this reductive account of the people does not do them justice" (1957; 138).

Consider the scene, for instance, where the hypnotized Mangan overhears himself being ridiculed as an "object" by Ellie and Hesione (both of whom have previously been trifling with him), and then wakes in tears to protest to them that "there are things no decent woman would do to a man—like a man hitting a woman in the breast" (97–98). Although Mangan's authentic anguish makes it impossible for us to continue to regard him merely as a "bloated capitalist," Shaw has here suggested the real person lurking beneath the façade in a way rather more disturbing than the usual method in his plays. What Paul Lauter has termed the "subversion of stereotypes" (14) had always been the dramatist's technique for suggesting that neither life nor persons will conform to our preconceived notions of how things ought to be. Down with formulas, says Shaw: You never can tell. But "you never can tell," systematically applied, can itself become a formula; and occasionally Shaw's fondness for denying our expectations becomes too predictable to seem spontaneous. We read his plays waiting for the ineffectual youth to be revealed as a strong man, for the invincible king to emerge as the mama's boy of a dowdy queen, for the sentimental prostitute to turn into the Virgin mother, and vice versa. And if we are seldom disappointed by the skill with which the transformation is accomplished, we are nonetheless entitled to doubt whether *every* Hamlet is a Tamburlaine beneath the skin. Now in regard to Mangan, we have supposedly witnessed another neat inversion of roles: while he seems like an ogre, really he has a heart. But, in fact, the elements in the Boss's character remain confused, nicely confirming Hesione's dictum that "people dont have their virtues and vices in sets: they have them anyhow: all mixed" (62). Though we may feel for Mangan when he weeps, we are jerked back to detachment when, in response to Hesione's genuine remorse, he can only snivel: "I'm a man aint I?" If the hard tyrant turns out to be a fool with feelings, the function of the inversion is to deepen rather than reverse our perceptions—Mangan does not cease to be dangerous because he is impotent, nor does he cease to be stupid when he becomes sympathetic. The very discomfort of our conflicting responses toward him offers a clue to the character's relevance to a larger dramatic point. On the one hand, we can afford to snicker: there is no future for the Mangans of this world. On the other hand, the laugh is on us: because of the Boss and men like him, there may be no future for anyone.

Still, the fact that characters are too complex to function neatly as carriers of thematic ballast is not totally an asset; for at times vivid personal interactions are not connected to the drama's overall meaning as clearly as in the foregoing scene. As a case in point, the second act concludes with an episode in which Hector calls in Lady Utterword to "manage" Randall, her jealous brother-in-law; and Ariadne unexpectedly rises to the occasion by humiliating Randall so viciously that Hector is shocked into involuntary sympathy with his rival for her attentions. One may defend the dramatic impact of this moment by pointing out that Randall's humiliation at the hands of Ariadne is not "reducible" to Pride being humbled by the strength of Empire; yet this still leaves unanswered the question of the integration of this occurrence into the play as a whole. If we see *Heartbreak House* as a study of the developing awareness of Ellie Dunn, the scene is superfluous because it tells us nothing about the girl, who is not present and never learns what has happened there. If we see the work in larger terms as a portrayal of the decline of Western culture, we can perhaps argue that this "jealousy trio" dramatizes in personal terms the spirit of divisive dominance whose political manifestations wreck civilizations; but in such an account the gap between the event itself and what it is presumed to signify seems disconcertingly wide. The fact is that in *Heartbreak House* Shaw often let his fancy run away with him; and while the resulting intractability of persons to their apparent symbolic functions makes the action full of bracing shocks of discovery, the same quality also accounts for some loose ends as well as the near impossibility of offering an integrated account of the entire result. More than is usually the case in discussing Shaw, the critic must come to grips not only with the play the dramatist wrote, but with the metaplay one suspects he was trying to write. The discussion here will approach *Heartbreak House* by comparing it with earlier Shavian works, in terms of which it is at once an outgrowth, a culmination, and a departure.

Moot Apocalypse

We have already seen that *Man and Superman, John Bull's Other Island,* and *Major Barbara* moved between the symbolic polarities of heaven and hell. A connection between *Heartbreak House* and these forerunners is suggested by the play's use of the same metaphorical framework. The first line is "God bless us!" (42); the last act finds Ellie wedded to the Captain "in heaven, where all true marriages are made" (131). In contrast, Shotover "sold himself to the devil in Zanzibar" (121); Ariadne has "the diabolical family fascination" (73); Hector wanders around like "a damned soul in hell" (110). The play's central conflicts are articulated in terms of an opposition between heavenly and infernal states—such as the contrast of Hector's aspirations to the materialism of the Mangans of the world: "I must believe that my spark, small as it is, is divine, and that the red light over their door is hell fire" (76). In addition, the drama uses allegorical devices suggestive of morality plays—the house built like a ship represents the political organism ("This soul's prison we call England"—138); the meaning of what occurs there is expanded to a religious frame of reference ("You are beneath the dome of heaven, in the house of God. What is true within these walls is true outside them"—65). Individual characters have preternatural overtones: Ellie is a hypnotist, Shotover's "demon daughters" (121) are the "mystical progeny" (121) of his strange marriage,[4] the Captain himself is "that supernatural old man" (71). Finally, *Heartbreak House* as a whole deals with the question basic to all morality plays—salvation versus damnation—explored in terms both of the individual and of the race.

In the drama's symbolic scheme, the burglar can be seen as a satire of the traditional Christian view of man's need for redemption from original sin. In fact, Billie sounds more like a bishop than a burglar when he speaks of having his "reward above" (103), refers to himself as one "scrambling out of the bottomless pit as it were" (104), and protests that he is being robbed of his salvation (104) when the others show no inclination to have him jailed. Like the fake "confessions" of Rummy Mitchens and Snobby Price in *Major Barbara*, the outlaw's comic lust for righteousness burlesques the conventional (religious and legal)

4. Not literally true. The West Indian Negress was Shotover's *first* wife (114); the two daughters are presumably the offspring of a second and more conventional union, which is never specifically mentioned. It is hard to imagine Lady Utterword as a mulatto.

system of salvation through expiation. Bill Walker, who in *Major Barbara* attempted to have himself "punished" to atone for a wrong act, is here succeeded by Billie Dunn, who employs a similar tactic as an ingenious ruse, forcing his captors to bribe him to depart rather than go through the inconvenience of prosecuting him. Whereas at least Bill offered to "pay" for his offense (striking Jenny Hill) by contributing a pound to the Salvation Army, Billie reverses the process by refusing to leave the burglarized premises until Hector gives *him* a pound. Thus this scene not only expresses a typical Shavian critique of the penal system, but also presents a parody in microcosm of the basic religious issues Shaw had attempted to resolve in *Major Barbara,* and to which events in the world have now forced him to return.

In seeking to discover larger thematic patterns inherent in the cumulative interactions of the characters, we might go back to a still earlier point in Shaw's development, to note that *Heartbreak House* is permeated by an atmosphere of illusions and pretenses —what Shaw in *The Quintessence of Ibsenism* called ideals. Indeed, if one remembers Don Juan's subsequent definition of hell as a place where "nothing is real. . . . That is the horror of damnation" (*Super* 88), Hesione's abode is easily recognized as a similar "Palace of Lies" (124).[5] Ellie's disillusionment in the first act turns on her discovery that Hector is untruthful; Mangan's remaining composure in the last act is broken by the assembled company's compulsion to flaunt their own fraudulence: "How are we to have any self-respect," he asks, "if we dont keep it up that we're better than we really are?" (130). Building on the foundation laid in the *Quintessence* and *Man and Superman,* Shaw in *Heartbreak House* presents his most elaborately developed dramatization of the psychology of illusion in human life.

The *Quintessence* defined an ideal as a "fancy picture" in-

5. The connnection between the atmosphere of "Don Juan in Hell" and *Heartbreak House* has also been noted by Wisenthal (1974; 137–138), though without relating the later play back to the *Quintessence.*

vented to rob life of terrors people had not the strength to face. Men resort to a myth of personal immortality because they cannot bear the thought of death; they disguise their domestic unhappiness by placing on the institution of marriage a pleasing mask of the ideal family. Since such pretenses remain safe from exposure only so long as everyone is united in covenantal obligation to maintain their truth, ideals must next become moral absolutes, principles, and duties in order for society to protect itself against the Shavian realist, that one man in a thousand whose skeptical honesty threatens the fools' paradise of the rest. By the time *Heartbreak House* was written, the use of ideals to intimidate had all but disappeared. Whereas the 1891 version of the realist might be ostracized for uttering disturbing truths about the British family system, the 1916 version moves in a liberated atmosphere where he is permitted, even encouraged, to speak his mind. At first this commendably tolerant state of affairs sounds like the fulfillment of all that late nineteenth-century progressives had been fighting for. But an important complication has arisen. Shaw's early essay held that the individual would thrive if society did not insist upon coercing him into conformity. His late play suggests, in contrast, that when society no longer imposes upon people, they proceed to find ways to impose upon themselves.

Of course, society may still slyly manipulate human beings to embrace those pretensions (such as dashing hero, captain of industry, bewitching siren) which will best ensure the perpetuation of the status quo. But though external pressures may entice persons to be what they often become, this process at the very least enables them to make fools of themselves on a much higher level than that which served to content the aboriginal idealist. The important point is that Shaw's former sociological analysis has come to include the possibility of a more personal focus: instead of being seen primarily as moral norms invoked by the community to suppress the realist who menaces its collective happiness, ideals can now be viewed also as private flatteries contrived by the individual to protect his own happiness. Psychologically, the resort to self-delusion is necessary because the person no less than the social organism suffers from a defect which is the Shavian analogue to the original sin of theological doctrine—the inability of human beings to live without happiness in an imperfect world. In the *Quintessence* social institutions contrived illusions to guard man's urge for contentment against the claims of truth; in *Heartbreak House* each man himself contrives to translate real life into the ideal forms his mind envisions. Eagerly embracing the call of a "refined and cultivated" Lucifer (*Super* 128) to sympathize with joy, love, happiness, and beauty (94), these people occupy the hell Don Juan described as "the home of the unreal and of the seekers for happiness" (99). Trapped in barren fancies, they are beyond understanding Shotover's distinction between the genuine happiness that comes from facing life's challenges bravely and the "accursed happiness" (114) of an escapism that leaves its possessors only "half alive" (132).

This is not to suggest that Shaw would deny to loveliness, beauty, and enchantment any valid function in life—rather he laments that human beings so often lack the capacity to put these qualities to creative use. Seen in the light of *Othello* (the play Ellie brings with her to the estate), the triangle of Hector, Ellie, and Hesione helps to make clear that falling in love can have a basis in reality even if the events surrounding it are not literally true. According to Ellie, the stories Othello told Desdemona are "not romance, exactly," but something that "might really happen" (57). When Hesione points out in response that some of Othello's tales *could* not have happened, Ellie holds nonetheless that "Othello was not telling lies"—that is, Shakespeare would have warned us had he wished his hero's account to be doubted (57). Convinced that "there are men who have done wonderful things," Ellie proceeds to tell of her own relationship with "Marcus," the heady joys of which Hesione surmises so evocatively: "How much better than the happiest dream! All life transfigured! No more wishing one had an interesting book to read, because life is so much happier than any book" (60). That the particular stories that Marcus/Hector has told her are false does not deprive Ellie's experience of all authenticity; for Hesione explains that Hector really *has* performed equally heroic deeds that he is too shy to mention. Long ago, Hesione too had been attracted by this "splendid" man (61). As she says to him a few minutes later: "We were frightfully in love with one another, Hector. It was such an enchanting dream that I have never been able to grudge it to you or anyone else since. I have invited all sorts of pretty women to the house on the chance of giving you another turn. But it has never come off" (73). Unfortunately, the characters are unable to make the most of these brief glories. It may be beside the point that Othello strangled Desdemona. But it is very much to the point that the Hushabyes attempt by compulsive flirtation to recapture their original delight, and that Ellie undergoes an acrid revulsion in which she promptly forgets that Hector has indeed done wonderful things. In short, life's revelatory moments, which should be the source of the characters' emotional growth, tend instead to become points of fixation to which they cling in terror of losing the happiness once so intensely—and briefly—possessed.

Converting such stubbornly regressive tendencies into genuine emotional growth depends upon the quality of consciousness by which a person explores—or evades—raw experience. Shaw sees the mediating power of imagination as a double-edged sword: on the one hand, a positive creative force increasing awareness of reality; and on the other, a negative fabricator of castles in the air (see above, p. 178). It was the second variety that Don Juan attacked when he spoke of "imagination resolved to starve rather than face . . . realities, piling up illusions to hide them, and calling itself cleverness, genius" (101), and that Larry Doyle castigated by suggesting that "an Irishman's heart is nothing but his imagination . . . [which] never lets him alone, never convinces him, never satisfies him; but . . . makes him that he cant face reality" (*Bull* 83–84). The term in this play corresponding to imagination is "invention," which similarly falls into two categories. Shotover as an inventor possessed great vital powers in his prime; on the other hand, Hector Hushabye's propensity to "tell lies to women" is also "a form of invention" (77). The two types of inventive faculty in turn are analogous to the two varieties of artistic creativity that Shaw characteristically discerned: the great art of genius illuminating the previously unknowable and the small art of cleverness hiding what we don't want to know. In *The Sanity of Art* (1895) Shaw had spoken of the superior artist who, "by supplying works of a higher beauty and a higher interest than have yet been perceived, succeeds after a brief struggle with its strangeness, in adding this fresh extension of sense to the heritage of the race" (316). But if art may be an instrument of self-knowledge, it may also be the handmaiden of illusion, making self-deception glamorous. Sidney Trefusis in *An Unsocial Socialist* had demanded "an end to the silly confusion, under the one name of Art, of the tomfoolery and make-believe of our play hours with the higher methods of teaching men to know themselves" (160). The "make-believe" of art had always been the handmaiden of retrogressive idealism —in the *Quintessence,* poets wove lovely veils to hide "the unbearable face of the truth" (28); in *Man and Superman* Juan recounts his temptation by "the artist, with his love songs and his paintings and his poems" (111). The idea surfaces again in *Heartbreak House,* where Shotover complains of being deluded by "singers and poets" as well as pretty daughters.

To be sure, the actual artistic skills exercised by the persons in this play are thoroughly trivial: Ellie sings and copies paintings for cash; Randall sketches, strums the piano, and plays the flute. Yet in a sense the entire play is a portrayal of the artistic imagination whereby the characters attempt to wrest order and meaning from daily life's succession of random details. And while their taste for histrionics might suggest membership in an actors' guild, Shaw's people may be more appropriately viewed as practitioners of, as well as participants in, the more pretentious art of literature. Mazzini's parents were poets, "like the Brownings" (51); it is suggested that "Alfred" Mangan was named after Tennyson (98); Randall, the hero of a medieval ballad, has jealous rages like Othello's (117); Hector/Marcus is Homeric warrior and Shakespearean hero; Ariadne and Hesione both have counterparts in classical mythology.[6] Such names provide more than clues to literary ancestry, for the characters themselves have a hand in fabricating the tall tales whose roles they enact. Each of them is a surrogate author who finds figures of speech indispensable in a world lacking a clear perspective from which reliable judgments may be formed, thus making something understandable—if at all—only in terms of something else. The bizarre nature of some of the implied comparisons makes evident that more is involved here than the common human tendency to talk in metaphors: Hastings's head resembled the figurehead on the Captain's ship (44); Shotover's happiness is like the sweetness of rotting fruit (114); Randall's having his heart broken is like having his head shampooed (136), and so forth. Shotover's metaphor of the house as ship, the controlling image of the play, is an example of the great art that reveals profound affinities between separate entities. But the persons in the play are for the most part devotees of an inferior art, employing their imaginative faculties to translate psychologically unpalatable facts into appealing fictive constructs. Hector turns his life into a romantic novel with Marcus as its hero; Mangan models his speech on movie idols (64); Hesione's walk on the heath with the Boss becomes her version of the love-night of Tristan and Isolde (108). What the society described in the *Quintessence* hired artists to do for it, these men and women attempt to do for themselves.

The corruption of art into the service of the bad side of idealism results in a state of dreamlike inertia which at times becomes

6. For a discussion of the significance of names in this play and elsewhere in Shaw's works, see Nethercot's Appendix to *Men and Supermen:* "What's in a Name" (291–308).

the play's metaphor for its own atmosphere. Deriving ultimately from Larry Doyle's outburst against the enervating effects of the Irish climate ("Oh, the . . . dreaming, dreaming, dreaming, dreaming!"—*Bull* 84), a conversation between Ellie and Shotover reveals that "dreaming" here connotes an aura of deep enchantment suffusing all the negative qualities the word "ideals" has previously indicated in Shaw's work. For instance, conventional idealism sought to provide contentment by recourse to illusions: dreaming, according to Shotover, is "to be easily pleased and deceived" (114). Traditional ideals were attempts to ignore the realities of life; Ellie wants the Captain to dream so that he will "never be in the real world when we talk together" (114). Adherence to the standard ideals precluded the freedom to pursue progressive goals; loss of dreams will mean for Ellie "having to fight and do things" (114). Repressive ideals attempted to thwart the spirit of a creative vitality that resists being bound by conventions and duties; so the ostensible pleasures of poetry, art, and romance—in short, of dreams—serve to enervate the powerful will on which the realist's strength once depended. The former idealistic morality prevented certain socially disapproved actions; the new idealistic fantasies forestall all action by diverting the energies of potential agents into a titillating numbness.

Heartbreak House evokes a mixture, so typical of dreams, of the impossible and the matter-of-fact. For instance, the burglar who breaks into the house turns out to be a pirate who once robbed the Captain, as well as the former spouse of the housekeeper. While both Shotover and Guinness are irked to meet this scapegrace again, neither is the slightest bit taken aback by the bizarre coincidences that conspired to produce Billie in the flesh at this time and place. Similarly, the audience roars when in the same act Hector enters wearing a wild Arab costume, which no one on stage even seems to notice. The fact that such fabulous occurrences seem entirely credible to these characters is Shaw's comment on the very unreality of the world they inhabit. Yet the psychic fantasy of this dream-play is not *merely* deceptive and false. Dreams are at times delightful, but at other times disquieting; they are not only disguises but also revelations of truths that lie beneath the threshold of consciousness; their very improbabilities may convey oblique intimations of reality. Thus Mangan's prissy fear that he might have been buried alive while hypnotized presages what will actually happen to him in the gravel pit. Lady Utterword's bootless insistence that her relatives should want to kiss her suggests her need to convince herself, by arousing affection in others, that she possesses a heart to be broken. "Now is it likely I'd kill any man on purpose" (86), asks Guinness when Mazzini accuses her of having murdered the hypnotized Mangan; yet upon discovering the true identity of the burglar a few minutes later, she turns to Mazzini and asks: "Why didnt you shoot him, sir? If I'd known who he was, I'd have shot him myself" (107). As a last example of this quality of unexpected truths, the Captain's impassioned prognosis of the shipwreck arouses only the response that "nothing will happen." Immediately, however, a "dull distant explosion is heard"; Hector asks what it is; Shotover replies, "Something happening" (139). This telescoping into three lines of the movement from Edwardian complacence to the First World War provokes literal-minded critics to complain of awkward transitions; but is it likely that verisimilitude is the effect Shaw was aiming at? Such startling disruptions of dramatic expectation are the vehicle of a fantasy which distorts truth in some ways just as surely as it reveals unexpected truths in others.

It is because dreams are surreal and not merely false that *Heartbreak House* can be an eschatological drama. Don Juan formerly described hell to Ana as a place where "you call your appearance beauty, your emotions love, your sentiments heroism, your aspirations virtue" (*Super* 99–100); and from one point of view this is exactly what the inhabitants of Hesione's dream-villa are doing. Unfortunately for their peace of mind, however, they have not Juan's assurance that there are "no hard facts to contradict" them (100). In earlier Shavian comedy, the world itself was the inescapable reality that subverted the ideals imposed on individuals by society as a whole. But now, just as idealistic illusions develop within the consciousness of characters who have elected to ignore the outside world, so each of them in turn has a counterbalancing impulse that resists total acceptance of his own self-delusion. Like Lady Utterword after an absence of twenty-three years, they are drawn to the house and trapped there because the strange ambiance of the place both soothes and threatens them. And the degree of discomfort experienced in these surroundings is actually a measure of the good fortune that at times causes a person's assumed role and genuine impulses to dissolve into indistinguishable layers of the same psyche. Is Hesione a sadistic witch or "the most sympathetic woman in the world" (60)? Is Ellie a "miserable little matrimonial adventurer" (93) or a young woman growing into maturity? Is Shotover a sage or a dreamer? In none of these cases is it a matter of *choosing* one or the other description, for Shaw has somehow been able to suggest the authentic person hovering somewhere in the interstices of appearances.

If one accepts Juan's criterion that "the truly damned are those who are happy in hell" (*Super* 87), then the dwellers in Heartbreak House are not smug enough to be utterly beyond hope. They may, like Shotover, be "tired of life" (114); but their spirits are not dead. Into the dream of the play they have projected not only that side of their consciousness which seeks to escape into unreality, but also the side whose restless and half-sought brushes with truth serve to make the dreamers more than merely a damned lot. For this reason, the play does not dramatize merely a progressive stripping of illusions that devalues people until they are only a "heap of squeezed lemons" (82). In the last act Hesione calls Mangan a fool; but Hector's rebuke—"Do not scorn the man. We are all fools" (133)—suggests both that the blight is universal and that no one is denied a residual dignity. When in a final litany these figures present the negative view of themselves ("A crazy old sea captain . . . a sluttish female . . . all heartbroken imbeciles"), Mazzini objects that they are rather "a favorable specimen of what is best in our English culture" (135). While ironic in one sense, this remark is literally accurate in another; for not one of those mentioned is devoid of intelligence, sympathy, or insight. Indeed, if most of them did not have more than the usual amount of these qualities, there would be no heartbreak in their turning out, finally, to be so helplessly cut off from one another and the world.

Despite the ray of hope for the characters, the wills of these incipient realists have been sufficiently infected so that it is with a greatly diminished optimism that Shaw returns to invoke the doctrines of salvation advocated in earlier works. In the course of *Heartbreak House*'s exhaustive retrospect, Shaw's previously developed views of self-realization are reintroduced, re-examined, and rejected as solutions to the quest for an authentic basis of affirmation. The most conspicuous sign of a change lies in what has happened to the Shavian model of the efficient man: the two characters in *Heartbreak House* with the greatest reputation for efficiency seem like travesties of the pragmatic heroes from Bluntschli onward. Boss Mangan's administrative accomplishments are peculiar, to say the least—his idea of a "triumph of practical business" is to be ignorant of how to run his own machinery while knowing how to "stick a ramrod into the other fellow's" (128). As an alternative to the Boss, Lady Utterword proposes her imperialist husband, "governor of all the crown colonies in succession" (46). Hastings clearly has executive power—"wooden yet enterprising" (44); "able to work sixteen hours a day at the dullest detail, and actually [liking] it" (116); and clearly capable of saving the country provided he is allowed "a good supply of bamboo to bring the British native to his senses" (129). Yet Shotover's reaction to this prospect (that the country "had better be lost"—129) suggests the dramatist's view that Hastings is only a Mangan who knows what he's doing. As a political man, Shaw tended to be increasingly susceptible to the appeal of the Hastingses of the world; as an artist, he understood that "any fool can govern with a stick in his hand. . . . It is not God's way" (129). An efficient numskull is not the answer.

Even were Hastings the savior his wife thinks, we could hardly fail to notice that he never appears on stage. If the characters in the play represent a wide range of human activities, the spectrum of inactivity is even more remarkable. That Mangan's factories run better without him is only the beginning. What is Randall's occupation? Hector is "at home all day" (110). The Captain, who strives to unite strength with wisdom, can supply "nothing but echoes. The last shot was fired years ago" (138). It is not novel for Shavian drama to treat situations where intelligent persons do not act, while those who do act are not intelligent. But *John Bull's Other Island* was the only previous play in which this dichotomy represented more than a critique of individual shortcomings. For now when Hector rebukes Mazzini—"What's the good of thinking. . . . Why didnt you do something?" (137) —he is not so much attacking the soldier-poet's personal incapacity for action as articulating a sense of civilized man's powerlessness to improve his own desperate condition. Mazzini's reply is poignant:

I joined societies and made speeches and wrote pamphlets. That was all I could do. But, you know, though the people in the societies thought they knew more than Mangan, most of them wouldnt have joined if they had known as much. You see they had never had any money to handle or any men to manage. Every year I expected a revolution, or some frightful smash-up: it seemed impossible that we could blunder and muddle on any longer. But nothing happened, except, of course, the usual poverty and crime and drink that we are used to. Nothing ever does happen. It's amazing how well we get along, all things considered. (137)

While this speech can be seen as middle-class culture's lament for its own inability to expire, the impending doom, for Shaw, is finally less attributable to some mistaken and replaceable "ism" than to a malaise rooted in human nature itself.

In examining the process by which Shaw reached this position from the contrary premise of so many previous works, one first detects a loss of faith in his earlier belief that people can be educated to develop a social conscience by outward extension of their own self-interest. The doctrine of individualism of *The Quintessence of Ibsenism* had been based on the conviction that genuine self-realization involves the growth of a concern for humanity. A point central to Shaw's treatment of *Emperor and Galilean*—that respect for one's fellows results from a man's "overflow of his conviction of his own worth" (58)—becomes the source of another of Shotover's revelations to Ellie:

A man's interest in the world is only the overflow from his interest in himself. When you are a child your vessel is not yet full; so you care for nothing but your own affairs. When you grow up, your vessel overflows; and you are a politician, a philosopher, or an explorer and adventurer. In old age the vessel dries up: there is no overflow: you are a child again. I can give you the memories of my ancient wisdom: mere scraps and leavings; but I no longer really care for anything but my own little wants and hobbies. (112–113)

Just as Maximus could not "fill the prior conviction [of Julian] even to fullness, much less to overflowing" (*Quint* 58), so the Captain's exhortations fail to stimulate his auditors to the exercise of faculties they do not possess. And whereas Emperor Julian was viewed by Shaw as a stubborn spirit whose inadequacies the perfect Ibsenite could presumably avoid, Shotover himself is the prophet who—lamentably—comes *nearest* to the goal he can no longer reach. The other characters by and large are too egotistical to conceive that their own self-interest is more than a purely private matter. Ostensibly, a man's instinct is still directed toward ensuring his own survival: Mangan boasts that he is "a man that knows how to take care of himself" (83). For Shaw, such "taking care" of self entails taking a lively interest in mankind—a responsibility that hardly weighs heavily on the minds of characters in a play whose dialogue contains not one *direct* reference to the fact that the world is at war. The whole posture of pragmatic truculence is mocked when we see that Mangan's means of self-preservation is to crawl off with Billie Dunn into the gravel pit (where Shotover's dynamite is stored) as the bombs are about to fall. When this happens, Mazzini, who ought to know better, feels that the Boss and the burglar "are acting very sensibly; and it is they who will survive" (141).

If the Captain's philosophy owes something to the discussion of *Emperor and Galilean,* his failure to implement it suggests the plight of Wotan in *The Perfect Wagnerite.* Like Wotan, Shotover is a conjuror: the god can slay Hunding with a wave of his hand; the Captain can design a ship with a magnetic keel that sucks up submarines (77). Wotan's vision must be won through battle with the rapacious Alberic; Shotover's is thwarted because he is unable to overcome ideological adversaries like Mangan, whose soul is as greedy and stunted as that of Wagner's dwarf. Just as Wotan had to compel obedience to the law from persons "unable to comprehend the thought of the lawgiver" (*Wag* 175), so Shotover on the high seas had to control "men so degraded that they wouldnt obey me unless I swore at them and kicked them and beat them with my fists" (111). In both cases, authority is forced to compromise: to manage his men, Shotover tricked them into believing that he had made a pact with Satan; to gain the necessary temporal power, Wotan pretended to honor the concept of the law symbolized by Fricka. As a result, Godhead was stymied: "Its resort to law finally cost it half its integrity" (*Wag* 174–175). Shotover too is impotent: the dynamite he stores is finally as useless to him as possession of the ring was to Wotan; to make matters worse, the old man is harried by daughters more like Circe than like Brynhild. If Andrew Undershaft's mission had been to learn to command the wealth of Alberic, then Shotover by comparison is a superannuated Wotan vainly in search of a Siegfried. And the play's aura of enticing illusions—the political, romantic, and artistic ideals embodied by the characters—suggests that no less an enchanter than Loki himself is stage-managing the collapse of this bourgeois Valhalla.

In an attempt to resolve Wotan's tragic dilemma, Shaw had created his own Don Juan, whose words from the climax of the hell scene of *Man and Superman* will be easily recalled:

DON JUAN. . . . The philosopher is Nature's pilot. And there you have our difference: to be in hell is to drift: to be in heaven is to steer.
THE DEVIL. On the rocks, most likely.
DON JUAN. Pooh! Which ship goes oftenest on the rocks or to the bottom? the drifting ship or the ship with a pilot on board?

(128)

The sitting room in *Heartbreak House* is designed to resemble a ship's gallery, and Shotover is the pilot on board; but a decade and a war have radically altered the emphasis of the navigational metaphor. The first ship drifted because it lacked a helmsman entirely; this one is imperiled because its captain is not equal to his responsibilities.

HECTOR. And this ship that we are all in? This soul's prison we call England?
CAPTAIN SHOTOVER. The captain is in his bunk, drinking bottled ditchwater; and the crew is gambling in the forecastle. She will strike and sink and split. Do you think the laws of God will be suspended in favor of England because you were born in it?

(138)[7]

For Juan, "to be in hell is to drift: to be in heaven is to steer"; for Shotover, damnation will overtake the ship of a "drifting skipper" unless Englishmen learn their business of "navigation" (139). But whereas Juan strove actively to advance the Life Force, the people of *Heartbreak House*—excepting perhaps Shotover and Ellie—rely instead on Mazzini's "theory of an overruling Providence" (137). If man is incompetent, the wish goes, someone else must be running the show. But for Shaw, the show stops if man stops running the something else: "One of the ways of Providence with drunken skippers is to run them on the

7. These two passages have been contrasted by so many critics that specific acknowledgment seems unnecessary.

rocks" (138). When Juan had pointed out that the "drifting ship" is the one that "goes oftenest on the rocks," he was arguing theoretically and with confidence the same point Shotover is driven to invoke by the horror of a concrete crisis. The Captain may be a philosopher, but he is not Nature's pilot.

We have already dealt with *Man and Superman* as the first play of a trilogy whose later components were attempted solutions to the increasingly difficult dilemmas into which Shaw had worked himself. If *Heartbreak House* is now seen as the successor to *John Bull's Other Island* and *Major Barbara,* then the main figures in each part of the resulting tetralogy come into focus as manifestations of a single basic consciousness. Just as March-banks, Dick Dudgeon, and Caesar were portrayals of the same fundamental awareness at different stages of life, so Tanner, Keegan, Undershaft, and Shotover may be viewed as *one* hero whose increasing age suggests the maturing of the dramatist's own vision as he progresses from play to play. Tanner is in his thirties, Keegan is fifty, Undershaft is described as "elderly" (*Barb* 257). The "ancient" (43) Shotover is a cumulative and composite figure with many of the qualities of the protagonists who preceded him. Like Tanner, he is an impressive rhetorician whose specialty is the jeremiad on the condition of England. Like Tanner's spiritual counterpart, Don Juan, the Captain is con-temptuous of the pursuit of happiness and strives instead to ad-vance the purpose of life. His similarities to Keegan are more striking—both have had experiences of a mystical nature (the ex-priest's confession of a dying Hindu, Shotover's marriage to a West Indian Negress) and avoid painful contact with their fellows by offering no resistance to (and even tacitly encourag-ing) the notion that they are mad. The resemblances to Undershaft are most significant, and only begin with the tan-talizing similarity in names.[8] Both men believe in the materialistic

8. For a discussion of the possible significance of Undershaft's name, see Weintraub, " 'Shaw's *Divine Comedy':* Addendum," *Shaw Review,* II, 5 (1958), 21–22.

premise—Undershaft manufactures cannons, Shotover produces engines of slaughter as well as "life-saving inventions" (77) for which the market is depressed. But an exploration of the analogy will reveal a shift in perspective: if *Major Barbara* had been the culmination of nineteenth-century optimism, *Heartbreak House* is the harbinger of twentieth-century despair.

Shaw cannot retain faith in the lofty culmination of life foreseen in *Man and Superman,* because he now sees that ultimately it comes to rest on the false foundation of might espoused in *Major Barbara. Heartbreak Houses's* pivotal passages boldly repudiate its predecessor's sentimental synthesis. Shotover has walked into a room to find Hector (who thinks he is alone) "with his arms stretched out and his fists clenched" (74):

CAPTAIN SHOTOVER. That sort of strength is no good. You will never be as strong as a gorilla.
HECTOR. What is the dynamite for?
CAPTAIN SHOTOVER. To kill fellows like Mangan.
HECTOR. No use. They will always be able to buy more dynamite than you.
CAPTAIN SHOTOVER. I will make a dynamite that he cannot explode.
HECTOR. And that you can, eh?
CAPTAIN SHOTOVER. Yes: when I have attained the seventh degree of concentration.
HECTOR. Whats the use of that? You never do attain it.
CAPTAIN SHOTOVER. What then is to be done? Are we to be kept for ever in the mud by these hogs to whom the universe is nothing but a machine for greasing their bristles and filling their snouts?
(74–75)

It is here that Shotover emerges as an older, less effectual, and wiser version of Andrew Undershaft. Their goals are the same. Undershaft wants "command of life and command of death" (*Barb* 287); Shotover is convinced that "we must win powers of life and death" (75) over the capitalistic and amoristic degenerates. But in the conversation with Hector the whole premise of *Major Barbara* is reviewed and rejected. The Captain says it all: "You will never be as strong as a gorilla." Play the brutes' game, and the brutes win; the Mangans "will always be able to buy more dynamite" than the Shotovers. The Captain's one hope of victory lies in a qualitative leap to "a dynamite that [the others] cannot explode"; but this in turn depends on the mysterious "seventh degree of concentration," which is never attained. Shotover's final agonizing question posits a dead future to which Shaw for the first time seems almost willing to consent.

In this changed world Shaw can no longer place his confidence where formerly it would have rested—in the sane selfishness of the independent man. Shotover is clearly right when he says, "Decent men are like Daniel in the lion's den: their survival is a miracle; and they do not always survive" (75). When Hector offers the hope that the Mangans and Randalls and Billie Dunns may be "too stupid to use their power," the Captain explains that the real function of such power is the negative one of intimidating those who do not possess it: "Do not deceive yourself: they do use it. We kill the better half of ourselves every day to propitiate them. The knowledge that these people are there to render all our aspirations barren prevents us having the aspirations" (76). What then *are* decent men to do: crawl off and congratulate themselves on how much more *high-minded* Archimedes was than the soldier who split him open?[9] Shaw certainly did not think so—his whole life's work might be described as an attempt to hand Archimedes a sword. His last major hero, Undershaft, had repudiated Christendom's glorification of submission and urged instead an active battle: "killing" for him was "the only way of saying Must" (*Barb* 331). Similarly, when Hector nobly condescends to spare wicked people, Shotover reminds him that "you cant spare them until you have the power to kill them. At present they have the power to kill you" (76). This is the kind of rebuttal that Cusins would have called "damnably

9. Note Shaw's bitter comment on British war hysteria: "One felt that the figure of St George and the Dragon on our coinage should be replaced by that of the soldier driving his spear through Archimedes" (*Heart* 17, Pref).

discouraging"; here it is even more so, because Shaw is bereft of confident alternatives.

It is Hector himself who has succeeded in prying the older man loose from the Gospel of St. Andrew:

CAPTAIN SHOTOVER. What are they that they should judge us? Yet they do, unhesitatingly. There is enmity between our seed and their seed. They know it and act on it, strangling our souls. They believe in themselves. When we believe in ourselves, we shall kill them.

HECTOR. It is the same seed. You forget that your pirate has a very nice daughter. Mangan's son may be a Plato: Randall's a Shelley. What was my father?

CAPTAIN SHOTOVER. The damndest scoundrel I ever met. . . .

HECTOR. Precisely. Well, dare you kill his innocent grandchildren?

CAPTAIN SHOTOVER. They are mine also.

HECTOR. Just so. We are members one of another. . . . (75)

The thrust of Hector's final line here is less "All men are brothers" than "One touch of nature makes the whole world kin." The difficulty is not that evil men may be better than they seem, but that good men may only flatter what they imagine to be a difference between themselves and the "human vermin" (75) they want to destroy. When Hector says, "Give me the power to kill them; and I'll spare them in sheer—", Shotover interrupts laconically with the words "Fellow feeling?" (75–76). Hector can afford to be dispassionate about the two men being discussed when he asks the Captain, "Are Mangan's bristles worse than Randall's lovelocks?" (75); but the reader can go one better and ask whether Randall's lovelocks are worse than Hector's lies, or Mangan's bristles than Shotover's booze. Perhaps all men deserve the right to live because all men are equally corrupt; in any case, one cannot kill "fellows like Mangan" (74) without becoming a fellow like Mangan. Whereas Undershaft asserted, "I am a millionaire. That is my religion" (279), Shotover concedes that "money is not made in the light" (79). Here Shaw faces squarely the truth he had avoided about Andrew Undershaft's profession: what is the point of exhorting the "right" people to acquire power, if power and the wrong people inevitably gravitate together?

All of Shaw's artistic career had been an exploration of the possibility of uniting power and wisdom, action and thought, efficiency and aspiration. The achievement of such a synthesis results in the state of salvation; the plays that depict it, such as *Man and Superman* and *Major Barbara,* are instances of Shavian comedy. On the other hand, a separation between opposing elements results in the state of damnation; and the plays depicting that, such as *John Bull's Other Island* and *Saint Joan,* are instances of Shavian tragedy. (What is involved here is Shaw's expression of inner conviction, not a choice of "genres" in the conventional sense.) *Heartbreak House* is a tragedy because isolation prevails. In the preface Shaw laments that in prewar Europe "power and culture were in separate compartments" (5); some of that essay's subtitles simply list the two sides of a dichotomy: "Little Minds and Big Battles" (21–22), or "The Dumb Capables and the Noisy Incapables" (22–24). The play itself dramatizes the preface's contrast between "Heartbreak House and Horseback Hall" (3), to which are added several other disjunct oppositions—the "thinking Dunns and the drinking Dunns" (105), love and will, money and the soul. Unfortunately, the questions raised by these implied clashes can be answered only in the negative, or at best by other questions:

CAPTAIN SHOTOVER. Is there no thunder in heaven?
HECTOR. Is there no beauty, no bravery, on earth?   (78)

Where reconciliation is impossible, one can only revert to Father Keegan's metaphor of the world as a hell which no amount of pragmatic combativeness can successfully integrate with the life of the spirit. Thus Shaw's long-sought salvational synthesis of might and mind becomes impossible because he sees mankind caught between the antinomies of soulless strength and strengthless soul.

The possibility of a positive resolution emerging in spite of these tragic implications depends upon the developing conscious-

ness of the play's initially ingenuous heroine, Ellie Dunn. Like
Barbara Undershaft, Ellie is less a "leading lady" than a point
of resistance upon which the pressure of the drama's conflicts
comes to bear. Barbara, with an antipathy for Bodger that foreshadows Ellie's revulsion toward rum, reproached Cusins with
"breaking [her] heart" (299) when he connived to aid in exposing her innocence concerning the Army's dependence on a
distiller's cash. Ellie, beginning similarly as an innocent "bound
in honor and gratitude" (56) to marry Mangan, undergoes at
Hector's hands an instant "heartbreak," to which she reacts
with a cynical resolve to wrest back the capital Mangan stole
from her father. Desmond MacCarthy objects to the "thunder-
ing impossibility of her sudden transformation" from green girl
to knowing woman (151), but this is to take Ellie's progress at
her own evaluation. Shaw is more likely to depict such disillusionment as a stage in a process rather than a terminal state—note
Undershaft's comment to Barbara ("You have learnt something.
That always feels at first as if you had lost something"—316),
or Joan of Arc's reaction to her own discouragement ("I am
wiser now; and nobody is any the worse for being wiser"—118–
119).[10] Thus it is not surprising that he treats Ellie's bitterness as
the expression of an adolescent desolation. No sooner has she
found out about Mangan than she begins editorializing about
us "women" (83); exhibiting her suffering assertively to Hesione
("dont think that because youre on velvet . . . women who are
in hell can take it as easily as you"—94); and indulging in such
profound self-revelations as "I was quite a nice girl this morning,
and am now neither a girl nor particularly nice" (94). An occasional involuntary breakthrough like her whimper to Hesione
("You have stolen my babies"—96) indicates the extent to which
the tough attitudinizing is a veneer over pathetically hurt feel-

10. When preparing the manuscript of his first novel for publication
over forty years after the fact, Shaw silently inserted a line—"Men easily
mistake the shock of disillusion for the impact of brute truth" (*Imm* 125)
—to make clear his mature judgment of the cynical tastes of his teen-
age hero.

ings. Hesione is predictably indulgent when she suggests in response to Ellie's initial vexation that "it's only life educating you, pettikins" (62).

To enable Ellie to struggle through her crisis to a new perception, Captain Shotover acts as the tutor who gently punctures the girl's pretensions while retaining complete respect for her as a person. Taking her paradoxical assertion that she is marrying for money to save her soul, he asks why she doesn't resort to theft instead. But Ellie, who is sophisticated enough to distinguish legality from morality, remains unimpressed with this appeal to "old-fashioned" honesty. Furthermore, when the Captain tries to warn that "if you sell yourself, you deal your soul a blow that all the [material pleasures] in the world wont heal" (111), she counters by asking why *he* sold himself to the devil in Zanzibar. It is in the ensuing account of his plight as ship's captain that Shotover most clearly echoes Wotan's resort to imposture in compelling obedience from creatures too stupid to "understand the aims of a god" (*Wag* 174):

CAPTAIN SHOTOVER. . . . Foolish people took young thieves off the streets; flung them into a training ship where they were taught to fear the cane instead of fearing God; and thought theyd make men and sailors of them by private subscription. I tricked these thieves into believing I'd sold myself to the devil. It saved my soul from the kicking and swearing that was damning me by inches.
ELLIE. . . . I shall pretend to sell myself to Boss Mangan to save my soul from the poverty that is damning *me* by inches.
CAPTAIN SHOTOVER. Riches will damn you ten times deeper. Riches wont save even your body.
ELLIE. Old-fashioned again. We know now that the soul is the body, and the body the soul. They tell us they are different because they want to persuade us that we can keep our souls if we let them make slaves of our bodies. I am afraid you are no use to me, Captain.
CAPTAIN SHOTOVER. What did you expect? A Savior, eh? Are you old-fashioned enough to believe in that? (111–112)

While Ellie's conviction of the damning effects of poverty suggests Undershaft at his most trenchant, Shotover is more conscious than Barbara's father appeared to be concerning the ultimately self-defeating nature of the compromises a man makes to gain mastery over his circumstances. Thus the Captain offers his own previous action not as a cause to be embraced but as a mistake to be avoided in all cases where a person has a choice (as Ellie does). And whereas Barbara came to see that "turning our backs on Bodger and Undershaft is turning our backs on life" (338), Ellie eventually comes to learn from the Captain that "your soul sticks to you if you stick to it; but the world has a way of slipping through your fingers" (110). No longer enticed by Mangan's money, she pledges troth to Shotover in the last act: "I, Ellie Dunn, give my broken heart and my strong sound soul to its natural captain, my spiritual husband and second father" (131–132). Robert Brustein treats this scene as a portrayal of how Ellie is driven to nearly total despair "when she contracts a spiritual marriage with Captain Shotover, and learns that his wisdom and purpose proceed primarily from the rum bottle" (226). But such a reading alters Shaw's emphasis—Ellie's spiritual marriage" takes place *after* she has learned of the Captain's tippling. Yet there is no denying that her search for "life with a blessing" (132) is a more fragile goal than Juan's search for the Superman. Likewise, her symbolic union with Shotover seems an attenuated synthesis indeed when compared with the trinities of fused forces that dominated Shaw's previous major works.[11]

Ellie's pilgrimage as Shavian prototype involves her deepening grasp of the play's key concept, heartbreak. Initially experiencing it as a searing disillusionment, she has already sensed a false note in her rage at Hector's duplicity when she says a few moments later: "I have a horrible fear that my heart is broken, but that heartbreak is not like what I thought it must be" (62).

11. Compare Wisenthal (1974): "One might think, then, that the union between Ellie and Shotover offers grounds for hope. . . . But this union does not dominate the end of the play in the way that the other unions dominate the endings of *Man and Superman* and *Major Barbara*" (149).

By the beginning of the next act, Ellie has come to see that heart-break lay not in the shock of discovery which ended her innocence, but rather in her new awareness that a unique experience in life is gone forever: "I know that what has happened to me with Marcus will not happen to me ever again" (94–95). After witnessing (and to some extent inflicting) the anguish that convinces even Hesione that Mangan has a heart (98), the girl generalizes from her particular disappointment to a feeling of loss pervasive in human life: "[Heartbreak] is a curious sensation: the sort of pain that goes mercifully beyond our powers of feeling. When your heart is broken, your boats are burned: nothing matters any more. It is the end of happiness and the beginning of peace" (108). These poignant words deeply vex Lady Utterword, whose own fear that she has *no* heart enables Ellie to understand that an inability to experience desolation is the only suffering devoid of meaning. Strengthened by this new insight, she can admit to Shotover her error in thinking that heartbreak meant she "should never feel happy again" (115). When the Captain suggests in reply that total self-sufficiency belongs to those who are "only happy when they are stripped of everything, even of hope" (115), Ellie agrees: "I feel now as if there was nothing I could not do, because I want nothing" (115). The alternative to fulfilling one's heart's desire is not the sniveling misery of Mangan or the howling of Randall when Ariadne "twists his heart" (136), but rather the strength—again in Shotover's words—to "let the heart break in silence" (134).

This state of resignation will seem too powerful to have arisen from the trivial incident of Ellie's initial disillusionment only if we forget that Hector's mendacity was but the starting point from which she gradually outgrows her private grievance to become educated to the utmost implications of her experience. Subsequently hurt, angered, and enlightened by several more characters (Mangan—81–83, Hesione—93–96, Ariadne—108–109, and Shotover—113–114), she develops as both participant and onlooker a more sympathetic view of the plight of human limitations struggling to cope with a "cruel, damnable world" (94—Hesione's phrase) which drives men to succumb to the happiness of illusions in order to possess the illusion of happiness. In progressing from her piqued query—"But how can you love a liar?" (61)—to the calm knowledge that there is "nothing real in the world" (129), Ellie has acquired a spirit of forgiveness large enough to discover a blessing "even on the lies of Marcus" (132). The bleaker her understanding of human motives becomes, the more tolerant of human frailty she grows, to the extent of being able to affirm the genuineness of the "beautiful black hair" (129) that Hesione earlier admitted to be false (96). If this gesture suggests in turn that Ellie has now learned to play the game along with the others, she nonetheless brings to such participation a more profound awareness of what is at stake. For her consciousness has come to rest not in the need to pretend that illusion *is* reality, but in the grace to accept the finality of life's irreconcilable, conflicting claims.

It was the Commander in "Don Juan in Hell" who quipped that hope is a "form of moral responsibility" (93). Having dearly welcomed such responsibility during most of his life, Shaw now admits the possibility that the cessation of hope may be a more authentic salvation than that which previous goal-directed strivings sought in vain to achieve. Yet when he also volunteered the comment that the impulse behind Caesar's assertion that "he who has never hoped can never despair" (*Caes* 183) might be diabolic rather than divine (*SSS* 133), Shaw was acknowledging that negation has dangers of its own. For just as love is aped by romance, just as the greater imagination is aped by the lesser, so a genuine resignation to life without hope can be imitated by the "absurdist" sentimentality that equates despair with wisdom. Hence the ambiguity of the play's conclusion. As these paragons of a diminished humanity greet the impending air raid, is their elation authentic or only a parading beside the abyss? Hesione hails the event with an ingratiating simile to the effect that the sound of the Zeppelins is "like Beethoven" (140); but Ellie's reply—"By thunder, Hesione: it *is* Beethoven" (140)—more daringly stakes everything on an assertion of the exact equivalence of the mind's metaphors and external reality. This act of faith ventures the gamble that all art must take: everything depends now on whether Ellie is a great artist or a little one. If Ellie's is the art that illuminates reality, then we can rejoice with her that in this ecstatic crisis the bombers *are* music, that Hector at last becomes "Marcus" (141), that those who expose themselves openly to danger are saved while prudent souls perish, and that the characters achieve a state of authentic negation beyond tragedy. But if Ellie's metaphor is instead the medium of an art that deceives, then her words "Set fire to the house, Marcus" (141) will suggest rather that it is only in moments of glamorized illusion that destruction seems beautiful, that exposing themselves to gratuitous danger is the assemblage's grotesque parody of the Captain's courage in facing necessary risks at sea (113), and that Hector's turning on the lights to leave them all "blazing to the skies" (141) is the vain finale of a *Götterdämmerung* in which Valhalla cannot catch fire.

Though Ellie seemed previously to fit Shotover's description of a self-sufficient soul who could be happy only when stripped of hope, the end of the play finds her welcoming the prospect of a new air raid with the words "I hope so" (142). Since hoping for extinction may be no less sentimental than hoping for progress, it remains dubious whether Shaw finds his people finally to be in a state of grace or more irretrievably damned than ever. For despite Ellie's belief that "life must come to a point sometime" (137), Hector's conviction that "we are useless, dangerous, and ought to be abolished" (124), and Shotover's prophecy of the "smash of the drunken skipper's ship on the rocks" (138), it is possible that the apocalypse itself may be only another illusion. Is the former belief in Providence as a panacea any *more* credulous than the certainty that now hails the blind might of the bombers as an instrument of divine judgment? The conclusion may be seen as an anticlimax in which nothing happens, really—the bombs miss the house, having dealt a glancing blow to the sensibilities of a group of people who for the most part remain in much the same situation as before. On the other hand, there is no denying that Mangan and Billie Dunn ("the two practical men of business"—142) have been killed and the nearby rectory has been destroyed—events critics have interpreted to affirm that the survival of the species depends on the death of capitalism and the rebirth of religion. Yet the moral salvaging operation thus implied serves less to solve a problem than to underscore a dilemma, for Ellie Dunn still remains "radiant at the prospect" (142) that the Zeppelins will return the following night. The dramatist does not choose between these alternative prospects, whose clashing implications point to a division in his own mind. Shaw's own despair is the greater because his hope is not dead. He exhorts us to renewed efforts even as his play's mighty music celebrates the death of the race.

PART FOUR

9   Epilogue

▄▀

Lilith's Retrospective Prophecy (*Back to Methusaleh,
Saint Joan, In Good King Charles's Golden Days*)

In the concluding speech from *Back to Methuselah* (1918–
1920), Lilith reviews her career as vital impetus in the universe:
" 'I brought life into the whirlpool of force, and compelled my enemy, Matter, to obey a living soul. But in enslaving Life's enemy I
made him Life's master; for that is the end of all slavery; and
now I shall see the slave set free and the enemy reconciled, the
whirlpool become all life and no matter' " (254). This statement
metaphorically recapitulates Shaw's own development. The reign
of matter corresponds to the primacy of efficiency over aspiration
in his earliest period. Compelling matter "to obey a living soul"
recalls the attempt, in such works as *Candida* and *The Perfect
Wagnerite,* to expand pragmatism to embrace a higher purpose
in life—a process that culminates in the vision of "Don Juan in
Hell." The discovery that "in enslaving Life's enemy I made him
Life's master" registers the failure of *John Bull's Other Island*
and *Major Barbara* to preserve *Man and Superman*'s synthesis
from contingencies that threaten to destroy it. After the collapse
of the vision in *Heartbreak House,* Shaw reluctantly concluded
that the only way to preserve the soul from the flesh was to dis-
engage one from the other so that the whirlpool might "become
all life and no matter." In cerebrating for 296 of their 300 years,
the barely corporeal Ancients in "As Far as Thought Can Reach"
have taken the first step toward becoming "vortices" who will

transform Don Juan's goal of spending "eons in contemplation" (*Super* 100) from a sprite's declaration of intent into a directive for everyday living.

Despite the inspirational rhetoric designed to bring this "meta-biological pentateuch" (*Back* iii) to an affirmative conclusion, Lilith's peroration is a thinly disguised acknowledgment of the defeat that has finally overwhelmed Shaw's eschatological quest. For while she may speak of fording "this last stream that lies between flesh and spirit" (253), Lilith is building a barricade instead of a bridge. Her goal of moving to "the whirlpool of pure intelligence that, when the world began, was a whirlpool in pure force" (253) is less a resolution than a retreat from the challenge of achieving harmonious interrelationship between spirit and matter. The extent of Shaw's commitment to this pessimistic conclusion is debatable, for a "Postscript" added in 1944 returns to his more characteristic doctrine of a Life Force "struggling towards its goal of godhead by *incarnating* itself in creatures with knowledge and power enough to control nature and circumstances" (263—italics mine). But the She-Ancient in the play confirms Lilith's tenet that "when the master [mind] has come to do everything through the slave [body], the slave becomes the master, since he cannot live without him" (245). Once freed from his "tyrannous body" (245), the Ancients look forward to an immortality of pure thought. The projected union of elements has broken down, and permanent separation is inevitable.

Shaw's post-*Methuselah* plays tend to be either ingenious re-statements of this basic dilemma (*Too True to Be Good,* 1931) or else abortive attempts to make a new beginning (*The Simpleton of the Unexpected Isles,* 1934). Although considerations of length preclude detailed treatment of Shaw's last dramatic phase, a brief discussion will suffice to establish the primacy of his fundamental pessimism even in plays that at first seem to contradict it, such as *Saint Joan* and *Good King Charles's Golden Days.* These two dramas give every appearance of representing basically comic actions, only to end by unexpectedly ratifying the meta-physics of Shavian tragedy.[1]

Saint Joan has often been treated as a "tragic" action marred by an inappropriate comic finale. Yet it seems to me that Joan without its epilogue would be a definite—albeit complex—instance of Shavian comedy. For Joan's death, no matter how horrible, would be tragic only in a scheme of values that holds personal survival to be of ultimate concern. If Joan were a realist in the sense of being a Shavian pragmatist, this would indeed be the case. But since her realism is instead that of an heroic idealist, the force of scenes I–VI depends not on her personal survival, but on the ultimate triumph of the higher goal to which she aspires. The body of the play is optimistic concerning the eventual victory of Joan's cause. Her "all or nothing" dedication to a divine call is contrasted favorably with the Philistinism of the "quiet and sensible" Dauphin (83), who merely wants to be let alone, or with the Machiavellian idealism of Warwick (the play's Burgoyne), who regards her death simply as a "political necessity" (123). Joan's statement that "the world is too wicked for me" (109) expresses her own resignation to her fate, not Shaw's criticism of her inability to adjust to "reality." Eager to "dare, and dare, and dare" (119) in the certainty that her loneliness is her strength, Joan resembles the "one in a thousand" Shaw described in the introduction to The Quintessence of Ibsenism. She embodies that book's conviction that "the supreme end shall be . . . not the abstract law but the living will" (Quint 122, 1913); even the Inquisitor finally acknowledges that the saint's "vision and freedom of the living soul" has prevailed over her judges' "blindness and bondage of the law" (162). Only on the most superficial level can Joan's condemnation by the Inquisition be regarded as a story of defeat. Warwick may gloat after the execution that "nothing remains, not a bone, not a nail, not a hair," but the executioner's statement that "her heart would not

1. As previously defined in this book. See above, pages 73n, 170–171, 184ff., 214, 226, 228, 256.

burn" (148) proclaims that Joan's spirit is not dead even though
her body has been destroyed.

Thus far *Saint Joan* could be considered simply a vivid "problem play" about a girl whose misfortune was to be born a
Protestant and a nationalist before her time. Her death at the
stake, the "last of her" (148) physically, is actually the first step
in the triumph of her spirit. But the epilogue—ostensibly dealing
with the triumph of Joan's "unbroken" soul (161)—is far more
pessimistic. Although the company assembled in Charles's dream
are willing to praise the saint, they hastily disappear into the
night when she proposes to return to them as a living woman
(162). Having been unable to destroy Joan, respectable society
canonizes her in the hope—unconscious, to be sure—that adoration will succeed where the flames failed. Without the epilogue,
we would have concluded that Joan's death was a necessary
catalyst for the evolution in consciousness that leads men at last
to recognize her greatness. But now Cauchon's great cry—"Must
then a Christ perish in torment *in every age* to save those that
have no imagination?" (158—italics mine)—implies a non-
teleological framework of eternal recurrence. Poor Joan would
have been born "before her time" no matter when she chanced
to live! In asking "O God that madest this beautiful earth, when
will it be ready to receive Thy saints? How long, O Lord, how
long?" (163), the saint foresees a future that will never escape
the bonds of history. Earth and heaven remain as eternally
separate in her vision as matter and the soul are in Lilith's.
Saint Joan is a tragedy, not in spite of, but *because* of, the epilogue.

Just as Joan is allied to the heroic idealist Shaw praised in the
first and final chapters of the *Quintessence,* so the hero of *Good
King Charles's Golden Days* recalls the Shavian pragmatist who
dominated his intervening discussion of Ibsen's plays. Armed
with double-edged empirical resourcefulness that enables him to
be both a deserter from the battle of Worcester and founder of
the Royal Society, the "merry monarch" is determined to avoid

the fate of his famous relatives, Mary Queen of Scots and Charles I. A clear understanding of his precarious position as king makes him justly contemptuous of the stupid courage of his brother James, the "man of principle" whose eventual downfall he correctly predicts. His characteristic remarks are those of the self-reliant, efficient man: "I must do the best I can with what I know" (194) or "We must forgive our enemies when we can afford to" (225). Like Bluntschli and other heroes of early Shavian drama, Charles has a simple boast: "I keep my head on my shoulders. It takes a man of brains to do that" (197). (The unstated significance of his being fifty years old in the play is suggested by his father's dates: 1600–1649). Moreover, the action of the long first act shows his wits working humanely as well as shrewdly. By creatively "unsettling" (201) the minds of George Fox, Godfrey Kneller, and Isaac Newton, the king manages to reconcile these gifted fanatics with a skill that makes the first act (five-sixths of the play's length) as much a depiction of the triumph of its hero as the first six scenes of *Saint Joan* were a portrayal of the triumph of its heroine.

Yet the later play's brief closing act (223–234) has a deflating impact analogous to that of *Joan*'s epilogue. When Newton's housekeeper had originally asked, "How do you live?" Charles had replied, "By my wits, Mistress Basham: by my wits" (167). This image of a man at ease with his own success is undercut by the concluding scene with his wife, which gives us a new sense of the king's view of his own limitations. Here we see a Charles who is bored with the atmosphere of the court, who must constantly maneuver to keep at bay competing factions united only in their designs on his and Catherine's lives, and who regards his fabled sexual involvements as no more than consolatory diversions from the awareness of his political impotence. While the assertion that Charles was "no king" because he had "no faith, no principles" (190) was merely laughable when made by his stolid brother, the same sentiment is in fact now expressed in Charles's own admission, "I am no real king . . . the utmost I can do is to keep my crown on my head and my head on my shoulders" (232). This is clearly an acknowledgment of defeat by one who, like Wotan in *The Perfect Wagnerite,* has been forced by circumstances into assuming a role that is at variance with his deepest impulses.[2]

A potential agent playing the part of detached observer, Charles is cognizant of the problem that is also central in *Saint Joan,* the need to reconcile individual uniqueness with social cohesion: "No two consciences are the same. . . . What is right for one is wrong for the other. Yet they cannot live together without laws; and a law is something that obliges all to do the same thing" (232). As a real king, Charles might have been able to do more about this dilemma than utter apothegms. As a figurehead, however, all he can do is "enjoy myself and let the people see me doing it, and leave things as they are, though things as they are will not bear thinking of by those who know what they are" (229–230). The coda-like second act reveals the victory of his clever pragmatism to be as illusory as that of Joan's heroic idealism. Joan's total commitment to a spiritual vocation led to her physical death. Charles's strategy of ensuring physical survival has emasculated his spiritual force. His ironic description of himself—"Oh! Oh! Oh! The merry monarch!" (226)—expresses a poignant awareness that nothing *fails* like success. This is exactly the realization to which the heroine came at the end of the epilogue to *Saint Joan.*

In using the contrasting moral stances of Joan and Charles to portray the same basic dilemma, Shaw does not imply any

2. While Charles's reference near the beginning to "so damaged a character as mine" (166) is a clear allusion to his reputation as a libertine, the same phrase can also be seen as an oblique reference to his divided nature. The poignancy of the king's predicament is underscored when the Frenchwoman, Louise de Keroualle, praises him as "very spiritual" and then corrects herself: "Clever, you call it. I am always in trouble with my English" (219). The irony here is that Charles is indeed "spiritual" in the English as well as the French sense of the word, but has fallen so far short of actualizing his potential that Louise's coincidentally appropriate description seems only an amusing blunder.

criticism of these figures for failing to embody a synthesis of power and wisdom, thought and deed, action and ideal. Permanent division between these specific properties follows necessarily from Lilith's general pronouncement of the ultimate separation of spirit and matter. When Warwick says that "the practical problem would seem to be how to save [Joan's] soul without saving her body" (102), he unwittingly echoes Lilith's point that the soul's salvation depends on "redemption from the flesh" (*Back* 253). Likewise, Joan's own posthumous comment—"I was not in my right mind until I was free of the body" (152)—suggests that she has moved in the direction of Lilith's "vortex freed from matter" (*Back* 253). Charles's amorous pastimes bring him to a similar conclusion: "I am done with all bodies. They are all alike. . . . It is the souls and the brains that are different." When he adds that "in the end one learns to leave the body out" (224–225), he too paraphrases Lilith's goal of life disentangled "from the matter that has always mocked it" (*Back* 253). And he anticipates the hermaphrodite in *Farfetched Fables* (1948), who insists: "I dont want to be a body: I want to be a mind and nothing but a mind" (120). Originally, the Superman was conceived as a being who would unite flesh and spirit; now a youth in the "Sixth and Last Fable" (122) holds that twentieth-century humanity were mere "black beetles compared to the supermen who evolved into the disembodied" (*Far* 126). In short, the human dichotomy can be escaped only by canceling out one of its elements. The failure of Joan and Charles arises not from any defect for which they could be held accountable as individuals, but from an isolation of faculties which Shaw sees as inherent in man's nature. Since each of them is limited to supplying only one component of a hypothetical higher being capable of uniting their qualities, both characters finally become specific historical manifestations of Lilith's general metaphysical dilemma. In light of this essentially negative vision, how strange that the criticism that still prevents many from taking Shaw seriously is his supposed superficial optimism!

The Tragic Optimist

My attempt to depict Shaw's intellectual odyssey from *Immaturity* (1879) to *Farfetched Fables* (1948) is now essentially complete. Some readers may object at this point that Shaw's handling of major themes—the nature of self-realization, the conflict between idealism and realism, the dichotomy between matter and spirit, and so forth—constitutes neither a systematic body of doctrine nor an original contribution to the history of ideas. In regard to the first point, my aim throughout has been to present Shaw's developing awareness, not to produce a set of propositions comprising a Shavian metaphysic. As for the second criticism, I have already shown how concepts that Shaw is commonly assumed to have borrowed from Bergson or Nietzsche had in fact been emerging in his own works for years before he read these philosophers. The matter of "sources" is a red herring in any case; for the real test of a creative writer's use of pre-existent ideas is whether his mind has engaged such materials with sufficient depth to make them live in his own art. Isak Dinesen's remark—"God so loved the Giraffe that He created them" (302) —delights us not because we mistake her for the inventor of the theological and Platonic premises it contains, but because she has linked these notions so penetratingly that her utterance has the *force* of an original insight. Even if every "Shavian" concept could be irrefutably traced to a definite external source, the power of the works generated by the interaction of Shaw's intellectual concerns and his artistic imagination would by no means be diminished. While his plays may not succeed as attempts to create a dramatized philosophy, they nonetheless constitute a remarkable achievement in philosophic drama.

Other readers may readily grant the resourcefulness with which Shaw has explored metaphysical questions through the medium of his art, but then protest that the whole fabric of his vision is tainted by his failure to come to grips with the problem of "radical evil" in human nature. This is perhaps the most serious and persistent charge leveled against Shaw's world-view. In a statement still quoted approvingly by anti-Shavians, Christopher Caudwell wrote that Shaw typifies the bourgeois intellectual's belief that "whatever he conceives as absolute truth and justice—vegetarianism or equal incomes or anti-vaccination—can be imposed on the world by successful argument" (11). Behind this allegation lies the image of Shaw the Fabian optimist awaiting progress, the proclaimer of panaceas like the Superman, the believer in an imperfect God who created cancer and Jack the Ripper by mistake.[3] Nowhere in his plays can one find an Iago: his most reprehensible characters—such as Mangan and de Stogumber—are well-intentioned dolts who are driven to "evil" actions by social pressures they do not understand.

Admittedly, Shaw's argument that essentially benevolent human impulses have been thwarted by institutionalized ideals would appear to have an obvious Achilles' heel. For if the concept of a transcendent deity is rejected, who is responsible for creating such institutions if not "beneficent" man himself? How can we be sure that viciousness and spite were not among the "half-satisfied passions" that set the human imagination in pursuit of dogmatic absolutes in the first place (*PP* xvi–xvii)? Shaw had invoked this very difficulty to embarrass his ideological adversaries: "Kropotkin, too optimistically, as I think, disposes of the average man by attributing his unsocialism to the pressure of the corrupt system under which he groans. Remove that pressure, and he will think rightly, says Kropotkin. But if the natural man be indeed social as well as gregarious, how did the corruption and oppression under which he groans ever arise?" (*EFS* 82). He goes on to argue in this early Fabian essay (1891) that the same selfishness that caused primitive man to seek domination over his fellows would impel better-informed nineteenth-century individualists to realize that their private interests are vitally bound up with the health of society as a whole. But as it eventually became apparent that no such process of humane self-

3. See, for example, "The Humanitarians and the Problem of Evil" (*Back* liii-lv).

assertion was actually occurring, Shaw ignored the implications of his own critique of Kropotkin and relied instead on distinguishing between the benevolent ends institutions were intended to serve and the pernicious effects they often produce. To be sure, *The Quintessence of Ibsenism* had argued plausibly that illusions originating in a seemingly harmless urge to disguise painful realities often end up being converted into idols clamoring for human sacrifices. But while Shaw's thesis is convincing as far as it goes, one can only regret that he avoided taking the crucial next step that would have required him to confront the Nietzschean position that human lust for power is the *primary* cause—not an unfortunate side effect—of the creation of conventional ideals.[4]

4. Though Shaw had not read Nietzsche at the time the *Quintessence* was written, the two writers offer closely parallel arguments defining ideals as respectable lies employed to disguise human weaknesses. But *The Genealogy of Morals* makes clear Nietzsche's view that the main purpose of idealism is not to enable frail creatures to escape consciousness of themselves, but rather to enable a slave class to wage psychological warfare against an heroic aristocracy: "Would anyone care to learn something about the way in which ideals are manufactured? Does anyone have the nerve? . . . Well then, go ahead! There's a chink through which you can peek into this murky shop. . . . I can't see a thing, but I hear all the more. There's a low, cautious whispering in every nook and corner. I have a notion these people are lying. All the sounds are sugary and soft. . . . They are transmuting weakness into merit. . . . Impotence, which cannot retaliate, into kindness; pusillanimity into humility; submission before those one hates into obedience to One of whom they say that he has commanded this submission—they call him God. The inoffensiveness of the weak, his cowardice, his ineluctable standing and waiting at doors, are being given honorific titles such as patience; to be *unable* to avenge oneself is called to be *unwilling* to avenge oneself— even forgiveness . . . I'm sure they are quite miserable, all these whisperers and smalltime counterfeiters, even though they huddle close together for warmth. But they tell me that this very misery is the sign of their election by God, . . . that this misery is perhaps also a preparation, a test, a kind of training, . . . something for which eventually they will be compensated with tremendous interest—in gold? No, in happiness. They call this *bliss*. . . . Now they tell me that not only are they better than the mighty of this earth, whose spittle they must lick (not from fear—

Yet Shaw's failure in this instance results more from the promptings of his hortatory conscience than from lack of awareness. His insistence that "defeatism is the wretchedest of policies" (*SSS* 79) often seems an attempt to keep a stiff upper lip in the midst of perceptions that threatened to produce a "discouragement" like that which killed the "Elderly Gentleman" in *Methuselah*. Shaw's later efforts at positive thinking arose from a strictly pragmatic conviction that he "must not darken counsel" (*Quint* 10, 2d Pref) so long as it is not certain that the human experiment is doomed. Beginning *Everybody's Political What's What?* (1944) during the Second World War, Shaw gave to his opening chapter the title: "Is Human Nature Incurably Depraved?" The octogenarian prophet's conclusion is that, while it may be that the "unchanging human heart" is "desperately wicked," it is also possible that ignorance rather than malice is at the root of the ills of civilization, that the hell Father Keegan found on earth is nonetheless "paved with good intentions" (2). This was not the first warning he had given against ceding the battle without a fight: "If there be no will, we are lost. That is a possibility for our crazy little empire, if not for the universe; and as such possibilities are not to be entertained without despair, we must, whilst we survive, proceed on the assumption that we have still energy enough to not only will to live, but to will to live better" (*Super* 204, Rev Hdbk). This utilitarian counsel is entirely consonant with the pragmatic perspective that had always been at the core of Shaw's philosophy. For just as obsession with life's inevitable "misfortune and mortality" (*Super* xxxi) diminishes ability to confront preventable pitfalls, so the temptation to in-

---

by no means—but because God commands us to honor our superiors), but they are even better off, or at least they will be better off someday. But I've had all I can stand. The smell is too much for me. This shop where they manufacture ideals seems to me to stink of lies. . . . Would you ever guess, if you only listened to their words, that these are men bursting with hatred? . . . *There can be no doubt that these weaklings, too, want a chance to be strong, to have their kingdom come*" (1956; 180–182—italics mine).

voke original sin as an explanatory principle for the state of civilization only serves to justify fatal passivity in the face of problems demanding immediate constructive action. As an elderly sage, Shaw was increasingly determined to hold clearly before us the magnitude of the basic choice modern man faces—whether to believe in human depravity or in politics. But this is a very different matter from his claiming—as Caudwell charged—that reformist prescriptions could be imposed on the world by mere argument. On the contrary, from *Major Barbara* onward, Shaw was more inclined to remind us that the inspired proposals of all the wise men of history never produced the slightest practical effect (see *Barb* 221–222, Pref; *CP* vii–viii; *Far* 98, Pref).

The beginnings of this shift away from progressivism can be detected quite early in Shaw's career. I have shown in the third chapter how his first gropings beyond pragmatism coincided with a diminution of his short-range meliorism. His notes to *Caesar and Cleopatra* (1898) attacked the idea that there has been any such thing as "Progress" since the time of Caesar (195–196); one section of *The Revolutionist's Handbook* (1903) is actually entitled "Progress an Illusion" (188–193). The later book contains in addition a section ("The Conceit of Civilization"—194–200) that turns a sustained Swiftian wrath on man's pride in his achievements. Far from being a messianically utopian document, the *Handbook* in fact sounds the death knell of nineteenth-century optimism. By marshaling evidence that no "moral progress whatever has been made in historic time" (201), Shaw attacks the "political program-maker" who relies on "some prescription for bettering us" (188). Then all progressive "isms" (including his own) are rejected in the light of the conclusion that "man will return to his idols and his cupidities, in spite of all 'movements' and all revolutions, until his nature is changed" (192). Thus the postulate of a "Superman" arises not from confidence in humanity, but from despair that the hill Difficulty "will never be climbed by Man as we know him" (188).

To be sure, we need not take Shaw's use of Nietzsche's term

at face value. Practically speaking, he was invoking prophecy as a means of sharpening criticism: the Superman was less a utopian's expectation of what the future would bring than a humanist's exhortation to a wayward species. But the increasing frequency with which he later found it necessary to argue against such metaphors as Swift's Yahoo (*Heart* 26, Pref; *Gen* 25, Pref; *EPWW* 2) or Shakespeare's "Angry Ape" (*Heart* 26, Pref; *Simp* 3, Pref; *Back* 271, Post) indicates growing frustration. Eventually, his belief that human nature will be transcended became linked with a warning that humanity is not necessarily the instrument by which this goal will be achieved. Hector Hushabye's premonition that "some new creation will come to supplant us as we have supplanted the animals" (*Heart* 124) foreshadows Lilith's threat that "from the moment I . . . lose hope and faith in [mankind], they are doomed. . . . I may not spare them forever" (*Back* 254). Thus the assurance that the Life Force will win its "finally irresistible way" (*Far* 74) has as its corollary the belief that "Creative Evolution can replace us" (*SSS* 79). Man may no more be father to the Superman than the dinosaur was father to man.

The sources of Shaw's increasing disillusionment can be located historically not only in the world wars, but also in the peculiar "triumph" of socialism in English politics. Julian Kaye has argued that "the most bitter disappointment of Shaw's life" (186) was the aftermath of the Labour victory of 1929, which saw an ex-Fabian, Ramsey MacDonald, elected prime minister. In no position to implement socialist programs as head of a minority government, MacDonald was gradually compelled by events to form a coalition with the Conservatives in 1931—an action that led to his expulsion from the Labour party (Taylor 270–296). In an uneasy preface written in 1930 for a reprint of *Fabian Essays,* Shaw perceptively notes the direction of events:

[The old Fabians] have lived to see their political plans carried out with a success beyond all their reasonable hopes. The parliamentary Labor Party for which they bargained has been formed, and has already held office twice. The Treasury Bench has been filled with Socialists. Yet as far as Socialism is concerned it might as well have been filled by Conservative bankers and baronets. No industry has been nationalized; and the unemployed are bought off by doles in the disastrous old Roman fashion. The Party System, under which "it is the business of the Opposition to oppose", still obstructs so effectively that bills to which nobody objects, and which could be disposed of in half an hour, take up as many months as really contentious measures. Fundamental changes are impossible: only the tinkerings necessary to prevent the State machine from jamming and stopping are introduced and pushed through by mere force of circumstances. Labor Governments, like other governments, end in disappointment and reaction with their millennial promises unfulfilled; whilst the revolutionary Left and the Fascist Right are supplied with daily evidence as to the futility of parliamentary action at home, and the swift effectiveness of hard knocks abroad. (xi)[5]

His 1932 speech, "In Praise of Guy Fawkes," bitterly assails MacDonald and the whole parliamentary system. Moreover, Shaw's tone now betrays an *affective* commitment to inflammatory postulates he would previously have employed to jolt audiences out of their complacency (for example, "I am impatient for the catastrophe. . . . The only way in which [a dispute] can finally be settled . . . is by one party killing the other"—*P&P* 257–258). Between the essay and the speech occurred Shaw's visit to Russia, which left him an enthusiastic Stalinist convinced of the need for the "scientific" liquidation of the socially unfit—a measure he went on to advocate in prefaces to *On the Rocks* (1933) and *The Simpleton of the Unexpected Isles* (1934).[6]

5. Quoted from the "Jubilee Edition" of *Fabian Essays* (London: George Allen & Unwin, 1948 [repr. 1950]). This useful volume reprints prefatory material from all previous editions, as well as a postscript written by Shaw in 1947.

6. Katherine Haynes Gatch (143–144) has argued that Shaw was no more serious when he proposed this in *On the Rocks* than Swift had been when he proposed eating babies in "A Modest Proposal." But Shaw returns to his own immodest proposal too persistently (for instance, the

These apparently conflicting tendencies—on the one hand, to apologize for totalitarian regimes as emergency expedients; on the other, to posit a cosmology that threatens to dispense with man altogether—are allied in the sense that both are desperate detours around the challenge of creating a viable politics. The first position's acceptance of brutal short-term solutions is a betrayal of Shaw's earlier conviction that efficiency must be exercised within a humane frame of reference; the second's reliance on the very long run is all too easily converted into an excuse for the very inaction he intended to oppose. His references to "the next million light years" (*Far* 63, Pref) sound suspiciously like a frustrated humanist's attempt to hedge his bets without formally repudiating his philosophy. With unintended irony, the writer who had used Captain Shotover so effectively to warn against the danger of trusting to the "theory of an overruling Providence" (*Heart* 137) goes on in his own last works to equate divine Providence directly with his own theory of the Life Force (*Back* 267, Post; *SSS* 78; *Far* 65, Pref).[7]

---

praise for the Russian Cheka throughout his late writings) for the likelihood of a satiric intention to remain plausible. Gatch bases her argument upon two observations: (1) the preface to *Rocks* contains an impassioned plea for toleration, and (2) Shaw habitually "could not . . . countenance cruelty" (144). Concerning the first point, the relevant sections of the preface in question plead for toleration of freedom of speech, not freedom of action. As for the second, Shaw's other writings indicate that his detestation of *punitive* or revengeful killing by no means precluded his approval of euthanasia for the incorrigibly unfit. This position, anticipated as early as *Caesar and Cleopatra*, is reaffirmed later in such works as *Barb* 239–240, Pref; *Crim* 195–201; and *EPWW* 281–283.

7. Yet if we consider that Shaw's political thinking was formed during the 1880's, it is remarkable how perceptive his later pronouncements sometimes are. Though too eager to drop the phrase, "by the people," from the Gettysburg Address, his preface to *The Apple Cart* (1929) is a forceful exposure of bourgeois democracy's enslavement by hidden plutocratic interests. Though overly indulgent toward Mussolini and Hitler, his "Preface on Bosses," written for *The Millionairess* (1936), shows awareness of the danger as well as the attractions of strong rulers. Some of his specific suggestions—such as a "coupled vote" requiring that men and women be elected in equal numbers to legislative bodies (*Charles* 157–

Nevertheless, the strong idealist taint in Shaw's later thought cannot be attributed to a sentimental disinclination to face the realities of human nature. Rarely if ever in the last forty years of his life does Shaw go further than to claim that man has "good impulses as well as bad ones" (*And* 80, Pref). But he differs from most commentators in defining bad impulses, not in terms of conventional moral categories, but in terms of regression to an earlier or lower stage in the evolutionary process. On this point he remained consistent throughout his life. In a paper on acting delivered in 1889, he told his audience that "each of us has not only the bird and fish in him, but also—and how much more strongly!—the savage, the barbarian, the hunter and slayer, the warrior, the murderer, the thief, the coward, and the fanatic" (*P&P* 18). *Caesar and Cleopatra* (1898) is full of comparisons of violent persons to jackals, tigers, and other wild animals. In "Killing for Sport" (1914), he attributes fascination with hunting to "subhuman" impulses (*CP* 143) rather than fiendish evil. In 1935, Hitler's persecution of the Jews is condemned as a manhunt that "revives a primitive instinct incompatible with civilization" (*Mill* 121, Pref). Here Shaw anticipates the attempts of later writers such as Konrad Lorenz and Arthur Koestler to explain human aggression. The point of his seeing "sinful" acts as the result of the Life Force's errors is not to minimize the often horrible effects of such behavior, but to call attention to the necessity for coping with a biological heritage all have in common: "Beware how you pretend that war does not interest and excite you more than printing, or that the thought of bringing down a springing tiger with a well-aimed shot does not interest you more than the thought of cleaning your teeth. Men may be as the poles asunder in their speculative views. In their actual nervous and emotional reactions they are 'members one of another' to a much greater extent than they choose to

---

159, Pref)—anticipate more recent "radical" proposals. Shaw's mind remained able to respond resourcefully to new facts except when the latter threatened the very foundations of his world view.

confess" (*CP* 145). By using an evolutionary instead of a moralistic framework, Shaw encourages people to recognize their own destructive impulses and to resist being tempted either into the self-righteous assumption that such tendencies are *other* people's problem, or else into the despair that arises when a belief in original sin is unaccompanied by faith in traditional dogmas of redemption.

Thus Shaw's denial of human depravity does not make him an optimist about man: atavism was as discouraging for him as sin is for the theologian. Furthermore, he sees clearly that the effects of subhuman savagery can be compounded by those of an all-too-human folly. Perhaps we are now in a better position to appreciate the essentially negative force of his apparently consoling assertion to the effect that "hell is paved with benevolence, which most people, the proverb being too deep for them, misinterpret as unfulfilled intentions" (*Unsoc* 101). While this premise allows ignorance (in all its manifestations and disguises) to supplant sin as a master principle to explain the state of the world, the belief that man is ignorant provides legitimate grounds for hope only if one believes that man is educable as well. Since it is at exactly this point that Shaw's faith tended to break down, his determination to view human nature as basically well-meaning makes his perception of human misdeeds all the more poignant: "There are no villains in [*Saint Joan*]. Crime, like disease, is not interesting: it is something to be done away with by general consent, and that is all about it. It is what men do at their best, with good intentions, and what normal men and women find that they must and will do in spite of their intentions, that really concern us" (*Joan* 49–50, Pref). The horror of Joan's death is heightened rather than diminished because her fate is brought about by men who are not "cruel by nature" (158). Similarly, the "Denshawai incident" would have been a less appalling absurdity had it resulted from mere depravity instead of bureaucratic panic.[8] For

8. See *Bull* 49–63, Pref. The incident began in a brawl when a party of officers from the British Army of Occupation entered the village of

Shaw the insoluble problem is not the wickedness of man, but his littleness.

Barring man's transformation into a higher being, Shaw can only fall back on his once confident belief that "many of the most detestable human vices are not radical, but are mere reactions of our institutions on our very virtues" (*Super* 188, Rev Hdbk). Should this indeed be the case, we would have some grounds for hoping that the effects of man's benevolent impulses have been only temporarily impeded by a reliance upon the political, moral, and religious absolutes that have so often concealed the effects of his viciousness and folly. At times Shaw is sanguine about the possible results of liberating the human spirit from artificial system: "I see plenty of good in the world working itself out as fast as the idealists will allow it"—that is, as soon as we found our institutions on a "genuinely scientific natural history" (*PP* xvi-xvii). But even in these earlier and more optimistic writings, he does not deny that such hopes involve a gamble: "If human nature . . . is really degenerating, then human society will decay; and no panic-begotten penal measures can possibly save it" (*Wag* 222). In any case, his point is that we have nothing to lose by running the risk. If it should turn out that men's traditional ideals have perverted their "natural compassion" (*Joan* 128) into "civilized" horrors like the Denshawai massacre or the burning of Joan, then the spontaneous operation of the human will may result in an improvement. If on the other hand such liberation only serves to release vile impulses from customary legal restraints, then people might as well go to hell in an honest orgy of self-destruction instead of

---

Denshawai and began shooting the pigeons upon which the natives depended for their livelihood. Hysterical overreaction proceeded to transform this scuffle into a judicial massacre ending in "four hanged, two [sentenced] to penal servitude for life, one to fifteen years penal servitude, six to seven years penal servitude, three to imprisonment for a year with hard labor and fifty lashes, and five to fifty lashes" (55). Shaw makes British rule in Egypt look ridiculous simply by quoting verbatim from the fatuous "official" documents relating to the case.

pretending to submit to higher authorities projected by their own imaginations. Even if Hobbes was closer than Rousseau to the truth about human nature, Shaw would still hold that insofar as man is good, conventional ideals prevent him from becoming better; while insofar as he is evil, they prevent him from facing the evil in himself. There is no surer way to let the devil get the better of us than by refusing to give him his due (*Marr* 279).[9]

In Shaw's view, human salvation ultimately hinges on the capacity of the species to come to terms with retrograde elements of its biological and cultural heritage. Although his advocacy of Lamarckian volitionism has convinced everyone that he is no scientist, Shaw's wrongheadedness concerning the mechanism of natural selection should not obscure his valid perception—in which he resembles other vitalists such as Teilhard de Chardin—that man is the creature in whom evolution has finally become conscious of itself. As Erich Kahler has noted, once the human stage has been reached, evolution "passes over from a mainly physical to a mainly psychic and mental level" (6). So although the notion that an organism can will its own improvement is not a convincing explanation of how a one-celled creature became a two-celled creature, "Creative Evolution" may have a great deal to do with the question: is humanity capable of any further self-development? Our real hope rests not in the growth of miraculous new organs or a lifespan of 300 years, but in the creation of a *consciousness* that will enable us to "conclude an amnesty with Nature wide enough to include even those we know the worst of: namely, ourselves" (*Cash* 249, Note). Having begun by holding that the individual must survive in order to be saved,

9. Compare the Bishop in *Getting Married* (1908): "If we are going to discuss ethical questions we must begin by giving the devil fair play. . . . We always assume that the devil is guilty: and we wont allow him to prove his innocence, because it would be against public morals if he succeeded. We used to do the same with prisoners accused of high treason. And the consequence is that we overreach ourselves; and the devil gets the better of us after all. Perhaps thats what most of us intend him to do" (279).

Shaw ends by holding that the species must be saved in order to survive. Are we essentially a race of Julians, who will destroy ourselves by fixation on the limitations of the past, or of Wotans, who will surpass ourselves by commitment to the possibilities of the future? Will mankind, like the self-realized Shavian hero, play an active role in its own self-transcendence? Or will it be superseded instead when the Life Force demolishes both man and the cycle of eternal recurrence that has thus far constituted the history of the "unchanging human heart"?

I have already suggested how Shaw's tendency to leapfrog over humanity into a remote cosmological future is, from one point of view, open to criticism; but it is also worth noting that, from a different perspective, Shaw's long-range optimism is an indispensable component of his tragic view of man. Lilith's claim— "Of life only is there no end" (*Back* 254)—heralds a victory for evolution that is fully compatible with a defeat for mankind. By definition, there can be no tragedy *of* life, but there is tragedy *in* life whenever we become cut off from participation in the vital process—whether by succumbing to the inertia that follows in the wake of discouragement, or by allowing ourselves to be "used by personally minded men for purposes which [we] recognize to be base" (*Super* xxxi). Shaw's earlier confidence that "the spirit of man is the will of the gods" (*Caes* 87) had obviously become very attenuated by the time he wrote, "It always comes to that: leave it to God. . . . All we know is that He leaves much of it to us; and we make a shocking mess of it" (*Buoy* 46). Indeed, the most characteristic heroes of the later plays—Joan, Aubrey, Prola, Charles—all intuit that man's self-division may forever preclude his self-realization. Thus the eventual triumph of the evolutionary process is no more reassuring from humanity's point of view than the Crucifixion was a blessed event from the point of view of the damned thief. Shaw's long-range optimism, very nearly the opposite of faith in *human* progress, underscores the ironic prospect that man's fate is to play a tragic role in the divine comedy of the cosmos.

References Cited

Abbott, Anthony S. *Shaw and Christianity*. New York: Seabury, 1965.

Albert, Sidney P. "'In More Ways Than One': *Major Barbara's* Debt to Gilbert Murray." *Educational Theatre Journal*, 20 (May 1968), 123–140.

Belmont, Eleanor Robson. *The Fabric of Memory*. New York: Farrar, Straus, 1957.

Bentley, Eric [Russell]. *Bernard Shaw*. Amended Edition. Norfolk: New Directions, 1957.

——. *A Century of Hero-Worship*. Philadelphia: Lippincott, 1944.

——. *The Playwright as Thinker*. New York: Reynal & Hitchcock, 1946.

Berst, Charles A. *Bernard Shaw and the Art of Drama*. Urbana: University of Illinois Press, 1973.

Bringle, Jerald. "The First Unpleasant Play by Bernard Shaw: An Analysis of the Formation and Evolution of *Widowers' Houses*." Doctoral dissertation, New York University, 1970.

Brustein, Robert. *The Theatre of Revolt*. Boston: Little, Brown, 1964.

Bunyan, John. *The Pilgrim's Progress*. London: Penguin, 1965.

Burton, Richard. *Bernard Shaw: The Man and the Mask*. New York: Henry Holt, 1916.

Carpenter, Charles A. *Bernard Shaw & the Art of Destroying Ideals: The Early Plays*. Madison: Wisconsin University Press, 1969.

Caudwell, Christopher. *Studies in a Dying Culture*. London: John Lane, The Bodley Head, 1938 (repr. 1947).

Chesterton, G. K. *George Bernard Shaw*. Expanded edition, 1935. Reprint, New York: Devin Adair, 1950.

Colbourne, Maurice. *The Real Bernard Shaw*. Boston: Bruce Humphries, 1931.

Collis, J. S. *Shaw*. London: Jonathan Cape, 1925.

Costello, Donald P. *The Serpent's Eye: Shaw and the Cinema.* Notre Dame: University of Notre Dame Press, 1965.

Crompton, Louis. *Shaw the Dramatist.* Lincoln: University of Nebraska Press, 1969.

Daiches, David. *A Critical History of English Literature.* 2 vols. 2d ed. New York: Ronald Press, 1970.

Dietrich, R. F. *Portrait of the Artist as a Young Superman: A Study of Shaw's Novels.* Gainesville: University of Florida Press, 1969.

Dinesen, Isak. *Out of Africa.* New York: Random House, 1938.

Dukore, Bernard F. "Toward an Interpretation of *Major Barbara.*" *Shaw Review,* VI, 2 (1963), 62–70.

Eliot, T. S. *Essays on Elizabethan Drama.* 1932. Reprint, New York: Harvest-Harcourt, 1960.

Fabian Essays in Socialism. London: Walter Scott, 1889.

Fabian Essays [in Socialism]. "Jubilee Edition." London: Allen & Unwin, 1948 (repr. 1950).

Fabian Tracts. Vol. I (nos. 1–47), Vol. II (nos. 48–95). Nendeln: Kraus Reprint, 1969.

Farmer, Henry George. *Bernard Shaw's Sister and Her Friends.* Leiden: E. J. Brill, 1959.

Fergusson, Francis. *The Idea of a Theatre.* 1949. Reprint, New York: Anchor-Doubleday, 1953.

Gatch, Katherine Haynes. "The Last Plays of Bernard Shaw: Dialectic and Despair." In *English Stage Comedy,* ed. W. K. Wimsatt, Jr. (*English Institute Essays,* 1954), pp. 126–147. New York: Columbia University Press, 1955.

Henderson, Archibald. *George Bernard Shaw: His Life and Works.* Cincinnati: Stewart & Kidd, 1911.

——. *George Bernard Shaw: Man of the Century.* New York: Appleton, 1956.

Hook, Sidney. "Heroic Vitalism" (review of Eric Bentley's *A Century of Hero-Worship*). *The Nation,* 159 (7 October 1944), 412–414.

Hoy, Cyrus. "Shaw's Tragicomic Irony: From 'Man and Superman' to 'Heartbreak House.'" *Virginia Quarterly Review,* 47 (1971), 57–78.

Ibsen, Henrik. *The Collected Works of Henrik Ibsen.* Ed. William Archer. 11 vols. London: Heinemann, 1907.

Irvine, William. *The Universe of G.B.S.* New York: McGraw-Hill, 1949.

James, William. *Pragmatism.* Cleveland: Meridian-World, 1965.

Joad, C. E. M. *Shaw*. London: Gollancz, 1949.

Kahler, Erich. *Out of the Labyrinth: Essays in Clarification*. New York: Braziller, 1967.

Kaufmann, R. J., ed. *G. B. Shaw: A Collection of Critical Essays*. Twentieth Century Views. Englewood Cliffs: Prentice-Hall, 1965.

Kaye, Julian B. *Bernard Shaw and the Nineteenth-Century Tradition*. Norman: University of Oklahoma Press, 1958.

Knight, G. Wilson. "Shaw's Integral Theatre." *The Golden Labyrinth: A Study of British Drama*. London: Phoenix House, 1962. Reprinted in Kaufmann, ed., 119–129.

Kronenberger, Louis, ed. *Shaw: A Critical Survey*. Cleveland: World, 1953.

Lauter, Paul. " 'Candida' and 'Pygmalion': Shaw's Subversion of Stereotypes." *Shaw Review*, III, 3 (1960), 14–19.

Laver, James. *Manners and Morals in the Age of Optimism: 1848–1914*. New York: Harper & Row, 1966.

Lerner, Alan Jay. "Pygmalion and My Fair Lady." *Shaw Review*, I, 10 (1956), 4–7.

MacCarthy, Desmond. *Shaw*. London: MacGibbon & Kee, 1951.

McBriar, A. M. *Fabian Socialism and English Politics, 1884–1918*. Cambridge: Cambridge University Press, 1962.

McDowell, Frederick P. W. "Politics, Comedy, Character, and Dialectic: The Shavian World of *John Bull's Other Island.*" *PMLA*, LXXXII (1967), 542–553.

Meisel, Martin. *Shaw and the Nineteenth-Century Theater*. Princeton: Princeton University Press, 1963.

Nethercot, Arthur. *Men and Supermen*. 2d ed. New York: Benjamin Blom, 1966.

Nietzsche, Friedrich. *The Birth of Tragedy* and *The Genealogy of Morals*. Trans. Francis Golffing. New York: Anchor-Doubleday, 1956.

——. *The Portable Nietzsche*. Ed. Walter Kaufmann. New York: Viking, 1954.

Ohmann, Richard H. *Shaw: The Style and the Man*. Middletown: Wesleyan University Press, 1962.

Ozy [pseud.]. "The Dramatist's Dilemma: An Interpretation of *Major Barbara.*" *Shaw Review*, II, 4 (1958), 18–24.

Pearson, Hesketh. *G.B.S.: A Postscript*. New York: Harper, 1950.

Perry, Ralph Barton. *The Thought and Character of William James*. 2 vols. Boston: Little, Brown, 1935.

Priestley, J. B. *Literature and Western Man.* London: Heinemann, 1960.

Shaw, Charlotte, ed. *Selected Passages from the Works of Bernard Shaw.* London: Constable, 1912.

Shaw, George Bernard. *The Author's Apology from Mrs. Warren's Profession.* New York: Brentano's, 1905.

——. *Cashel Byron's Profession.* Ed. Stanley Weintraub. Carbondale: Southern Illinois University Press, 1968.

——. *Collected Letters: 1874–1897.* Ed. Dan H. Laurence. New York: Dodd, Mead, 1965.

——. *The Complete Prefaces of Bernard Shaw.* London: Hamlyn, 1965.

——. "The Fabian Society: What It Has Done and How It Has Done It." Fabian Tract No. 41. London, 1892.

——. *How to Become a Musical Critic.* Ed. Dan H. Laurence. London: Hart-Davis, 1960.

——. *The Irrational Knot. Our Corner,* V–IX (April 1885–February 1887). London.

——. *John Bull's Other Island* and *Major Barbara.* New York: Brentano's, 1907.

——. *Love among the Artists. Our Corner,* X–XII (November 1887–December 1888). London.

——. *Man and Superman.* New York: Brentano's, 1904.

——. *My Dear Dorothea.* Ed. Stephen Winsten. New York: Vanguard, 1956.

——. *The Perfect Wagnerite.* Chicago: Herbert S. Stone, 1899.

——. *The Perfect Wagnerite.* 2d ed. London: Constable, 1902.

——. *The Perfect Wagnerite.* 2d ed. (expanded). New York: Brentano's, 1909.

——. *The Perfect Wagnerite.* 3d ed. Leipzig: Tauchnitz, 1913.

——. *Platform and Pulpit.* Ed. Dan H. Laurence. New York: Hill & Wang, 1961.

——. *Plays Pleasant and Unpleasant.* 2 vols. Chicago: Herbert S. Stone, 1898.

——. *The Quintessence of Ibsenism.* Boston: Benjamin R. Tucker, 1891.

——. *The Quintessence of Ibsenism.* 2d ed. New York: Brentano's, 1913.

——. *The Religious Speeches of Bernard Shaw.* Ed. Warren S. Smith. University Park: Pennsylvania State University Press, 1963.

——. *The Sanity of Art.* New York: Benjamin R. Tucker, 1908.

——. *Selected Non-Dramatic Writings of Bernard Shaw*. Ed. Dan. H. Laurence. Boston: Houghton Mifflin, 1965.

——. *Shaw on Religion*. Ed. Warren Sylvester Smith. New York: Dodd, Mead, 1967.

——. *Shaw on Theatre*. Ed. E. J. West. New York: Hill & Wang, 1958.

——. *Standard Edition of the Works of Bernard Shaw*. 37 vols. London: Constable, 1931–1950.

——. *Three Plays for Puritans*. Chicago: Herbert S. Stone, 1901.

Styan, J. L. *The Dark Comedy: The Development of Modern Comic Tragedy*. 2d ed. Cambridge: Cambridge University Press, 1968.

Taylor, A. J. P. *English History: 1914–1945*. New York and Oxford: Oxford University Press, 1965.

Wagner, Richard. *The Ring of the Nibelung*. Trans. Stuart Robb. New York: Dutton, 1960.

Watson, Barbara Bellow. *A Shavian Guide to the Intelligent Woman*. London: Chatto and Windus, 1964.

Weintraub, Stanley. *Journey to Heartbreak: The Crucible Years of Bernard Shaw: 1914–1918*. New York: Weybright and Talley, 1971.

——. " 'Shaw's *Divine Comedy*': Addendum." *Shaw Review, II*, 5 (1958), 21–22.

Wellek, René. *A History of Modern Criticism: 1750–1950*. Vol. IV: *The Late Nineteenth Century*. New Haven: Yale University Press, 1965.

Wells, H. G. *Journalism and Prophecy*. Ed. W. Warren Wager. Boston: Houghton Mifflin, 1964.

West, Alick. *George Bernard Shaw: A Good Man Fallen among Fabians*. New York: International Publishers, 1950.

Wilson, Colin. *Bernard Shaw: A Reassessment*. New York: Atheneum, 1969.

Wilson, Edmund. "Bernard Shaw at Eighty." *The Triple Thinkers*. New York: Oxford, 1938. Reprinted in Kronenberger, ed., 126–152.

Winsten, Stephen. *Jesting Apostle: The Private Life of Bernard Shaw*. New York: Dutton, 1957.

Wisenthal, J. L. *The Marriage of Contraries: Bernard Shaw's Middle Plays*. Cambridge: Harvard University Press, 1974.

Wisenthal, J. L. "The Underside of Undershaft: A Wagnerian Motif in *Major Barbara*." *Shaw Review*, XV, 2 (1972), 56–64.

Woodbridge, Homer E. *George Bernard Shaw: Creative Artist.* Crosscurrents: Modern Critiques. Carbondale: Southern Illinois University Press, 1963.

Young, Stark. "Heartbreak Houses." *Immortal Shadows.* New York: Scribner's, 1948. Reprinted in Kronenberger, ed., 232–235.

Index

293

Shaw's Moral Vision

Designed by R. E. Rosenbaum.
Composed by York Composition Co., Inc.,
in 11 point Intertype Baskerville, 2 points leaded,
with display lines in monotype Baskerville.
Printed letterpress from type by York Composition Co.
on Warren's Number 66 Antique Text, 50 lb. basis
Bound by John H. Dekker & Sons, Inc.

Library of Congress Cataloging in Publication Data
(For library cataloging purposes only)
Turco, Alfred.
  Shaw's moral vision.

  Bibliography: p.
  Includes index.
  1. Shaw, George Bernard, 1856–1950—Criticism
and interpretation. I. Title.
PR5367.T8   822'.9'12   75-36524
ISBN 0-8014-0965-9